I0212571

UNIVERSAL CLASSICS
LIBRARY

ILLUSTRATED
WITH PHOTOGRAVURES
ON JAPAN VELLUM
HAND PAINTED
REPRODUCTIONS
AND FULL PAGE
PORTRAITS
OF
AUTHORS

M. WALTER DUNNE
PUBLISHER
NEW YORK AND LONDON

Copyright, 1901,

By

M. WALTER DUNNE,

Publisher

IDEAL EMPIRES
AND REPUBLICS

ROUSSEAU'S SOCIAL CONTRACT

MORE'S UTOPIA

BACON'S NEW ATLANTIS

CAMPANELLA'S CITY OF THE SUN

WITH AN INTRODUCTION BY

CHARLES M. ANDREWS, Ph.D.
Professor of History, Bryn Mawr College

WILDSIDE PRESS

COPYRIGHT, 1901,
BY
M. WALTER DUNNE,
PUBLISHER

ILLUSTRATIONS

(v)

INTRODUCTION

T HE term Utopia, as generally used, refers to those
ideal states which are impossible of realization, both
because they are peopled by ideal human beings
uninfluenced by personal jealousies or individual passions,
and because they are based, with but little regard for
the complexities and varieties of real society, upon what
the writer thinks ought to be, rather than upon the collective experience of mankind. More broadly speaking,
however, the term need not be confined to these "fantastic pictures of impossible societies," or "romantic accounts of fictitious states," as they have been called, but
may be applied to any social, intellectual, or political
scheme which is impracticable at the time when it is conceived and presented. Thus enlarged, the field may be
made to include schemes as diverse as More's *Utopia*,
Campanella's *City of the Sun*, Cabet's *Icarie*, and Morris's
News from Nowhere; Rousseau's society of the *Social
Contract;* and modern socialistic and communistic organi-
zations, such as the *Co-operative Commonwealth* of Law-
rence Grönlund, popularized by Bellamy in *Looking
Backward*, and Flürcheim's *Money Island.*

Utopias have generally made their appearance during
periods of great social and political unrest, and it is, therefore, no accident that after Plato's *Republic*, written during dark days in the history of Athens, all Utopias should
have fallen in the period from the beginning of the sixteenth century to the present time. The Middle Ages,
with their fixed institutions, their blind faith, and their
acceptance of authority were not a suitable seed-ground
for the growth of Utopian schemes. Any ideals that
were conceived were of a religious character, based upon
conceptions of the past and hopes of the future: those of

the past combined the pagan notion of a golden age with the Christian's concept of an age of innocence, giving rise to the doctrine that man had fallen from a perfect life whose simple rules were based on natural law; those of the future looked forward to the re-establishment of Christ's kingdom on earth. Such doctrines were characteristic of a period in which there existed no true idea of human progress.

But in the period following the Middle Ages, when mediæval institutions were breaking down and men were awakening to the fact that governments had become corrupt and tyrannical, and social relations unjust and immoral, it was natural that they should find comfort and satisfaction in casting into romantic or ideal form their conception of what society ought to be. Excellent examples of such Utopias are to be found among the works of sixteenth century writers, who prompted by the new spirit of inquiry constructed ideal conditions that should eliminate the evils of their age. The earliest, More's *Utopia* (1516), presents the lofty ideals of the Oxford reformers, and stands as the greatest literary effort of the time; Vives, a versatile Catholic humanist, in 1531 erected in his *De Corruptis Artibus* and *De Tradendis Discipliniis* an ideal academy, a pedagogical Utopia, founded on the highest educational, scientific, and moral considerations;* Doni in *I Mundi celesti, terrestri, et infernali* (1552–53) satirized in Utopian form the political and social vices of Italy; and a little later, in 1605, under the pseudonym, Mercurius Britannicus, Joseph Hall, made Bishop of Norwich in 1641, published a moral satire, *Mundus Alter et Idem*, in tone rather Rabelaisian than ideal.

As the seventeenth century advanced, the spirit of free inquiry grew bolder, overthrowing the philosophy of Aristotle, and leading men to study the operations of nature in order to discover the fundamental principles that underlay the constitution of the universe. Three writers, in harmony with the spirit of the age, conceived philosophical and intellectual Utopias, in which by means of the new methods of scientific experimentation the social and intellectual order was to be remodeled. Campa-

* *Handbuch der Pädagogik*, Vol. VII., p. 425.

nella, a Dominican monk of Calabria, began in 1602 his *Civitas Solis*, which he published in 1623; Bacon in the *Novus Atlantis*, written before 1617 and published in 1627, exhibited a state of which the most striking feature was a college "instituted for the interpreting of nature and the production of great and marvelous works for the benefit of man;" and Comenius, after issuing his *Conatuum Pansophicorum Dilucidatio* in 1639, went to England to form a "Universal College" for physical research on the lines suggested by Bacon in the *New Atlantis.**** But in the turmoil of the Civil War the *Pansophia* of Comenius was lost, and hopes of a Universal College soon vanished.

During the next hundred years political questions supplanted philosophical. Harrington's *Oceana* dedicated to Cromwell in 1656, was not a romance, but "the first sketch in English political science of a written constitution limiting sovereignty," † "the only valuable model of a commonwealth," as Hume calls it. Hume himself, a century later (1752), in his *Essays, Moral and Political*, Part II., commenting on Plato, More, and Harrington, presented his "Idea of a Perfect Commonwealth," and believed that in his *Utopia* he had discovered a form of government to which he himself could not in theory formulate "any considerable objection."

In France also, writers were coming forward with schemes of a perfect government. Vairasse d'Allais, in *La République des Sévarambes*, a part of his *Histoire des Sévarambes*, 1672, pictured a monarchy, with the state owning land and wealth and the people dwelling in huge osmasies like Fourier's *phalanstères*. Fénélon in Book X. of the *Télémaque*, which contains his account of the kingdom of Salente, described a perfect state under the authority of a perfect king.

But Utopias advocating monarchy are rare. With the realization of the evils of the state system of the eighteenth century, thought took a new direction. Morelly in *Naufrage des îles flottantes ou la Basiliade de Pilpai*, 1753, declared that the existing conditions were corrupt,

---

* Keatinge: *The Great Didactic of Comenius*, p. 45.

† Dwight in "Political Science Quarterly," 1887, p. 17.

attacked the law of property, and tried to demonstrate
the necessity of placing society under the law of nature
and truth,— ideas more fully developed in his *Code de la
Nature*, 1755. This appeal to the law of nature showed
the prevailing political concept of the period. The eyes
of the reformers were now turned to the natural principles of social order and government, and in 1762 Rousseau gave to the world, in the *Contrat Social* his scheme
of the state founded on social compact. Mably went
further than Rousseau, and in his various writings from
1765 to 1784 denounced private property, inheritance and
right of bequest, commerce, credit, the arts and sciences,
libraries, museums, and the like. Finding his ideal
among the Greeks, he viewed the Spartan era as a
golden age, and extolled poverty as the mother of frugality
and the virtues. He preached not only equality and
equal education for all, but a federal state and community of goods. If Rousseau inspired Robespierre and St.
Just, it is equally true that Mably and Pechméja (*Télèphe*,
1784) inspired Marat, Babœuf, and Buonarrotti. Although
during the French Revolution men acted rather than
dreamed, yet in the teachings of Maréchal, Marat, and
the Girondist Brissot de Warville, and in the speeches
of St. Just and Robespierre, we find embodied Utopian
ideals regarding man and his fundamental rights. The
adoption of the constitution of 1793 was as truly an attempt to found a Utopia as was the forming of the
" Society of Equals," through which Babœuf hoped to
hasten a communistic millenium.

The French Revolution so shattered society that
writers of Utopias, who before had had little real expectation of seeing their theories applied, now worked
to remodel the social and industrial order. The followers of St. Simon established an experimental community in 1826; in 1840 a *phalanstère* of Fourier was set
up at Brook Farm in America; at New Lanark, before
the close of the eighteenth century, Robert Owen had
tried his economic Utopia, and in 1825 was experiment-
ing at New Harmony in Pennsylvania. In 1848 great
national workshops were set up in Paris; and in Algiers
Marshal Bugeaud endeavored to establish a military

colony on a communistic basis. Cabet copied More's *Utopia* in his *Voyage en Icarie*, and gave it a better trial at Nauvoo in Illinois in 1849 than had Frank, Münster, and Münzer in Germany in the sixteenth century. But after Cabet's *Icarie*, except in a few cases such as Lytton's *Coming Race*, Bellamy's *Looking Backward*, and Secrétan's *Mon Utopie*, which were little more than literary pastimes, and such experimental communities as the Christian Commonwealth near Columbus, Georgia, and the Ruskin Colony in the same state, both of which have failed, the history of Utopias is the history of scientific socialism, and is not to be dealt with here.

Of all the Utopias the most famous are the four selected for presentation in this volume, for not only are they great creations of the imagination, but they stand in the first rank of literary productions; and two of them, those of More and Rousseau, have surpassed all others in influence. The work of More is further distinguished by the fact that it was the first of the modern productions of the kind, and also the first to bear the familiar title of *Utopia*. Sir Thomas More was born in 1478. He early became a student of law and the new learning, and though his later years were spent in the practice of law, diplomacy, and statecraft, he remained to the end of his life devoted to learning and religion. That he was a keen observer of the social conditions of his time the *Utopia* proves; for it contains not only a picture of an ideal community, but a severe indictment of the disorders attending the great social and economic transformation from an agricultural to an industrial and commercial state through which England was passing. New conditions of industry and commerce had made impossible the retention of the old manorial system; villenage was disappearing and the villeins were becoming copy-holders; agriculture was ceasing to be profitable under the old methods; money was taking the place of payments in kind; and the dispersion of the manorial tenantry was increasing vagabondage and the number of the unemployed. The old towns, too, like Norwich, Exeter, York, Winchester, and Southampton, with their narrow gild restrictions were falling **into** decay, and were making way for new industrial centers like Birmingham, Manchester, Leeds, and Sheffield. More important still was the introduction, in many of the counties, of the inclosure system. Landlords, discovering that farming was more profitable when done on a large scale, and that sheep raising brought even larger returns than agriculture, turned arable lands into pasture, thus depopulating the old villages, setting adrift large number of villeins to find work wherever they could, and bringing great distress and misery to the people. Such were the conditions that inspired More in his *Utopia*, the first book of which is a treatise on the evils of the time.

The second book of the *Utopia* presents as a remedy for all ills an ideal state in which there are no drones and of which the key-note is moderation. With the exception of the very learned, the inhabitants of the new state are all producers, who devote six hours of each day to labor and the remaining to social and intellectual pleasures; who avoid war and all luxuries; and whose king, chosen by themselves and for life, lives like a common citizen, governing not in the interest of the few, but for the happiness of the many. In his treatment of labor, questions of criminal law, education, public health, and freedom of speech, More strikes a very modern note; but though he showed himself, like the other Oxford reformers, a lover of liberty, justice, truth, and toleration, and though he rose to be Chancellor of England, he made no effort to apply as a politician the doctrines he had advanced as a philosopher. Possibly, as Master of the Court of Requests, or Court of Poor Men's Causes, he may have dispensed the justice of the *Utopia;* but in other matters, notably that of religion, he did not in practice rise to the height he had attained in his thought. He opposed Lutheranism, and while not persecuting the Protestants, as has been charged, battled with heresy till his death. In fact, the second book of the *Utopia* at its best but reflects the character of a noble man, whose mind revolted against the injustice and inequalities of his age.

Both Campanella's *City of the Sun* and Bacon's *New Atlantis*, notwithstanding their differences in setting and treatment, represent an awakened interest in a new philosophy. Unlike Sir Thomas More, neither Campanella nor Bacon concerned himself much with the economic or social questions of his time. Campanella was from boyhood a student of logic and physics. Bacon, led partly by personal inclination, and partly by the fact that in the greater prosperity of the age of Elizabeth, social conditions had become less exigent, turned his attention to politics and philosophy. The crisis reflected in the Utopias of these writers were, therefore, revolutions, not in society, but in philosophical thought and method. Influenced by Bernhard Telesius (1508–88), the great Italian opponent of the doctrines of Aristotle, Campanella, like Bacon saw the need of a fundamental reform of natural philosophy, and the substitution for analogies and abstract generalizations of the sounder method of exact observation. Unwilling to employ principles established arbitrarily, they based all conclusions on careful and scientific experimentation. Before Campanella was twenty-five years old he had published a series of works supporting the contention that men can understand the world only through the senses. Bacon, born in 1561, seven years earlier than Campanella, although from boyhood eager to accomplish by means of a new philosophy something of practical benefit for humanity, was slower in publishing his views. Whereas the *City of the Sun*, written after the *De Sensu Rerum, Philosophia Sensibus Demonstrata*, and *De Investigatione Rerum*, presents a social and philosophical scheme worked out in minute detail, the *New Atlantis*, written before the publication of the *Novum Organum* and the *Instauratio Magna*, is but a sketch of the results Bacon would like to have attained, rather than a demonstration of the methods necessary for their attainment. Campanella's work is, so far as it goes, complete; Bacon's is only a fragment which probably he never intended to perfect.

Campanella, born in southern Calabria in 1568, became at a very early age a Dominican monk and was interested rather in physics than in theology. By attacking the prevailing Aristotelian philosophy, he soon roused enemies against him, and was imprisoned on the charge of conspiring to overthrow the Kingdom of Naples and found a republic. He was seven times tortured during twenty-seven years of confinement in fifty different prisons, and was often deprived of the means of study and writing. After his release in 1626, he withdrew to France; and in 1639, died in a convent of his order. The *Civitas Solis seu idea reipublicae philosophicæ*, written in prison, is believed to have been the beginning of a large work, of which the first part was to deal with the laws of nature, the second with the manners and customs of men, the third with the organization of the state, the fourth with the economic bases of society. It was, as Campanella himself says, the counterpart of Plato's *Republic*, and on its scientific side was based on Telesius. It formulated for the first time a complete socialistic system on a scientific foundation,* and, in France especially, furnished a model for later ideal communities.

The city with its seven walls, its compact organization, its carefully divided labors, and rigorous discipline reflect the monastic experiences of the writer; but the principles, in accordance with which the state is governed, the social relation determined, and industry controlled, are such as to interest men in all ages. Collectively, the inhabitants labor for the common good; individually, each seeks the perfecting of his body and soul, the care of the young children, and the worship of God. Government is intrusted to the wisest and ablest, and laws are made and administered only so far as they promote the object for which all are laboring. The essences of life are equality, sacrifice of self for the community, the banishment of egotism; and peculiar features are the community of wives and goods, common meals, state control of produce, and of children after a certain age, dislike of commercial exchange, depreciation of money, love of all for manual labor, and the high regard which all show for intellectual and artistic pursuits. It is a remarkable fact that in spite of Campanella's sufferings his work should not only show no trace of bitterness, but should maintain consistently the loftiest ideals.

Less purely Utopian in conception than the *City of the Sun* is Bacon's *Atlantis*, and almost entirely wanting is

* Sigwart, *Kleine Schriften*, p. 151.

it in the communistic extravagances of Campanella's work. It contains an expression of the scientific views of Bacon and his opinion regarding the duty of the state toward science. More than this it describes his tastes in conduct and dress, and is characterized by a spirit of hospitality, kindliness, and courtesy, which betrays his sympathetic nature. As has been well said "there is no single work of his which has so much of himself in it." Unlike More, who would limit the population, Bacon, as the institutions of the Tirsan shows, would have families large; and unlike other writers of his age, he gives a prominent part and attractive character to Joabin, a Jew. But the chief interest of the author centers in Solomon's House, the College of the Six Days Works, a state institution governed by an official body, and founded for the purpose of discovering "the causes and secret motions of things." Here Bacon gives a list of those experiments and observations, which he hoped would increase knowledge, ameliorate the conditions of life, improve the physical well-being of man, and enlarge the bounds of the human empire. In medicine, surgery, meteorology, food, and mechanical contrivances he anticipates many of the improvements of later times. It has been generally supposed that "this noblest foundation that ever was on earth" suggested the foundation and program of the Royal Society in England and of similar societies abroad.

From Campanella and Bacon to Rousseau is a long reach not only in time, but in thought also; and nothing could be more foreign to the philosophy advocated by the earlier writers than the *a priori* methods of Rousseau, and his disregard of history, observation, and induction. Taking ideas that had been floating about in Europe for two centuries, he presented them, with great charm and vigor of style, as a set of positive principles governing the organization of the state. Nor did he invent an island of Utopia, a City of the Sun, or a far away Atlantis in which to apply his principles, but he declared that they were capable of universal application, and that they indicated what every government would be if it were stripped of the artificial garb of civilization. His vague generalizations and impracticable doctrines were the more effective because not embodied in a romantic form, for each doctrine applied directly to the man who read it and was applied by him to the state that was oppressing him. Rousseau fascinated the multitude because he seemed to appeal, not to their imagination, but to their reason, and seemed to say that the state of the *Social Contract* was what France ought to be and might be, if only the people of France had their rights.

The central idea of the *Social Contract* is the absolute authority of the people. Rousseau declares that the existing situation is but a degeneration from a more perfect order, when man, born free, was possessed of natural liberty and governed by natural law; and that this degeneration had begun when man exchanged natural liberty for civil liberty, and natural law for positive law. Rousseau further holds that government and the state are the result of a social compact, a common agreement between individuals who voluntarily yield themselves to be subject to the common will; that such body politic is composed of equal members possessed of absolute authority; that sovereignty residing in the people can neither be delegated to representatives nor modified by contract with a king; and that the will of the majority, as expressed by universal suffrage, determines the form the government should take, and can at any time change the government if it desires. The result of such ideas was to lead the people to believe that existing institutions had no right to exist; that sovereignty rightfully belonged not to the king but to them; and that a government which had usurped sovereignty could be set aside.

But Rousseau's Utopia was based on four fallacies: first, the essential goodness of man; secondly, the original freedom and equality of man; thirdly, the possession by man of inherent political rights; and fourthly, the compact between individuals as the basis of the State Yet its doctrines found a firm rooting among the people of the period after Rousseau, both in France and in America, and rights of man and an original compact became the shibboleths of statesmen for half a century Rousseau's Utopia, unlike the ideal states that had gone before, appealed to the masses of the people already ripe for revolution, became a standard around which they were to rally, an article of faith for which they were to fight. In this respect, the *Social Contract* is no longer a Utopia, but a creed, of that class to which Calvin's *Institutes* belong With the rise of the historical school, however, its doctrines have vanished, much as did those of Aristotle before the attacks of Campanella and Bacon. Latter-day Utopias are not founded on *a priori* deductions; they generally have a scientific basis.

The systematic study of Utopias cannot but be fruitful of results. Fantastic though many of the systems are, each is nevertheless a mirror of the prevailing thought of the period in which it is written and a key to the ideals of the best men. To write properly the history of Utopias from the time of Sir Thomas More to the present is to write the history of the progress of human thought in the last five centuries.

Charles M. Andrews.

CONTENTS

BOOK IV.

PREFATORY NOTE.

THIS little treatise is extracted from a larger work undertaken at an earlier time without consideration of my capacity, and long since abandoned. Of the various fragments that might be selected from what was accomplished, the following is the most considerable and appears to me the least unworthy of being offered to the public. The rest of the work is no longer in existence.

BOOK I.

INTRODUCTORY NOTE.

I wish to inquire whether, taking men as they are and laws as they can be made, it is possible to establish some just and certain rule of administration in civil affairs. In this investigation I shall always strive to reconcile what right permits with what interest prescribes, so that justice and utility may not be severed.

I enter upon this inquiry without demonstrating the importance of my subject. I shall be asked whether I am a prince or a legislator that I write on politics. I reply that I am not; and that it is for this very reason that I write on politics. If I were a prince or a legislator, I should not waste my time in saying what ought to be done; I should do it or remain silent.

Having been born a citizen of a free State,* and a member of the sovereign body, however feeble an influence my voice may have in public affairs, the right to vote upon them is sufficient to impose on me the duty of informing myself about them; and I feel happy, whenever I meditate on governments, always to discover in my researches new reasons for loving that of my own country.

---

* Rousseau, born at Geneva in 1712, was a CITIZEN, that is, a member of the sovereign body enjoying full political rights. He was proud of his membership of this close aristocracy. Rousseau believed that the SOCIAL CONTRACT would be well received in his native city on account of the praise bestowed on aristocratic government; but the work was burned, and in 1763 he renounced his citizenship.—ED.

CHAPTER I.

SUBJECT OF THE FIRST BOOK.

MAN is born free, and everywhere he is in chains. Many a one believes himself the master of others, and yet he is a greater slave than they. How has this change come about? I do not know. What can render it legitimate? I believe that I can settle this question.

If I considered only force and the results that proceed from it, I should say that so long as a people is compelled to obey and does obey, it does well; but that, so soon as it can shake off the yoke and does shake it off, it does better; for, if men recover their freedom by virtue of the same right by which it was taken away, either they are justified in resuming it, or there was no justification for depriving them of it. But the social order is a sacred right which serves as a foundation for all others. This right, however, does not come from nature. It is therefore based on conventions. The question is to know what these conventions are. Before coming to that, I must establish what I have just laid down.

CHAPTER II.

PRIMITIVE SOCIETIES.

THE earliest of all societies,* and the only natural one, is the family; yet children remain attached to their father only so long as they have need of him for their own preservation. As soon as this need ceases, the natural bond is dissolved. The children being freed from the obedience which they owed to their father, and the father from the cares which he owed to his children, become equally independent. If they remain united, it is no

---

* Rousseau's endeavor in chapters 2 to 4 is to establish that freeborn men have fallen into slavery.— ED.

(4)

longer naturally but voluntarily; and the family itself is kept together only by convention.

This common liberty is a consequence of man's nature. His first law is to attend to his own preservation, his first cares are those which he owes to himself; and as soon as he comes to years of discretion, being sole judge of the means adapted for his own preservation, he becomes his own master.

The family is, then, if you will, the primitive model of political societies; the chief is the analogue of the father, while the people represent the children; and all, being born free and equal, alienate their liberty only for their own advantage. The whole difference is that, in the family, the father's love for his children repays him for the care that he bestows upon them; while, in the State, the pleasure of ruling makes up for the chief's lack of love for his people.

Grotius* denies that all human authority is established for the benefit of the governed, and he cites slavery as an instance. His invariable mode of reasoning is to establish right by fact. A juster method might be employed, but none more favorable to tyrants.

It is doubtful, then, according to Grotius, whether the human race belongs to a hundred men, or whether these hundred men belong to the human race; and he appears throughout his book to incline to the former opinion, which is also that of Hobbes. In this way we have mankind divided like herds of cattle, each of which has a master, who looks after it in order to devour it.

Just as a herdsman is superior in nature to his herd, so chiefs, who are the herdsmen of men, are superior in nature to their people. Thus, according to Philo's account, the Emperor Caligula reasoned, inferring truly enough from this analogy that kings are gods, or that men are brutes.

The reasoning of Caligula is tantamount to that of Hobbes and Grotius. Aristotle, before them all, had

* Grotius (b. 1582, d. 1645). See Book I. 3 of his *De Jure Belli et Pacis*. Hallam (*Lit. of Europe*, III, 4) denies that Grotius confounded right with fact, though he concedes that the latter's theological prejudices led him to carry too far the principle of obedience to government.—ED.

likewise said that men are not naturally equal, but that some are born for slavery and others for dominion.

Aristotle was right, but he mistook the effect for the cause. Every man born in slavery is born for slavery; nothing is more certain. Slaves lose everything in their bonds, even the desire to escape from them; they love their servitude as the companions of Ulysses loved their brutishness. If, then, there are slaves by nature, it is because there have been slaves contrary to nature. The first slaves were made such by force; their cowardice kept them in bondage.

I have said nothing about King Adam nor about Emperor Noah, the father of three great monarchs who shared the universe, like the children of Saturn with whom they are supposed to be identical. I hope that my moderation will give satisfaction; for, as I am a direct descendant of one of these princes, and perhaps of the eldest branch, how do I know whether, by examination of titles, I might not find myself the lawful king of the human race? Be that as it may, it cannot be denied that Adam was sovereign of the world, as Robinson was of his island, so long as he was its sole inhabitant; and it was an agreeable feature of that empire that the monarch, secure on his throne, had nothing to fear from rebellions, or wars, or conspirators.

CHAPTER III.

THE RIGHT OF THE STRONGEST.

THE strongest man is never strong enough to be always master, unless he transforms his power into right, and obedience into duty. Hence the right of the strongest — a right apparently assumed in irony, and really established in principle. But will this phrase never be explained to us? Force is a physical power; I do not see what morality can result from its effects. To yield to force is an act of necessity, not of will; it is at most an act of prudence. In what sense can it be a duty?

Let us assume for a moment this pretended right. I say that nothing results from it but inexplicable non-sense; for if force constitutes right, the effect changes with the cause, and any force which overcomes the first succeeds to its rights. As soon as men can disobey with impunity, they may do so legitimately; and since the strongest is always in the right, the only thing is to act in such a way that one may be the strongest. But what sort of a right is it that perishes when force ceases? If it is necessary to obey by compulsion, there is no need to obey from duty; and if men are no longer forced to obey, obligation is at an end. We see then, that this word RIGHT adds nothing to force; it here means nothing at all.

Obey the powers that be. If that means, Yield to force, the precept is good but superfluous; I reply that it will never be violated. All power comes from God, I admit; but every disease comes from him too; does it follow that we are prohibited from calling in a physician? If a brigand should surprise me in the recesses of a wood, am I bound not only to give up my purse when forced, but am I also morally bound to do so when I might conceal it? For, in effect, the pistol which he holds is a superior force.

Let us agree, then, that might does not make right, and that we are bound to obey none but lawful authorities. Thus my original question ever recurs.

CHAPTER IV.

SLAVERY.

SINCE no man has any natural authority over his fellow-men, and since force is not the source of right, conventions remain as the basis of all lawful authority among men.*

* Having shown that political authority does not spring from the law of nature, and that force is not a source of right, Rousseau reverts to his statement in chapter I. that all lawful authority rests on conventions, and he now proceeds to consider what conventions are legitimate.—(ED.)

If an individual, says Grotius, can alienate his liberty and become the slave of a master, why should not a whole people be able to alienate theirs, and become subject to a king? In this there are many equivocal terms requiring explanation; but let us confine ourselves to the word ALIENATE. To alienate is to give or sell. Now, a man who becomes another's slave does not give himself; he sells himself at the very least for his subsistence. But why does a nation sell itself? So far from a king supplying his subjects with their subsistence, he draws his from them; and, according to Rabelais, a king does not live on a little. Do subjects, then, give up their persons on condition that their property also shall be taken? I do not see what is left for them to keep.

It will be said that the despot secures to his subjects civil peace. Be it so; but what do they gain by that, if the wars which his ambition brings upon them, together with his insatiable greed and the vexations of his administration, harass them more than their own dissensions would? What do they gain by it if this tranquillity is itself one of their miseries? Men live tranquilly also in dungeons; is that enough to make them contented there? The Greeks confined in the cave of the Cyclops lived peacefully until their turn came to be devoured.

To say that a man gives himself for nothing is to say what is absurd and inconceivable; such an act is illegitimate and invalid, for the simple reason that he who performs it is not in his right mind. To say the same thing of a whole nation is to suppose a nation of fools; and madness does not confer rights.

Even if each person could alienate himself, he could not alienate his children; they are born free men; their liberty belongs to them, and no one has a right to dispose of it except themselves. Before they have come to years of discretion, the father can, in their name, stipulate conditions for their preservation and welfare, but not surrender them irrevocably and unconditionally; for such a gift is contrary to the ends of nature, and exceeds the rights of paternity. In order, then, that an arbitrary government might be legitimate, it would be necessary that the people in each generation should have the option of accepting or rejecting it; but in that case such a government would no longer be arbitrary.

To renounce one's liberty is to renounce one's quality as a man, the rights and also the duties of humanity. For him who renounces everything there is no possible compensation. Such a renunciation is incompatible with man's nature, for to take away all freedom from his will is to take away all morality from his actions. In short, a convention which stipulates absolute authority on the one side and unlimited obedience on the other is vain and contradictory. Is it not clear that we are under no obligations whatsoever toward a man from whom we have a right to demand everything? And does not this single condition, without equivalent, without exchange, involve the nullity of the act? For what right would my slave have against me, since all that he has belongs to me? His rights being mine, this right of me against myself is a meaningless phrase.

Grotius and others derive from war another origin for the pretended right of slavery. The victor having, according to them, the right of slaying the vanquished, the latter may purchase his life at the cost of his freedom; an agreement so much the more legitimate that it turns to the advantage of both.

But it is manifest that this pretended right of slaying the vanquished in no way results from the state of war. Men are not naturally enemies, if only for the reason that, living in their primitive independence, they have no mutual relations sufficiently durable to constitute a state of peace or a state of war. It is the relation of things and not of men which constitutes war; and since the state of war cannot arise from simple personal relations, but only from real relations, private war—war between man and man—cannot exist either in the state of nature, where there is no settled ownership, or in the social state where everything is under the authority of the laws.

Private combats, duels, and encounters are acts which do not constitute a state of war; and with regard to the private wars authorized by the Establishments of Louis IX., king of France, and suspended by the Peace of God, they were abuses of the feudal government, an absurd system if ever there was one, contrary both to the principles of natural right and to all sound government.

War, then, is not a relation between man and man, but a relation between State and State, in which individuals are enemies only by accident, not as men, nor even as citizens, but as soldiers; not as members of the fatherland, but as its defenders. In short, each State can have as enemies only other States and not individual men, inasmuch as it is impossible to fix any true relation between things of different kinds.

This principle is also conformable to the established maxims of all ages and to the invariable practice of all civilized nations. Declarations of war are not so much warnings to the powers as to their subjects. The foreigner, whether king, or nation, or private person, that robs, slays, or detains subjects without declaring war against the government, is not an enemy, but a brigand. Even in open war, a just prince, while he rightly takes possession of all that belongs to the State in an enemy's country, respects the person and property of individuals; he respects the rights on which his own are based. The aim of war being the destruction of the hostile State, we have a right to slay its defenders so long as they have arms in their hands; but as soon as they lay them down and surrender, ceasing to be enemies or instruments of the enemy, they become again simply men, and no one has any further right over their lives. Sometimes it is possible to destroy the State without killing a single one of its members; but war confers no right except what is necessary to its end. These are not the principles of Grotius;* they are not based on the authority of poets, but are derived from the nature of things, and are founded on reason.

With regard to the right of conquest, it has no other foundation than the law of the strongest. If war does not confer on the victor the right of slaying the van-

*GROTIUS treats of declarations of war in *De Jure* III. 3. The reference to the authority of poets is a sneer at Grotius, borrowed probably from Hobbes (Review and Conclusion) and Locke I. 11. Mackintosh and Hallam have defended Grotius by pointing out that he quotes poets as witnesses, not as authorities.—ED.

quished, this right, which he does not possess, cannot be the foundation of a right to enslave them. If we have a right to slay an enemy only when it is impossible to enslave him, the right to enslave him is not derived from the right to kill him; it is, therefore, an iniquitous bargain to make him purchase his life, over which the victor has no right, at the cost of his liberty. In establishing the right of life and death upon the right of slavery, and the right of slavery upon the right of life and death, is it not manifest that one falls into a vicious circle?

Even if we grant this terrible right of killing everybody, I say that a slave made in war, or a conquered nation, is under no obligation at all to a master, except to obey him so far as compelled. In taking an equivalent for his life the victor has conferred no favor on the slave; instead of killing him unprofitably, he has destroyed him for his own advantage. Far, then, from having acquired over him any authority in addition to that of force, the state of war subsists between them as before, their relation even is the effect of it; and the exercise of the rights of war supposes that there is no treaty of peace. They have made a convention. Be it so; but this convention, far from terminating the state of war, supposes its continuance.

Thus, in whatever way we regard things, the right of slavery is invalid, not only because it is illegitimate, but because it is absurd and meaningless. These terms, SLAVERY and RIGHT, are contradictory and mutually exclusive. Whether addressed by a man to a man, or by a man to a nation, such a speech as this will always be equally foolish: "I make an agreement with you wholly at your expense and wholly for my benefit, and I shall observe it as long as I please, while you also shall observe it as long as I please."

CHAPTER V.

That It Is Always Necessary to Go Back to a First Convention.

IF I should concede all that I have so far refuted, those who favor despotism would be no farther advanced. There will always be a great difference between subduing a multitude and ruling a society. When isolated men, however numerous they may be, are subjected one after another to a single person, this seems to me only a case of master and slaves, not of a nation and its chief; they form, if you will, an aggregation, but not an association, for they have neither public property nor a body politic. Such a man, had he enslaved half the world, is never anything but an individual; his interest, separated from that of the rest, is never anything but a private interest. If he dies, his empire after him is left disconnected and disunited, as an oak dissolves and becomes a heap of ashes after the fire has consumed it.

A nation, says Grotius, can give itself to a king. According to Grotius, then, a nation is a nation before it gives itself to a king. This gift itself is a civil act, and presupposes a public resolution. Consequently, before examining the act by which a nation elects a king, it would be proper to examine the act by which a nation becomes a nation; for this act, being necessarily anterior to the other, is the real foundation of the society.

In fact, if there were no anterior convention, where, unless the election were unanimous, would be the obligation upon the minority to submit to the decision of the majority? And whence do the hundred who desire a master derive the right to vote on behalf of ten who do not desire one? The law of the plurality of votes is itself established by convention, and presupposes unanimity once at least.

(12)

CHAPTER VI.

THE SOCIAL PACT.

I ASSUME that men have reached a point at which the obstacles that endanger their preservation in the state of nature overcome by their resistance the forces which each individual can exert with a view to maintaining himself in that state. Then this primitive condition cannot longer subsist, and the human race would perish unless it changed its mode of existence.

Now as men cannot create any new forces, but only combine and direct those that exist, they have no other means of self-preservation than to form by aggregation a sum of forces which may overcome the resistance, to put them in action by a single motive power, and to make them work in concert.

This sum of forces can be produced only by the combination of many; but the strength and freedom of each man being the chief instruments of his preservation, how can he pledge them without injuring himself, and without neglecting the cares which he owes to himself? This difficulty, applied to my subject, may be expressed in these terms:—

"To find a form of association which may defend and protect with the whole force of the community the person and property of every associate, and by means of which, coalescing with all, may nevertheless obey only himself, and remain as free as before." Such is the fundamental problem of which the social contract furnishes the solution.

The clauses of this contract are so determined by the nature of the act that the slightest modification would render them vain and ineffectual; so that, although they have never perhaps been formally enunciated, they are everywhere the same, everywhere tacitly admitted and recognized, until, the social pact being violated, each man regains his original rights and recovers his natural liberty while losing the conventional liberty for which he renounced it.

(13)

These clauses, rightly understood, are reducible to one only, viz, the total alienation to the whole community of each associate with all his rights; for, in the first place, since each gives himself up entirely, the conditions are equal for all; and, the conditions being equal for all, no one has any interest in making them burdensome to others.

Further, the alienation being made without reserve, the union is as perfect as it can be, and an individual associate can no longer claim anything; for, if any rights were left to individuals, since there would be no common superior who could judge between them and the public, each, being on some point his own judge, would soon claim to be so on all; the state of nature would still subsist, and the association would necessarily become tyrannical or useless.

In short, each giving himself to all, gives himself to nobody; and as there is not one associate over whom we do not acquire the same rights which we concede to him over ourselves, we gain the equivalent of all that we lose, and more power to preserve what we have.

If, then, we set aside what is not of the essence of the social contract, we shall find that it is reducible to the following terms: " Each of us puts in common his person and his whole power under the supreme direction of the general will; and in return we receive every member as an indivisible part of the whole."

Forthwith, instead of the individual personalities of all the contracting parties, this act of association produces a moral and collective body, which is composed of as many members as the assembly has voices, and which receives from this same act its unity, its common self (*moi*), its life, and its will. This public person, which is thus formed by the union of all the individual members, formerly took the name of CITY, and now takes that of REPUBLIC or BODY POLITIC, which is called by its members STATE when it is passive, SOVEREIGN when it is active, POWER when it is compared to similar bodies. With regard to the asssociates, they take collectively the name of PEOPLE, and are called individually CITIZENS, as participating in the sovereign power, and SUBJECTS, as sub-

jected to the laws of the State. But these terms are
often confused and are mistaken one for another; it is
sufficient to know how to distinguish them when they
are used with complete precision.

CHAPTER VII.

THE SOVEREIGN.

WE SEE from this formula that the act of association
contains a reciprocal engagement between the public and
individuals, and that every individual, contracting so to
speak with himself, is engaged in a double relation, viz,
as a member of the sovereign toward individuals, and as
a member of the State toward the sovereign. But we
cannot apply here the maxim of civil law that no one is
bound by engagements made with himself; for there is
a great difference between being bound to oneself and
to a whole of which one forms part.

We must further observe that the public resolution
which can bind all subjects to the sovereign in consequence of the two different relations under which each
of them is regarded cannot, for a contrary reason, bind
the sovereign to itself; and that accordingly it is contrary to the nature of the body politic for the sovereign
to impose on itself a law which it cannot transgress. As
it can only be considered under one and the same relation, it is in the position of an individual contracting with
himself; whence we see that there is not, nor can be,
any kind of fundamental law binding upon the body of
the people, not even the social contract. This does not
imply that such a body cannot perfectly well enter into
engagements with others in what does not derogate from
this contract; for, with regard to foreigners, it becomes a
simple being, an individual.

But the body politic or sovereign, deriving its existence only from the sanctity of the contract, can never
bind itself, even to others, in anything that derogates
from the original act, such as alienation of some portion

of itself, or submission to another sovereign. To violate
the act by which it exists would be to annihilate itself;
and what is nothing produces nothing.

So soon as the multitude is thus united in one body,
it is impossible to injure one of the members without
attacking the body, still less to injure the body without
the members feeling the effects. Thus duty and interest
alike oblige the two contracting parties to give mutual
assistance; and the men themselves should seek to combine in this twofold relationship all the advantages which
are attendant on it.

Now, the sovereign, being formed only of the individuals that compose it, neither has nor can have any
interest contrary to theirs; consequently the sovereign
power needs no guarantee toward its subjects, because it
is impossible that the body should wish to injure all its
members; and we shall see hereafter that it can injure
no one as an individual. The sovereign, for the simple
reason that it is so, is always everything that it ought
to be.

But this is not the case as regards the relation of subjects to the sovereign, which, notwithstanding the common interest, would have no security for the performance of their engagements, unless it found means to
ensure their fidelity.

Indeed, every individual may, as a man, have a particular will contrary to, or divergent from, the general
will which he has as a citizen; his private interest may
prompt him quite differently from the common interest;
his absolute and naturally independent existence may
make him regard what he owes to the common cause as
a gratuitous contribution, the loss of which will be less
harmful to others than the payment of it will be burdensome to him; and, regarding the moral person that constitutes the State as an imaginary being because it is
not a man, he would be willing to enjoy the rights of a
citizen without being willing to fulfil the duties of a
subject. The progress of such injustice would bring
about the ruin of the body politic.

In order, then, that the social pact may not be a vain
formulary, it tacitly includes this engagement, which can

alone give force to the others, that whoever refuses to obey the general will shall be constrained to do so by the whole body; which means nothing else than that he shall be forced to be free; for such is the condition which, uniting every citizen to his native land, guarantees him from all personal dependence, a condition that insures the control and working of the political machine, and alone renders legitimate civil engagements, which, without it, would be absurd and tyrannical, and subject to the most enormous abuses.

CHAPTER VIII.

THE CIVIL STATE.

THE passage from the state of nature to the civil state produces in man a very remakable change, by substituting in his conduct justice for instinct, and by giving his actions the moral quality that they previously lacked. It is only when the voice of duty succeeds physical impulse, and law succeeds appetite, that man, who till then had regarded only himself, sees that he is obliged to act on other principles, and to consult his reason before listening to his inclinations. Although, in this state, he is deprived of many advantages that he derives from nature, he acquires equally great ones in return; his faculties are exercised and developed; his ideas are expanded; his feelings are ennobled; his whole soul is exalted to such a degree that, if the abuses of this new condition did not often degrade him below that from which he has emerged, he ought to bless without ceasing the happy moment that released him from it for ever, and transformed him from a stupid and ignorant animal into an intelligent being and a man.

Let us reduce this whole balance to terms easy to compare. What man loses by the social contract is his natural liberty and an unlimited right to anything which tempts him and which he is able to attain: what he gains is civil liberty and property in all that he possesses. In

order that we may not be mistaken about these com-
pensations, we must clearly distinguish natural liberty,
which is limited only by the powers of the individual,
from civil liberty, which is limited by the general will;
and possession, which is nothing but the result of force
or the right of first occupancy, from property, which
can be based only on a positive title.

Besides the preceding, we might add to the acquisitions
of the civil state moral freedom, which alone renders
man truly master of himself; for the impulse of mere
appetite is slavery, while obedience to a self-prescribed
law is liberty.   But I have already said too much on
this head, and the philosophical meaning of the term
LIBERTY does not belong to my present subject.

CHAPTER IX.

REAL PROPERTY.

EVERY member of the community at the moment of its
formation gives himself up to it, just as he actually is,
himself and all his powers, of which the property that
he possesses forms part.   By this act, possession does not
change its nature when it changes hands, and become
property in those of the sovereign; but, as the powers of
the State (*cité*) are incomparably greater than those of
an individual, public possession is also, in fact, more
secure and more irrevocable, without being more legitimate, at least in respect of foreigners; for the State, with
regard to its members, is owner of all their property by
the social contract, which, in the State, serves as the
basis of all rights; but with regard to other powers, it
is owner only by the right of first occupancy which it
derives from individuals.

The right of first occupancy, although more real than that
of the strongest, becomes a true right only after the establishment of that of property.   Every man has by nature
a right to all that is necessary to him; but the positive
act which makes him proprietor of certain property

excludes him from all the residue. His portion having been allotted, he ought to confine himself to it, and he has no further right to the undivided property. That is why the right of first occupancy, so weak in the state of nature, is respected by every member of a State. In this right men regard not so much what belongs to others as what does not belong to themselves.

In order to legalize the right of first occupancy over any domain whatsoever, the following conditions are, in general, necessary: first, the land must not yet be inhabited by any one; secondly, a man must occupy only the area required for his subsistence; thirdly, he must take possession of it, not by an empty ceremony, but by labor and cultivation, the only mark of ownership which, in default of legal title, ought to be respected by others.

Indeed, if we accord the right of first occupancy to necessity and labor, do we not extend it as far as it can go? Is it impossible to assign limits to this right? Will the mere setting foot on common ground be sufficient to give an immediate claim to the ownership of it? Will the power of driving away other men from it for a moment suffice to deprive them for ever of the right of returning to it? How can a man or a people take possession of an immense territory and rob the whole human race of it except by a punishable usurpation, since other men are deprived of the place of residence and the sustenance which nature gives to them in common. When Nuñez Balboa on the seashore took possession of the Pacific Ocean and of the whole of South America in the name of the crown of Castile, was this sufficient to dispossess all the inhabitants, and exclude from it all the princes in the world? On this supposition such ceremonies might have been multiplied vainly enough; and the Catholic king in his cabinet might, by a single stroke, have taken possession of the whole world, only cutting off afterward from his empire what was previously occupied by other princes.

We perceive how the lands of individuals, united and contiguous, become public territory, and how the right of sovereignty, extending itself from the subjects to the land which they occupy, becomes at once real and personal; which places the possessors in greater dependence, and

makes their own powers a guarantee for their fidelity—
an advantage which ancient monarchs do not appear to
have clearly perceived, for, calling themselves only kings
of the Persians or Scythians or Macedonians, they seem
to have regarded themselves as chiefs of men rather than
as owners of countries. Monarchs of to-day call themselves more cleverly kings of France, Spain, England,
etc.; in thus holding the land they are quite sure of
holding its inhabitants.

The peculiarity of this alienation is that the community,
in receiving the property of individuals, so far from robbing them of it, only assures them lawful possession,
and changes usurpation into true right, enjoyment into
ownership. Also, the possessors being considered as
depositaries of the public property, and their rights being
respected by all the members of the State, as well as
maintained by all its power against foreigners, they have,
as it were, by a transfer advantageous to the public and
still more to themselves, acquired all that they have given
up—a paradox which is easily explained by distinguishing between the rights which the sovereign and the proprietor have over the same property, as we shall see
hereafter.

It may also happen that men begin to unite before
they possess anything, and that afterward occupying territory sufficient for all, they enjoy it in common, or share
it among themselves, either equally or in proportions
fixed by the sovereign. In whatever way this acquisition
is made, the right which every individual has over his
own property is always subordinate to the right which the
community has over all; otherwise there would be no
stability in the social union, and no real force in the
exercise of sovereignty.

I shall close this chapter and this book with a remark
which ought to serve as a basis for the whole social system; it is that instead of destroying natural equality, the
fundamental pact, on the contrary, substitutes a moral
and lawful equality for the physical inequality which
nature imposed upon men, so that, although unequal in
strength or intellect, they all become equal by convention and legal right.

BOOK II.

CHAPTER I.

THAT SOVEREIGNTY IS INALIENABLE.

THE first and most important consequence of the principles above established is that the general will alone can direct the forces of the State according to the object of its institution, which is the common good; for if the opposition of private interests has rendered necessary the establishment of societies, the agreement of these same interests has rendered it possible. That which is common to these different interests forms the social bond; and unless there were some point in which all interests agree, no society could exist. Now, it is solely with regard to this common interest that the society should be governed.

I say, then, that sovereignty, being nothing but the exercise of the general will, can never be alienated, and that the sovereign power, which is only a collective being, can be represented by itself alone; power indeed can be transmitted, but not will.

In fact, if it is not impossible that a particular will should agree on some point with the general will, it is at least impossible that this agreement should be lasting and constant; for the particular will naturally tends to preferences, and the general will to equality. It is still more impossible to have a security for this agreement; even though it should always exist, it would not be a result of art, but of chance. The sovereign may indeed say: " I will now what a certain man wills, or at least what he says that he wills "; but he cannot say: " What that man wills to-morrow, I shall also will," since it is absurd that the will should bind itself as regards the future, and since it is not incumbent on any will to

consent to anything contrary to the welfare of the being
that wills. If then, the nation simply promises to obey,
it dissolves itself by that act and loses its character as a
people; the moment there is a master, there is no longer
a sovereign, and forthwith the body politic is destroyed.

This does not imply that the orders of the chiefs cannot
pass for decisions of the general will, so long as the sovereign, free to oppose them, refrains from doing so. In
such a case the consent of the people should be inferred
from the universal silence. This will be explained at
greater length.

CHAPTER II.

That Sovereignty is Indivisible.

For the same reason that sovereignty is inalienable it
is indivisible; for the will is either general, or it is not;
it is either that of the body of the people, or that of
only a portion. In the first case, this declared will is an
act of sovereignty and constitutes law; in the second
case, it is only a particular will, or an act of magistracy
—it is at most a decree.

But our publicists, being unable to divide sovereignty
in its principle, divide it in its object. They divide it
into force and will, into legislative power and executive
power; into rights of taxation, of justice, and of war;
into internal administration and power of treating with
foreigners — sometimes confounding all these departments,
and sometimes separating them. They make the sovereign a fantastic being, formed of connected parts; it is
as if they composed a man of several bodies, one with
eyes, another with arms, another with feet, and nothing
else. The Japanese conjurers, it is said, cut up a child
before the eyes of the spectators; then, throwing all its
limbs into the air, they make the child come down again
alive and whole. Such almost are the juggler's tricks of
our publicists; after dismembering the social body by a
deception worthy of the fair, they recombine its parts,
nobody knows how.

This error arises from their not having formed exact notions about the sovereign authority, and from their taking as parts of this authority what are only emanations from it. Thus, for .example, the acts of declaring war and making peace have been regarded as acts of sovereignty, which is not the case, since neither of them is a law, but only an application of the law, a particular act which determines the case of the law, as will be clearly seen when the idea attached to the word LAW is fixed.

By following out the other divisions in the same way it would be found that, whenever the sovereignty appears divided, we are mistaken in our supposition; and that the rights which are taken as parts of that sovereignty are all subordinate to it, and always suppose supreme wills of which these rights are merely executive.

It would be impossible to describe the great obscurity in which this want of precision has involved the conclusions of writers on the subject of political right when they have endeavored to decide upon the respective rights of kings and peoples on the principles that they had established. Every one can see in chapters III. and IV. of the first book of Grotius, how that learned man and his translator Barbeyrac became entangled and embarrassed in their sophisms, for fear of saying too much or not saying enough according to their views, and so offending the interests that they had to conciliate. Grotius, having taken refuge in France through discontent with his own country, and wishing to pay court to Louis XIII., to whom his book is dedicated, spares no pains to despoil the people of all their rights, and, in the most artful manner, bestow them on kings. This also would clearly have been the inclination of Barbeyrac, who dedicated his translation to the king of England, George I. But unfortunately the expulsion of James II., which he calls an abdication, forced him to be reserved and to equivocate and evade in order not to make William appear a usurper. If these two writers had adopted true principles, all difficulties would have been removed, and they would have been always consistent; but they would have spoken the truth with regret, and would have paid court only to the people. Truth, however, does not lead to fortune, and the people confer neither embassies, nor professorships, nor pensions.

CHAPTER III.

WHETHER THE GENERAL WILL CAN ERR.

IT FOLLOWS from what precedes that the general will is always right and always tends to the public advantage; but it does not follow that the resolutions of the people have always the same rectitude. Men always desire their own good, but do not always discern it; the people are never corrupted, though often deceived, and it is only then that they seem to will what is evil.

There is often a great deal of difference between the will of all and the general will; the latter regards only the common interest, while the former has regard to private interests, and is merely a sum of particular wills; but take away from these same wills the pluses and minuses which cancel one another, and the general will remains as the sum of the differences.

If the people come to a resolution when adequately informed and without any communication among the citizens, the general will would always result from the great number of slight differences, and the resolution would always be good. But when factions, partial associations, are formed to the detriment of the whole society, the will of each of these associations becomes general with reference to its members, and particular with reference to the State; it may then be said that there are no longer as many voters as there are men, but only as many voters as there are associations. The differences become less numerous and yield a less general result. Lastly, when one of these associations becomes so great that it predominates over all the rest, you no longer have as the result a sum of small differences, but a single difference; there is then no longer a general will, and the opinion which prevails is only a particular opinion.

It is important, then, in order to have a clear declaration of the general will, that there should be no partial association in the State, and that every citizen should express only his own opinion.* Such was the unique and sublime institution of the great Lycurgus. But if there are partial associations, it is necessary to multiply their number and prevent inequality, as Solon, Numa, and Servius did. These are the only proper precautions for insuring that the general will may always be enlightened, and that the people may not be deceived.

CHAPTER IV.

The Limits of the Sovereign Power.

If the State or city is nothing but a moral person, the life of which consists in the union of its members, and if the most important of its cares is that of self-preservation, it needs a universal and compulsive force to move and dispose every part in the manner most expedient for the whole. As nature gives every man an absolute power over all his limbs, the social pact gives the body politic an absolute power over all its members; and it is this same power which, when directed by the general will, bears, as I said, the name of sovereignty.

But besides the public person, we have to consider the private persons who compose it, and whose life and liberty are naturally independent of it. The question, then, is to distinguish clearly between the respective rights of the citizens and of the sovereign,† as well as

* "It is true," says Machiavelli, "that some divisions injure the State, while some are beneficial to it; those are injurious to it which are accompanied by cabals and factions; those assist it which are maintained without cabals, without factions. Since, therefore, no founder of a State can provide against enmities in it, he ought at least to provide that there shall be no cabals." ("History of Florence," Book VII.).

† Attentive readers, do not, I beg you, hastily charge me with contradiction here. I could not avoid it in terms owing to the poverty of the language, but wait.

between the duties which the former have to fulfil in their capacity as subjects and the natural rights which they ought to enjoy in their character as men.

It is admitted that whatever part of his power, property, and liberty each one alienates by the social compact is only that part of the whole of which the use is important to the community; but we must also admit that the sovereign alone is judge of what is important.

All the services that a citizen can render to the State he owes to it as soon as the sovereign demands them; but the sovereign on its part, cannot impose on its subjects any burden which is useless to the community; it cannot even wish to do so, for, by the law of reason, just as by the law of nature, nothing is done without a cause.

The engagements which bind us to the social body are obligatory only because they are mutual; and their nature is such that in fulfilling them we cannot work for others without also working for ourselves. Why is the general will always right, and why do all invariably desire the prosperity of each, unless it is because there is no one but appropriates to himself this word EACH and thinks of himself in voting on behalf of all? This proves that equality of rights and the notion of justice that it produces are derived from the preference which each gives to himself, and consequently from man's nature; that the general will, to be truly such, should be so in its object as well as in its essence; that it ought to proceed from all in order to be applicable to all; and that it loses its natural rectitude when it tends to some individual and determinate object, because in that case, judging of what is unknown to us, we have no true principle of equity to guide us.

Indeed, so soon as a particular fact or right is in question with regard to a point which has not been regulated by an anterior general convention, the matter becomes contentious; it is a process in which the private persons interested are one of the parties and the public the other, but in which I perceive neither the law which must be followed, nor the judge who should decide. It would be ridiculous in such a case to wish to refer the matter for an express decision of the general will, which can be nothing but the decision of one of the parties, and which, consequently, is for the other party only a will that is foreign, partial, and inclined on such an occasion to injustice as well as liable to error. Therefore, just as a particular will cannot represent the general will, the general will in turn changes its nature when it has a particular end, and cannot, as general, decide about either a person or a fact. When the people of Athens, for instance, elected or deposed their chiefs, decreed honors to one, imposed penalties on another, and by multitudes of particular decrees exercised indiscriminately all the functions of government, the people no longer had any general will properly so called; they no longer acted as a sovereign power, but as magistrates. This will appear contrary to common ideas, but I must be allowed time to expound my own.

From this we must understand that what generalizes the will is not so much the number of voices as the common interest which unites them; for, under this system, each necessarily submits to the conditions which he imposes on others — an admirable union of interest and justice, which gives to the deliberations of the community a spirit of equity that seems to disappear in the discussion of any private affair, for want of a common interest to unite and identify the ruling principle of the judge with that of the party.

By whatever path we return to our principle we always arrive at the same conclusion, viz, that the social compact establishes among the citizens such an equality that they all pledge themselves under the same conditions and ought all to enjoy the same rights. Thus, by the nature of the compact, every act of sovereignty, that is, every authentic act of the general will, binds or favors equally all the citizens; so that the sovereign knows only the body of the nation, and distinguishes none of those that compose it.

What, then, is an act of sovereignty properly so called ? It is not an agreement between a superior and an inferior, but an agreement of the body with each of its members; a lawful agreement, because it has the social contract as its foundation; equitable, because it is common to all; useful, because it can have no other object than the general welfare; and stable, because it has the public force and the supreme power as a guarantee. So long as the subjects submit only to such conventions, they obey no one, but simply their own will; and to ask how far the respective rights of the sovereign and citizens extend is to ask up to what point the latter can make engagements among themselves, each with all and all with each.

Thus we see that the sovereign power, wholly absolute, wholly sacred, and wholly inviolable as it is, does not, and cannot, pass the limits of general conventions, and that every man can fully dispose of what is left to him, of his property and liberty by these conventions; so that the sovereign never has a right to burden one subject more than another, because then the matter becomes particular and his power is no longer competent.

These distinctions once admitted, so untrue is it that in the social contract there is on the part of individuals any real renunciation, that their situation, as a result of this contract, is in reality preferable to what it was before, and that, instead of an alienation, they have only made an advantageous exchange of an uncertain and precarious mode of existence for a better and more assured one, of natural independence for liberty, of the power to injure others for their own safety, and of their strength, which others might overcome, for a right which the social union renders inviolable. Their lives, also, which they have devoted to the State, are continually protected by it; and in exposing their lives for its defense, what do they do but restore what they have received from it? What do they do but what they would do more frequently and with more risk in the state of nature, when, engaging in inevitable struggles, they would defend at the peril of their lives their means of preservation? All have to fight for their country in case of need, it is true; but then no one ever has to fight for himself. Do we not gain, moreover, by incurring, for what insures our safety, a part of the risks that we should have to incur for ourselves individually, as soon as we were deprived of it?

CHAPTER V.

The Right of Life and Death.

It MAY be asked how individuals who have no right to dispose of their own lives can transmit to the sovereign this right which they do not possess. The question appears hard to solve only because it is badly stated. Every man has a right to risk his own life in order to preserve it. Has it ever been said that one who throws himself out of a window to escape from a fire is guilty of suicide? Has this crime, indeed, ever been imputed to a man who perishes in a storm, although, on embarking, he was not ignorant of the danger?

The social treaty has as its end the preservation of the contracting parties. He who desires the end desires also the means, and some risks, even some losses, are inseparable from these means. He who is willing to preserve his life at the expense of others ought also to give it up for them when necessary. Now, the citizen is not a judge of the peril to which the law requires that he should expose himself; and when the prince has said to him: "It is expedient for the State that you should die," he ought to die, since it is only on this condition that he has lived in security up to that time, and since his life is no longer merely a gift of nature, but a conditional gift of the State.

The penalty of death inflicted on criminals may be regarded almost from the same point of view; it is in order not to be the victim of an assassin that a man consents to die if he becomes one. In this treaty, far from disposing of his own life, he thinks only of securing it, and it is not to be supposed that any of the contracting parties contemplates at the time being hanged.

Moreover, every evil-doer who attacks social rights becomes by his crimes a rebel and a traitor to his country; by violating its laws he ceases to be a member of it, and even makes war upon it. Then the preservation of the State is incompatible with his own — one of the two must perish; and when a guilty man is executed, it is less as a citizen than as an enemy. The proceedings and the judgment are the proofs and the declaration that he has broken the social treaty, and consequently that he is no longer a member of the State. Now, as he has acknowledged himself to be such, at least by his residence, he ought to be cut off from it by exile as a violator of the compact, or by death as a public enemy; for such an enemy is not a moral person, he is simply a man; and this is a case in which the right of war is to slay the vanquished.

But, it will be said, the condemnation of a criminal is a particular act. Granted; but this condemnation does not belong to the sovereign; it is a right which that power can confer, though itself unable to exercise it. All my ideas are connected, but I could not expound them all at once.

Again, the frequency of capital punishments is always a sign of weakness or indolence in the government. There is no man so worthless that he cannot be made good for something. We have a right to kill, even for example's sake, only those who cannot be preserved without danger.

As regards the right to pardon or to exempt a guilty man from the penalty imposed by the law and inflicted by the judge, it belongs only to a power which is above both the judge and the law, that is to say, the sovereign; still its right in this is not very plain, and the occasions for exercising it are very rare. In a well-governed State there are few punishments, not because many pardons are granted, but because there are few criminals; the multitude of crimes insures impunity when the State is decaying. Under the Roman Republic neither the Senate nor the consuls attempted to grant pardons; the people even did not grant any, although they sometimes revoked their own judgments. Frequent pardons proclaim that crimes will soon need them no longer, and every one sees to what that leads. But I feel my heart murmuring and restraining my pen; let us leave these questions to be discussed by the just man who has not erred, and who never needed pardon himself.

CHAPTER VI.

THE LAW.

BY THE social compact we have given existence and life to the body politic; the question now is to endow it with movement, and will by legislation. For the original act by which this body is formed and consolidated determines nothing in addition as to what it must do for its own preservation.

What is right and conformable to order is such by the nature of things, and independently of human conventions. All justice comes from God, he alone is the source of it: but could we receive it direct from so lofty a source, we should need neither government nor laws. Without doubt there is a universal justice emanating from reason alone; but this justice, in order to be admitted among us, should be reciprocal. Regarding things from a human standpoint, the laws of justice are inoperative among men for want of a natural sanction; they only bring good to the wicked and evil to the just when the latter observe them with every one, and no one observes them in return. Conventions and laws, then, are necessary to couple rights with duties and apply justice to its object. In the state of nature, where everything is in common, I owe nothing to those to whom I have promised nothing; I recognize as belonging to others only what is useless to me. This is not the case in the civil state, in which all rights are determined by law.

But then, finally, what is a law? So long as men are content to attach to this word only metaphysical ideas, they will continue to argue without being understood; and when they have stated what a law of nature is, they will know no better what a law of the State is.

I have already said that there is no general will with reference to a particular object. In fact, this particular object is either in the State or outside of it. If it is outside of the State, a will which is foreign to it is not general in relation to it; and if it is within the State, it forms part of it; then there is formed between the whole and its part a relation which makes of it two separate beings, of which the part is one, and the whole, less this same part, is the other. But the whole, less one part, is not the whole, and so long as the relation subsists, there is no longer any whole, but two unequal parts; whence it follows that the will of the one is no longer general in relation to the other.

But when the whole people decree concerning the whole people, they consider themselves alone; and if a relation is then constituted it is between the whole object under one point of view and the whole object under another point of view, without any division at all. Then the matter respecting which they decree is general like the will that decrees. It is this act that I call a law.

When I say that the object of the laws is always general, I mean that the law considers subjects collectively, and actions as abstract, never a man as an individual nor a particular action. Thus the law may indeed decree that there shall be privileges, but cannot confer them on any person by name; the law can create several classes of citizens, and even assign the qualifications which shall entitle them to rank in these classes, but it cannot nominate such and such persons to be admitted to them; it can establish a royal government and a hereditary succession, but cannot elect a king or appoint a royal family; in a word, no function which has reference to an individual object appertains to the legislative power.

From this standpoint we see immediately that it is no longer necessary to ask whose office it is to make laws, since they are acts of the general will; nor whether the prince is above the laws, since he is a member of the State; nor whether the law can be unjust, since no one is unjust to himself; nor how we are free and yet subject to the laws, since the laws are only registers of our wills.

We see, further, that since the law combines the universality of the will with the universality of the object, whatever any man prescribes on his own authority is not a law; and whatever the sovereign itself prescribes respecting a particular object is not a law, but a decree, not an act of sovereignty, but of magistracy.

I therefore call any State a republic which is governed

by laws, under whatever form of administration it may be; for then only does the public interest predominate and the commonwealth count for something. Every legitimate government is republican;* I will explain hereafter what government is.

Laws are properly only the conditions of civil association. The people, being subjected to the laws, should be the authors of them; it concerns only the associates to determine the conditions of association. But how will they be determined? Will it be by a common agreement, by a sudden inspiration? Has the body politic an organ for expressing its will? Who will give it the foresight necessary to frame its acts and publish them at the outset? Or how shall it declare them in the hour of need? How would a blind multitude, which often knows not what it wishes because it rarely knows what is good for it, execute of itself an enterprise so great, so difficult, as a system of legislation? Of themselves, the people always desire what is good, but do not always discern it. The general will is always right, but the judgment which guides it is not always enlightened. It must be made to see objects as they are, sometimes as they ought to appear; it must be shown the good path that it is seeking, and guarded from the seduction of private interests; it must be made to observe closely times and places, and to balance the attraction of immediate and palpable advantages against the danger of remote and concealed evils. Individuals see the good which they reject; the public desire the good which they do not see. All alike have need of guides. The former must be compelled to conform their wills to their reason; the people must be taught to know what they require. Then from the public enlightenment results the union of the understanding and the will in the social body; and from that the close co-operation of the parts, and, lastly, the maximum power of the whole. Hence arises the need of a legislator.

---

* I do not mean by this word an aristocracy or democracy only, but in general any government directed by the general will, which is the law. To be legitimate, the government must not be combined with the sovereign power, but must be its minister; then monarchy itself is a republic. This will be made clear in the next book.

3

CHAPTER VII.

THE LEGISLATOR.

IN ORDER to discover the rules of association that are most suitable to nations, a superior intelligence would be necessary who could see all the passions of men without experiencing any of them; who would have no affinity with our nature and yet know it thoroughly; whose happiness would not depend on us, and who would nevertheless be quite willing to interest himself in ours; and, lastly, one who, storing up for himself with the progress of time a far-off glory in the future, could labor in one age and enjoy in another. Gods would be necessary to give laws to men.

The same argument that Caligula adduced as to fact, Plato put forward with regard to right, in order to give an idea of the civil or royal man whom he is in quest of in his work, the "Statesman." But if it is true that a great prince is a rare man, what will a great legislator be? The first has only to follow the model which the other has to frame. The latter is the mechanician who invents the machine, the former is only the workman who puts it in readiness and works it. "In the birth of societies," says Montesquieu, "it is the chiefs of the republics who frame the institutions, and afterward it is the institutions which mold the chiefs of the republics."

He who dares undertake to give institutions to a nation ought to feel himself capable, as it were, of changing human nature; of transforming every individual, who in himself is a complete and independent whole, into part of a greater whole, from which he receives in some manner his life and his being; of altering man's constitution in order to strengthen it; of substituting a social and moral existence for the independent and physical existence which we have all received from nature. In a word, it is necessary to deprive man of his native powers in order to endow him with some which are alien to him, and of which he cannot make use without the aid

(34)

of other people. The more thoroughly those natural powers are deadened and destroyed, the greater and more durable are the acquired powers, the more solid and perfect also are the institutions; so that if every citizen is nothing, and can be nothing, except in combination with all the rest, and if the force acquired by the whole be equal or superior to the sum of the natural forces of all the individuals, we may say that legislation is at the highest point of perfection which it can attain.

The legislator is in all respects an extraordinary man in the State. If he ought to be so by his genius, he is not less so by his office. It is not magistracy nor sovereignty. This office, which constitutes the republic, does not enter into its constitution; it is a special and superior office, having nothing in common with human government; for if he who rules men ought not to control legislation, he who controls legislation ought not to rule men; otherwise his laws, being ministers of his passions, would often serve only to perpetrate his acts of injustice; he would never be able to prevent private interests from corrupting the sacredness of his work.

When Lycurgus gave laws to his country, he began by abdicating his royalty. It was the practice of the majority of the Greek towns to intrust to foreigners the framing of their laws. The modern republics of Italy often imitated this usage; that of Geneva did the same and found it advantageous. Rome, at her most glorious epoch, saw all the crimes of tyranny spring up in her bosom, and saw herself on the verge of destruction, though uniting in the same hands legislative authority and sovereign power.

Yet the Decemvirs themselves never arrogated the right to pass any law on their sole authority. Nothing that we propose to you, they said to the people, can pass into law without your consent. Romans, be yourselves the authors of the laws which are to secure your happiness.

He who frames laws, then, has, or ought to have, no legislative right, and the people themselves cannot, even if they wished, divest themselves of this incommunicable right, because, according to the fundamental compact, it is only the general will that binds individuals, and we can never be sure that a particular will is comformable to the general will until it has been submitted to the free votes of the people. I have said this already, but it is not useless to repeat it.

Thus we find simultaneously in the work of legislation two things that seem incompatible — an enterprise surpassing human powers, and, to execute it, an authority that is a mere nothing.

Another difficulty deserves attention. Wise men who want to speak to the vulgar in their own language instead of in a popular way will not be understood. Now, there are a thousand kinds of ideas which it is impossible to translate into the language of the people. Views very general and objects very remote are alike beyond its reach; and each individual, approving of no other plan of government than that which promotes his own interests, does not readily perceive the benefits that he is to derive from the continual deprivations which good laws impose. In order that a newly formed nation might approve sound maxims of politics and observe the fundamental rules of state policy, it would be necessary that the effect should become the cause; that the social spirit, which should be the work of the institution, should preside over the institution itself, and that men should be, prior to the laws, what they ought to become by means of them. Since, then, the legislator cannot employ either force or reasoning, he must needs have recourse to an authority of a different order, which can compel without violence and persuade without convincing.

It is this which in all ages has constrained the founders of nations to resort to the intervention of heaven, and to give the gods the credit for their own wisdom, in order that the nations, subjected to the laws of the State as to those of nature, and recognizing the same power in the formation of man and in that of the State, might obey willingly, and bear submissively the yoke of the public welfare.

The legislator puts into the mouths of the immortals that sublime reason which soars beyond the reach of common men, in order that he may win over by divine

authority those whom human prudence could not move.
But it does not belong to every man to make the gods
his oracles, nor to be believed when he proclaims himself their interpreter. The great soul of the legislator is
the real miracle which must give proof of his mission.
Any man can engrave tables of stone, or bribe an oracle, or pretend secret intercourse with some divinity, or
train a bird to speak in his ear, or find some other clumsy
means to impose on the people. He who is acquainted
with such means only will perchance be able to assemble
a crowd of foolish persons; but he will never found an
empire, and his extravagant work will speedily perish
with him. Empty deceptions form but a transient bond;
it is only wisdom that makes it lasting. The Jewish law,
which still endures, and that of the child of Ishmael,
which for ten centuries has ruled half the world, still
bear witness to-day to the great men who dictated them;
and while proud philosophy or blind party spirit sees in
them nothing but fortunate impostors, the true statesman admires in their systems the great and powerful
genius which directs durable institutions.

It is not necessary from all this to infer with Warburton that politics and religion have among us a common
aim, but only that, in the origin of nations, one serves
as an instrument of the other.

CHAPTER VIII.

THE PEOPLE.

As AN architect, before erecting a large edifice, examines and tests the soil in order to see whether it can
support the weight, so a wise lawgiver does not begin
by drawing up laws that are good in themselves, but
considers first whether the people for whom he designs
them are fit to endure them. It is on this account that
Plato refused to legislate for the Arcadians and Cyrenians,
knowing that these two peoples were rich and could not
tolerate equality; and it is on this account that good laws

and worthless men were to be found in Crete, for Minos had only disciplined a people steeped in vice.

A thousand nations that have flourished on the earth could never have borne good laws; and even those that might have done so could have succeeded for only a very short period of their whole duration. The majority of nations, as well as of men, are tractable only in their youth; they become incorrigible as they grow old. When once customs are established and prejudices have taken root, it is a perilous and futile enterprise to try and reform them; for the people cannot even endure that their evils should be touched with a view to their removal, like those stupid and cowardly patients that shudder at the sight of a physician.

But just as some diseases unhinge men's minds and deprive them of all remembrance of the past, so we sometimes find, during the existence of States, epochs of violence, in which revolutions produce an influence upon nations such as certain crises produce upon individuals, in which horror of the past supplies the place of forgetfulness, and in which the State, inflamed by civil wars, springs forth so to speak from its ashes, and regains the vigor of youth in issuing from the arms of death. Such was Sparta in the time of Lycurgus, such was Rome after the Tarquins, and such among us moderns were Holland and Switzerland after the expulsion of their tyrants.

But these events are rare; they are exceptions, the explanation of which is always found in the particular constitution of the excepted State. They could not even happen twice with the same nation; for it may render itself free so long as it is merely barbarous, but can no longer do so when the resources of the State are exhausted. Then commotions may destroy it without revolutions being able to restore it, and as soon as its chains are broken, it falls in pieces and ceases to exist; henceforward it requires a master and not a deliverer. Free nations, remember this maxim: " Liberty may be acquired but never recovered. "

Youth is not infancy. There is for nations as for men a period of youth, or, if you will, of maturity, which they must await before they are subjected to laws; but it is not always easy to discern when a people is mature, and if the time is anticipated, the labor is abortive. One nation is governable from its origin, another is not so at the end of ten centuries. The Russians will never be really civilized, because they have been civilized too early. Peter had an imitative genius; he had not the true genius that creates and produces anything from nothing. Some of his measures were beneficial, but the majority were ill-timed. He saw that his people were barbarous, but he did not see that they were unripe for civilization; he wished to civilize them, when it was necessary only to discipline them. He wished to produce at once Germans or Englishmen when he should have begun by making Russians; he prevented his subjects from ever becoming what they might have been, by persuading them that they were what they were not. It is in this way that a French tutor trains his pupil to shine for a moment in childhood, and then to be forever a nonentity. The Russian Empire will desire to subjugate Europe, and will itself be subjugated. The Tartars, its subjects or neighbors, will become its masters and ours. This revolution appears to me inevitable. All the kings of Europe are working in concert to accelerate it.

CHAPTER IX.

THE PEOPLE (Continued).

As NATURE has set limits to the stature of a properly formed man, outside which it produces only giants and dwarfs; so likewise, with regard to the best constitution of a State, there are limits to its possible extent so that it may be neither too great to enable it to be well governed, nor too small to enable it to maintain itself single-handed. There is in every body politic a maximum of force which it cannot exceed, and which is often diminished as the State is aggrandized. The more the social bond is extended, the more it is weakened; and, in general, a small State is proportionally stronger than a large one.

A thousand reasons demonstrate the truth of this maxim. In the first place, administration becomes more difficult at great distances, as a weight becomes heavier at the end of a longer lever. It also becomes more burdensome in proportion as its parts are multiplied; for every town has first its own administration, for which the people pay; every district has its administration, still paid for by the people; next, every province, then the superior governments, the satrapies, the vice-royalties, which must be paid for more dearly as we ascend, and always at the cost of the unfortunate people; lastly comes the supreme administration, which overwhelms everything. So many additional burdens perpetually exhaust the subjects; and far from being better governed by all these different orders, they are much worse governed than if they had but a single superior. Meanwhile, hardly any resources remain for cases of emergency; and when it is necessary to have recourse to them the State trembles on the brink of ruin.

Nor is this all; not only has the government less vigor and activity in enforcing observance of the laws, in putting a stop to vexations, in reforming abuses, and in forestalling seditious enterprises which may be entered upon in distant places, but the people have less affection for their chiefs whom they never see, for their country, which is in their eyes like the world, and for their fellow-citizens, most of whom are strangers to them. The same laws cannot be suitable to so many different provinces, which have different customs and different climates, and cannot tolerate the same form of government. Different laws beget only trouble and confusion among the nations which, living under the same chiefs and in constant communication, mingle or intermarry with one another, and, when subjected to other usages, never know whether their patrimony is really theirs. Talents are hidden, virtues ignored, vices unpunished, in that multitude of men, unknown to one another, whom the seat of the supreme administration gathers together in one place. The chiefs, overwhelmed with business, see nothing themselves; clerks rule the State. In a word, the measures that must be taken to maintain the general authority, which so many officers at a distance wish to evade or impose upon, absorb all the public attention; no regard for the welfare of the people remains, and scarcely any for their defense in time of need; and thus a body too huge for its constitution sinks and perishes, crushed by its own weight.

On the other hand, the State must secure a certain foundation, that it may possess stability and resist the shocks which it will infallibly experience, as well as sustain the efforts which it will be forced to make in order to maintain itself; for all nations have a kind of centrifugal force, by which they continually act one against another, and tend to aggrandize themselves at the expense of their neighbors, like the vortices of Descartes. Thus the weak are in danger of being quickly swallowed up, and none can preserve itself long except by putting itself in a kind of equilibrium with all, which renders the compression almost equal everywhere.

Hence we see that there are reasons for expansion and reasons for contraction; and it is not the least of a statesman's talents to find the proportion between the two which is most advantageous for the preservation of the State. We may say, in general, that the former, being only external and relative, ought to be subordinated to the others, which are internal and absolute. A healthy and strong constitution is the first thing to be sought; and we should rely more on the vigor that springs from a good government than on the resources furnished by an extensive territory.

States have, however, been constituted in such a way that the necessity of making conquests entered into their very constitution, and in order to maintain themselves they were forced to enlarge themselves continually. Perhaps they rejoiced greatly at this happy necessity, which nevertheless revealed to them, with the limit of their greatness, the inevitable moment of their fall.

CHAPTER X.

The People (Continued.)

A BODY politic may be measured in two ways, viz, by the extent of its territory, and by the number of its people; and there is between these two modes of measurement a suitable relation according to which the State may be assigned its true dimensions. It is the men that constitute the State, and it is the soil that sustains the men; the due relation, then, is that the land should suffice for the maintenance of its inhabitants, and that there should be as many inhabitants as the land can sustain. In this proportion is found the maximum power of a given number of people; for if there is too much land, the care of it is burdensome, the cultivation inadequate, and the produce superfluous, and this is the proximate cause of defensive wars. If there is not enough land, the State is at the mercy of its neighbors for the additional quantity; and this is the proximate cause of offensive wars. Any nation which has, by its position, only the alternative between commerce and war is weak in itself; it is dependent on its neighbors and on events; it has only a short and precarious existence. It conquers and changes its situation, or it is conquered and reduced to nothing. It can preserve its freedom only by virtue of being small or great.

It is impossible to express numerically a fixed ratio between the extent of land and the number of men which are reciprocally sufficient, on account of the differences that are found in the quality of the soil, in its degrees of fertility, in the nature of its products, and in the influence of climate, as well as on account of those which we observe in the constitutions of the inhabitants, of whom some consume little in a fertile country, while others consume much on an unfruitful soil. Further, attention must be paid to the greater or less fecundity of the women, to the conditions of the country, whether more or less favorable to the population, and to the numbers which the legislator may hope to draw thither by his institutions; so that an opinion should be based not on what is seen, but on what is foreseen, while the actual state of the people should be less observed than that which it ought naturally to attain. In short, there are a thousand occasions on which the particular accidents of situation require or permit that more territory than appears necessary should be taken up. Thus men will spread out a good deal in a mountainous country, where the natural productions, viz, woods and pastures, require less labor, where experience teaches that women are more fecund than in the plains, and where with an extensive inclined surface there is only a small horizontal base, which alone should count for vegetation. On the other hand, people may inhabit a smaller space on the sea-shore, even among rocks and sands that are almost barren, because fishing can, in great measure, supply the deficiency in the productions of the earth, because men ought to be more concentrated in order to repel pirates, and because, further, it is easier to relieve the country, by means of colonies, of the inhabitants with which it is overburdened.

In order to establish a nation, it is necessary to add to these conditions one which cannot supply the place of any other, but without which they are all useless — it is that the people should enjoy abundance and peace; for the time of a State's formation is, like that of forming soldiers in a square, the time when the body is least capable of resistance and most easy to destroy. Resistance would be greater in a state of absolute disorder than at a moment of fermentation, when each is occupied with his own position and not with the common danger. Should a war, a famine, or a sedition supervene at this critical period, the State is inevitably overthrown.

Many governments, indeed, may be established during such storms, but then it is these very governments that destroy the State. Usurpers always bring about or select troublous times for passing, under cover of the public agitation, destructive laws which the people would never adopt when sober-minded. The choice of the moment for the establishment of a government is one of the surest marks for distinguishing the work of the legislator from that of the tyrant.

What nation, then, is adapted for legislation ? That which is already united by some bond of interest, origin, or convention, but has not yet borne the real yoke of the laws; that which has neither customs nor superstitions firmly rooted; that which has no fear of being overwhelmed by a sudden invasion, but which, without entering into the disputes of its neighbors, can single-handed resist either of them, or aid one in repelling the other; that in which every member can be known by all, and in which there is no necessity to lay on a man a greater burden than a man can bear; that which can subsist without other nations, and without which every other nation can subsist;* that which is neither rich nor poor and is self-sufficing; lastly, that which combines the stability of an old nation with the docility of a new one. The work of legislation is rendered arduous not so much by what must be established as by what must be destroyed; and that which makes success so rare is the impossibility of finding the simplicity of nature conjoined with the necessities of society. All these conditions, it is true, are with difficulty combined; hence few well-constituted States are seen.

There is still one country in Europe capable of legislation; it is the island of Corsica. The courage and firmness which that brave nation has exhibited in recovering and defending its freedom would well deserve that some wise man should teach it how to preserve it. I have some presentiment that this small island will one day astonish Europe.

* If of two neighboring nations one could not subsist without the other, it would be a very hard situation for the first, and a very dangerous one for the second. Every wise nation in such a case will endeavor very quickly to free the other from this dependence. The republic of Thlascala, inclosed in the empire of Mexico, preferred to do without salt rather than buy it of the Mexicans or even accept it gratuitously. The wise Thlascalans saw a trap hidden beneath this generosity. They kept themselves free; and this small State, inclosed in that great empire, was at last the instrument of its downfall.

CHAPTER XI.

The Different Systems of Legislation.

If we ask precisely wherein consists the greatest good of all, which ought to be the aim of every system of legislation, we shall find that it is summed up in two principal objects, LIBERTY and EQUALITY, liberty, because any individual dependence is so much force withdrawn from the body of the State; equality, because liberty cannot subsist without it.

I have already said what civil liberty is. With regard to equality, we must not understand by this word that the degrees of power and wealth should be absolutely the same; but that, as to power, it should fall short of all violence, and never be exercised except by virtue of station and of the laws; while, as to wealth, no citizen should be rich enough to be able to buy another, and none poor enough to be forced to sell himself,* which supposes, on the part of the great, moderation in property and influence, and, on the part of ordinary citizens, repression of avarice and covetousness.

It is said that this equality is a chimera of speculation which cannot exist in practical affairs. But if the abuse is inevitable, does it follow that it is unnecessary even to regulate it? It is precisely because the force of circumstances is ever tending to destroy equality that the force of legislation should always tend to maintain it.

But these general objects of every good institution ought to be modified in each country by the relations which arise both from the local situation and from the character of the inhabitants; and it is with reference to these relations that we must assign to each nation a particular system

* If, then, you wish to give stability to the State, bring the two extremes as near together as possible; tolerate neither rich people nor beggars. These two conditions, naturally inseparable, are equally fatal to the general welfare; from the one class spring tyrants, from the other, the supporters of tyranny; it is always between these that the traffic in public liberty is carried on; the one buys and the other sells.

of institutions, which shall be the best, not perhaps in
itself, but for the State for which it is designed. For
instance, if the soil is unfruitful and barren, or the
country too confined for its inhabitants, turn your attention to arts and manufactures, and exchange their products for the provisions that you require. On the other
hand, if you occupy rich plains and fertile slopes, if, in
a productive region, you are in need of inhabitants, bestow all your cares on agriculture, which multiplies men,
and drives out the arts, which would only end in depopulating the country by gathering together in a few spots
the few inhabitants that the land possesses.* If you
occupy extensive and convenient coasts, cover the sea
with vessels and foster commerce and navigation; you
will have a short and brilliant existence. If the sea on
your coasts bathes only rocks that are almost inaccessible,
remain fish-eating barbarians; you will lead more peace-
ful, perhaps better, and certainly happier lives. In a
word, besides the maxims common to all, each nation
contains within itself some cause which influences it in a
particular way, and renders its legislation suitable for
it alone. Thus the Hebrews in ancient times, and the
Arabs more recently, had religion as their chief object,
the Athenians literature, Carthage and Tyre commerce,
Rhodes navigation, Sparta war, Rome valor. The author
of the "Spirit of the Laws" has shown in a multitude
of instances by what arts the legislator directs his institutions toward each of these objects.

What renders the constitution of a State really solid
and durable is the observance of expediency in such a
way that natural relations and the laws always coincide,
the latter only serving, as it were, to secure, support,
and rectify the former. But if the legislator, mistaken in
his object, takes a principle different from that which
springs from the nature of things; if the one tends to
servitude, the other to liberty, the one to riches, the
other to population, the one to peace, the other to con-

* Any branch of foreign commerce, says the Marquis d'Argenson,
diffuses merely a deceptive utility through the kingdom generally; it
may enrich a few individuals, even a few towns, but the nation as a
whole gains nothing, and the people are none the better for it.

quests, we shall see the laws imperceptibly weakened and the constitution impaired; and the State will be ceaselessly agitated until it is destroyed or changed, and invincible nature has resumed her sway.

CHAPTER XII.

DIVISION OF THE LAWS.

IN ORDER that everything may be duly regulated and the best possible form given to the commonwealth, there are various relations to be considered. First, the action of the whole body acting on itself, that is, the relation of the whole to the whole, or of the sovereign to the State; and this relation is composed of that of the intermediate terms, as we shall see hereafter.

The laws governing this relation bear the name of political laws, and are also called fundamental laws, not without some reason if they are wise ones; for, if in every State there is only one good method of regulating it, the people which has discovered it ought to adhere to it; but if the established order is bad, why should we regard as fundamental laws which prevent it from being good? Besides, in any case, a nation is always at liberty to change its laws, even the best; for if it likes to injure itself, who has a right to prevent it from doing so?

The second relation is that of the members with one another, or with the body as a whole; and this relation should, in respect of the first, be as small, and, in respect of the second, as great as possible; so that every citizen may be perfectly independent of all the rest, and in absolute dependence on the State. And this is always effected by the same means; for it is only the power of the State that secures the freedom of its members. It is from this second relation that civil laws arise.

We may consider a third kind of relation between the individual man and the law, viz, that of punishable disobedience; and this gives rise to the establishment of criminal laws, which at bottom are not so much a particular species of laws as the sanction of all the others.

To these three kinds of laws is added a fourth, the most important of all, which is graven neither on marble nor on brass, but in the hearts of the citizens; a law which creates the real constitution of the State, which acquires new strength daily, which, when other laws grow obsolete or pass away, revives them or supplies their place, preserves a people in the spirit of their institutions, and imperceptibly substitutes the force of habit for that of authority. I speak of manners, customs, and above all of opinion—a province unknown to our politicians, but one on which the success of all the rest depends; a province with which the great legislator is occupied in private, while he appears to confine himself to particular regulations, that are merely the arching of the vault, of which manners, slower to develop, form at length the immovable keystone.

Of these different classes, political laws, which constitute the form of government, alone relate to my subject.

BOOK   III.

Before speaking of the different forms of government, let us try to fix the precise meaning of that word, which has not yet been very clearly explained.

CHAPTER I.

Government in General.

I warn the reader that this chapter must be read carefully, and that I do not know the art of making myself intelligible to those that will not be attentive.

Every free action has two causes concurring to produce it; the one moral, viz, the will which determines the act; the other physical, viz, the power which executes it. When I walk toward an object, I must first will to go to it; in the second place, my feet must carry me to it. Should a paralytic wish to run, or an active man not wish to do so, both will remain where they are. The body politic has the same motive powers; in it, likewise, force and will are distinguished, the latter under the name of legislative power, the former under the name of executive power. Nothing is, or ought to be, done in it without their co-operation.

We have seen that the legislative power belongs to the people, and can belong to it alone. On the other hand, it is easy to see from the principles already established, that the executive power cannot belong to the people generally as legislative or sovereign, because that power is exerted only in particular acts, which are not within the province of the law, nor consequently within that of the sovereign, all the acts of which must be laws.

The public force, then, requires a suitable agent to concentrate it and put it in action according to the directions of the general will, to serve as a means of communication

4   (49)

between the State and the sovereign, to effect in some manner in the public person what the union of soul and body effects in a man. This is, in the State, the function of the government, improperly confounded with the sovereign of which it is only the minister.*

What, then, is the government? An intermediate body established between the subjects and the sovereign for their mutual correspondence, charged with the execution of the laws and with the maintenance of liberty both civil and political.

The members of this body are called magistrates or KINGS, that is, GOVERNORS; and the body as a whole bears the name of PRINCE†. Those therefore who maintain that the act by which a people submits to its chiefs is not a contract are quite right. It is absolutely nothing but a commission, an employment, in which, as simple officers of the sovereign, they exercise in its name the power of which it has made them depositaries, and which it can limit, modify, and resume when it pleases. The alienation of such a right, being incompatible with the nature of the social body, is contrary to the object of the association.

Consequently, I give the name GOVERNMENT or supreme administration to the legitimate exercise of the executive power, and that of Prince or magistrate to the man or body charged with that administration.

It is in the government that are found the intermediate powers, the relations of which constitute the relation of the whole to the whole, or of the sovereign to the State. This last relation can be represented by that of the extremes of a continued proportion, of which the mean proportional is the government. The government receives from the sovereign the commands which it gives to the people; and in order that the State may be in stable equilibrium, it is necessary, everything being balanced,

---

* By restricting the function of the sovereign to legislation, Rousseau hampers himself in treating of governments. A sharp division between the legislative and the executive is impossible (*cf*. Austin, «Jurisprudence,» Part I. Lect. VI.).—ED.

† It is for this reason that at Venice the title of Most Serene Prince is given to the College, even when the Doge does not attend it.

that there should be equality between the product or the power of the government taken by itself, and the product or the power of the citizens, who are sovereign in the one aspect and subjects in the other.

Further, we could not alter any of the three terms without at once destroying the proportion. If the sovereign wishes to govern, or if the magistrate wishes to legislate, or if the subjects refuse to obey, disorder succeeds order, force and will no longer act in concert, and the State being dissolved falls into despotism or anarchy. Lastly, as there is but one mean proportional between each relation, there is only one good government possible in a State; but as a thousand events may change the relations of a people, not only may different governments be good for different peoples, but for the same people at different times.

To try and give an idea of the different relations that may exist between these two extremes, I will take for an example the number of the people, as a relation most easy to express.

Let us suppose that the State is composed of ten thousand citizens. The sovereign can only be considered collectively and as a body; but every private person, in his capacity of subject, is considered as an individual; therefore, the sovereign is to the subject as ten thousand is to one, that is, each member of the State has as his share only one ten-thousandth part of the sovereign authority, although he is entirely subjected to it.

If the nation consists of a hundred thousand men, the position of the subjects does not change, and each alike is subjected to the whole authority of the laws, while his vote reduced to one hundred-thousandth, has ten times less influence in their enactment. The subject, then, always remaining a unit, the proportional power of the sovereign increases in the ratio of the number of the citizens. Whence it follows that the more the State is enlarged, the more does liberty diminish.

When I say that the proportional power increases, I mean that it is farther removed from equality. Therefore, the greater the ratio is in the geometrical sense, the less is the ratio in the common acceptation; in the former, the ratio, considered according to quantity, is measured by the exponent, and in the other, considered according to identity, it is estimated by the similarity.

Now, the less the particular wills correspond with the general will, that is, customs with laws, the more should the repressive power be increased. The government, then, in order to be effective, should be relatively stronger in proportion as the people are more numerous.

On the other hand, as the aggrandizement of the State gives the depositaries of the public authority more temptations and more opportunities to abuse their power, the more force should the government have to restrain the people, and the more should the sovereign have in its turn to restrain the government. I do not speak here of absolute force, but of the relative force of the different parts of the State.

It follows from this double ratio that the continued proportion between the sovereign, the Prince, and the people is not an arbitrary idea, but a necessary consequence of the nature of the body politic. It follows, further, that one of the extremes, viz, the people, as subject, being fixed and represented by unity, whenever the double ratio increases or diminishes, the single ratio increases or diminishes in like manner, and consequently the middle term is changed. This shows that there is no unique and absolute constitution of government, but that there may be as many governments different in nature as there are States different in size.

If, for the sake of turning this system to ridicule, it should be said that, in order to find this mean proportional and form the body of the government, it is, according to me, only necessary to take the square root of the number of the people, I should answer that I take that number here only as an example; that the ratios of which I speak are not measured only by the number of men, but in general by the quantity of action, which results from the combination of multitudes of causes; that, moreover, if for the purpose of expressing myself in fewer words, I borrow for a moment geometrical terms, I am nevertheless aware that geometrical precision has no place in moral quantities.

The government is on a small scale what the body politic which includes it is on a large scale. It is a moral person endowed with certain faculties, active like the sovereign, passive like the State, and it can be resolved into other similar relations; from which arises as a consequence a new proportion, and yet another within this, according to the order of the magistracies, until we come to an indivisible middle term, that is, to a single chief or supreme magistrate, who may be represented, in the middle of this progression, as unity between the series of fractions and that of the whole numbers.

Without embarrassing ourselves with this multiplication of terms, let us be content to consider the government as a new body in the State, distinct from the people and from the sovereign, and intermediate between the two.

There is this essential difference between those two bodies, that the State exists by itself, while the government exists only through the sovereign. Thus the dominant will of the Prince is, or ought to be, only the general will, or the law; its force is only the public force concentrated in itself; so soon as it wishes to perform of itself some absolute and independent act, the connection of the whole begins to be relaxed. If, lastly, the Prince should chance to have a particular will more active than that of the sovereign, and if, to enforce obedience to this particular will, it should employ the public force which is in its hands, in such a manner that there would be, so to speak, two sovereigns, the one *de jure* and the other *de facto*, the social union would immediately disappear, and the body politic would be dissolved.

Further, in order that the body of the government may have an existence, a real life to distinguish it from the body of the State; in order that all its members may be able to act in concert and fulfill the object for which it is instituted, a particular personality is necessary to it, a feeling common to its members, a force, a will of its own tending to its preservation. This individual existence supposes assemblies, councils, a power of deliberating and resolving, rights, titles, and privileges which belong to the Prince exclusively, and which render the position of the magistrate more honorable in proportion as it is more arduous. The difficulty lies in the method of disposing, within the whole, this subordinate whole, in such a way that it may not weaken the general constitution in strengthening its own; that its particular force, intended for its own preservation, may always be kept distinct from the public force, designed for the preservation of the State; and, in a word, that it may always be ready to sacrifice the government to the people, and not the people to the government.

Moreover, although the artificial body of the government is the work of another artificial body, and has in some respects only a derivative and subordinate existence, that does not prevent it from acting with more or less vigor or celerity, from enjoying, so to speak, more or less robust health. Lastly, without directly departing from the object for which it was instituted, it may deviate from it more or less, according to the manner in which it is constituted.

From all these differences arise the different relations which the government must have with the body of the State, so as to accord with the accidental and particular relations by which the State itself is modified. For often the government that is best in itself will become the most vicious, unless its relations are changed so as to meet the defects of the body politic to which it belongs.

CHAPTER II.

THE PRINCIPLE WHICH CONSTITUTES THE DIFFERENT FORMS OF GOVERNMENT.

To EXPLAIN the general cause of these differences, I must here distinguish the Prince from the government, as I before distinguished the State from the sovereign.

The body of the magistracy may be composed of a greater or less number of members. We said that the ratio of the sovereign to the subjects was so much greater as the people were more numerous; and, by an evident analogy, we can say the same of the government with regard to the magistrates.

Now, the total force of the government, being always that of the State, does not vary; whence it follows that the more it employs this force on its own members, the less remains for operating upon the whole people.

Consequently, the more numerous the magistrates are, the weaker is the government. As this maxim is fundamental, let us endeavor to explain it more clearly.

We can distinguish in the person of the magistrate three wills essentially different: first, the will peculiar to the individual, which tends only to his personal advantage; secondly, the common will of the magistrates, which has reference solely to the advantage of the Prince, and which may be called the corporate will, being general in relation to the government, and particular in relation to the State of which the government forms part; in the third place, the will of the people, or the sovereign will, which is general both in relation to the State considered as the whole, and in relation to the government considered as part of the whole.

In a perfect system of legislation the particular or individual will should be inoperative; the corporate will proper to the goverment quite subordinate; and consequently the general or sovereign will always dominant, and the sole rule of all the rest.

On the other hand, according to the natural order, these different wills become more active in proportion as they are concentrated. Thus the general will is always the weakest, the corporate will has the second rank, and the particular will the first of all; so that in the government each member is, firstly, himself, next a magistrate, and then a citizen — a gradation directly opposed to that which the social order requires.

But suppose that the whole government is in the hands of a single man, then the particular will and the corporate will are perfectly united, and consequently the latter is in the highest possible degree of intensity. Now, as it is on the degree of will that the exertion of force depends, and as the absolute power of the government does not vary, it follows that the most active government is that of a single person.

On the other hand, let us unite the government with the legislative authority; let us make the sovereign the Prince, and all the citizens magistrates; then the corporate will, confounded with the general will, will have no more activity than the latter, and will leave the particular will in all its force. Thus the government, always with the same absolute force, will be at its minimum of relative force or activity.

These relations are incontestable, and other considerations serve still further to confirm them. We see, for example, that each magistrate is more active in his body than each citizen is in his, and that consequently the particular will has much more influence in the acts of government than in those of the sovereign; for every magistrate is almost always charged with some function of government, whereas each citizen, taken by himself, has no function of sovereignty. Besides, the more a State extends, the more is its real force increased, although it does not increase in proportion to its extent; but, while the State remains the same, it is useless to multiply magistrates, for the government acquires no greater real force, inasmuch as this force is that of the State, the quantity of which is always uniform. Thus the relative force or activity of the government diminishes without its absolute or real force being able to increase.

It is certain, moreover, that the dispatch of business is retarded in proportion as more people are charged with it; that, in laying too much stress on prudence, we leave too little to fortune; that opportunities are allowed to pass by, and that owing to excessive deliberation the fruits of deliberation are often lost.

I have just shown that the government is weakened in proportion to the multiplication of magistrates, and I have before demonstrated that the more numerous the people are, the more ought the repressive force to be increased. Whence it follows that the ratio between the magistrates and the government ought to be inversely as the ratio between the subjects and the sovereign; that is, the more the State is enlarged, the more should the government contract; so that the number of chiefs should diminish in proportion as the number of the people is increased.

But I speak here only of the relative force of the government, and not of its rectitude; for, on the other hand, the more numerous the magistracy is, the more does the corporate will approach the general will; whereas, under a single magistrate, this same corporate will is, as I have said, only a particular will.· Thus, what is lost on one side can be gained on the other, and the art of the legislator consists of knowing how to fix the point where the force and will of the government, always in reciprocal proportion, are combined in the ratio most advantageous to the State.

CHAPTER III.

CLASSIFICATION OF GOVERNMENTS.

WE HAVE seen in the previous chapter why the different kinds or forms of government are distinguished by the number of members that compose them; it remains to be seen in the present chapter how this division is made.

The sovereign may, in the first place, commit the charge of the government to the whole people, or to the greater part of the people, in such a way that there may be more citizens who are magistrates than simple individual citizens. We call this form of government DEMOCRACY.

Or it may confine the government to a small number, so that there may be more ordinary citizens than magistrates; and this form bears the name of ARISTOCRACY.

Lastly, it may concentrate the whole government in the hands of a single magistrate from whom all the rest derive their power. This third form is the most common, and is called MONARCHY, or royal government.

We should remark that all these forms, or at least the first two, admit of degrees, and may indeed have a considerable range; for democracy may embrace the whole people, or be limited to a half. Aristocracy, in its turn, may

restrict itself from a half of the people to the smallest
number indeterminately. Royalty even is susceptible of
some division. Sparta by its constitution always had two
kings; and in the Roman Empire there were as many as
eight Emperors at once without its being possible to say
that the Empire was divided. Thus there is a point at
which each form of government blends with the next;
and we see that, under three denominations only, the
government is really susceptible of as many different
forms as the State has citizens.

What is more, this same government being in certain
respects capable of subdivision into other parts, one administered in one way, another in another, there may
result from combinations of these three forms a multitude of mixed forms, each of which can be multiplied by
all the simple forms.

In all ages there has been much discussion about the
best form of government, without consideration of the
fact that each of them is the best in certain cases, and
the worst in others.

If, in the different States, the number of the supreme
magistrates should be in inverse ratio to that of the citizens, it follows that, in general, democratic government
is suitable to small States, aristocracy to those of moderate size, and monarchy to large ones. This rule follows immediately from the principle. But how is it
possible to estimate the multitude of circumstances which
may furnish exceptions?

CHAPTER IV.

DEMOCRACY.*

HE THAT makes the law knows better than any one how
it should be executed and interpreted. It would seem,
then, that there could be no better constitution than one
in which the executive power is united with the legislative; but it is that very circumstance which makes a

* Plato treated democracy as a debased form of commonwealth,
characterized by an excessive freedom tending to degenerate into
license ("Republic" VIII.).—ED.

democratic government inadequate in certain respects, because things which ought to be distinguished are not, and because the Prince and the sovereign, being the same person, only form as it were a government without government.

It is not expedient that he who makes the laws should execute them, nor that the body of the people should divert its attention from general considerations in order to bestow it on particular objects. Nothing is more dangerous than the influence of private interests on public affairs; and the abuse of the laws by the government is a less evil than the corruption of the legislator, which is the infallible result of the pursuit of private interests. For when the State is changed in its substance all reform becomes impossible. A people which would never abuse the government would likewise never abuse its independence; a people which always governed well would not need to be governed.

Taking the term in its strict sense, there never has existed, and never will exist, any true democracy. It is contrary to the natural order that the majority should govern and that the minority should be governed. It is impossible to imagine that the people should remain in perpetual assembly to attend to public affairs, and it is easily apparent that commissions could not be established for that purpose without the form of administration being changed.

In fact, I think I can lay down as a principle that when the functions of government are shared among several magistracies, the least numerous acquire, sooner or later, the greatest authority, if only on account of the facility in transacting business which naturally leads them on to that.

Moreover, how many things difficult to combine does not this government presuppose! First, a very small State, in which the people may be readily assembled, and in which every citizen can easily know all the rest; secondly, great simplicity of manners, which prevents a multiplicity of affairs and thorny discussions; next, considerable equality in rank and fortune, without which equality in rights and authority could not long subsist; lastly, little or no luxury, for luxury is either the effect of wealth or renders it necessary; it corrupts both the rich and the poor, the former by possession, the latter by covetousness; it betrays the country to effeminacy and vanity; it deprives the State of all its citizens in order to subject them one to another, and all to opinion.

That is why a famous author has assigned virtue as the principle of a republic, for all these conditions could not subsist without virtue; but through not making the necessary distinctions, this brilliant genius has often lacked precision and sometimes clearness, and has not seen that the sovereign authority being everywhere the same, the same principle ought to have a place in every well-constituted State, in a greater or less degree, it is true, according to the form of government.

Let us add that there is no government so subject to civil wars and internal agitation as the democratic or popular, because there is none which tends so strongly and so constantly to change its form, none which demands more vigilance and courage to be maintained in its own form. It is especially in this constitution that the citizen should arm himself with strength and steadfastness, and say every day of his life from the bottom of his heart what a virtuous Palatine said in the Diet of Poland: *Malo periculosam libertatem quam quietum servitium.*

If there were a nation of gods, it would be governed democratically. So perfect a government is unsuited to men.

CHAPTER V.

ARISTOCRACY.

WE HAVE here two moral persons quite distinct, viz, the government and the sovereign; and consequently two general wills, the one having reference to all the citizens, the other only to the members of the administration. Thus, although the government can regulate its internal policy as it pleases, it can never speak to the people except in the name of the sovereign, that is, in the name of the people themselves. This must never be forgotten.

The earliest societies were aristocratically governed. The heads of families deliberated among themselves about public affairs. The young men yielded readily to the authority of experience. Hence the names PRIESTS, ELDERS, SENATE, GERONTES. The savages of North America are still governed in this way at the present time, and are very well governed.

But in proportion as the inequality due to institutions prevailed over natural inequality, wealth or power * was preferred to age, and aristocracy became elective. Finally, the power transmitted with the father's property to the children, rendering the families patrician, made the government hereditary and there were senators only twenty years old.

There are, then, three kinds of aristocracy — natural, elective, and hereditary. The first is only suitable for simple nations; the third is the worst of all governments. The second is the best; it is aristocracy properly so-called.

Besides the advantage of the distinction between the two powers, aristocracy has that of the choice of its members; for in a popular government all the citizens are born magistrates; but this one limits them to a small number, and they become magistrates by election only;† a method by which probity, intelligence, experience, and all other grounds of preference and public esteem are so many fresh guarantees that men will be wisely governed.

Further, assemblies are more easily convoked; affairs are better discussed and are dispatched with greater order and diligence; while the credit of the State is better

* It is clear that the word *optimates* among the ancients did not mean the best, but the most powerful.

† It is very important to regulate by law the form of election of magistrates; for, in leaving it to the will of the Prince, it is impossible to avoid falling into hereditary aristocracy, as happened in the republics of Venice and Berne. In consequence, the first has long been a decaying State, but the second is maintained by the extreme wisdom of its Senate; it is a very honorable and a very dangerous exception.

maintained abroad by venerable senators than by an unknown or despised multitude.

In a word, it is the best and most natural order of things that the wisest should govern the multitude, when we are sure that they will govern it for its advantage and not for their own. We should not uselessly multiply means, nor do with twenty thousand men what a hundred chosen men can do still better. But we must observe that the corporate interest begins here to direct the public force in a less degree according to the rule of the general will, and that another inevitable propensity deprives the laws of a part of the executive power.

With regard to special expediences, a State must not be so small, nor a people so simple and upright, that the execution of the laws should follow immediately upon the public will as in a good democracy. Nor again must a nation be so large that the chief men, who are dispersed in order to govern it, can set up as sovereigns, each in his own province, and begin by making themselves independent so as at last to become masters.

But if aristocracy requires a few virtues less than popular government, it requires also others that are peculiarly its own, such as moderation among the rich and contentment among the poor; for a rigorous equality would seem to be out of place in it, and was not even observed in Sparta.

Besides, if this form of government comports with a certain inequality of fortune, it is expedient in general that the administration of public affairs should be intrusted to those that are best able to devote their whole time to it, but not, as Aristotle maintains, that the rich should always be preferred. On the contrary, it is important that an opposite choice should sometimes teach the people that there are, in men's personal merits, reasons for preference more important than wealth.

CHAPTER VI.

MONARCHY.

WE HAVE hitherto considered the Prince as a moral and collective person united by the force of the laws, and as the depositary of the executive power in the State. We have now to consider this power concentrated in the hands of a natural person, of a real man, who alone has a right to dispose of it according to the laws. He is what is called a monarch or a king.

Quite the reverse of the other forms of administration, in which a collective being represents an individual, in this one an individual represents a collective being; so that the moral unity that constitutes it is at the same time a physical unity, in which all the powers that the law combines in the other with so much effort are combined naturally.

Thus the will of the people, the will of the Prince, the public force of the State, and the particular force of the government, all obey the same motive power; all the springs of the machine are in the same hand, everything works for the same end; there are no opposite movements that counteract one another, and no kind of constitution can be imagined in which a more considerable action is produced with less effort. Archimedes, quietly seated on the shore, and launching without difficulty a large vessel, represents to me a skillful monarch, governing from his cabinet his vast States, and, while he appears motionless, setting everything in motion.

But if there is no government which has more vigor, there is none in which the particular will has more sway and more easily governs others. Everything works for the same end, it is true; but this end is not the public welfare, and the very power of the administration turns continually to the prejudice of the State.

Kings wish to be absolute, and from afar men cry to them that the best way to become so is to make themselves beloved by their people. This maxim is very fine,

and also very true in certain respects; unfortunately it will
always be ridiculed in courts. Power which springs from
the affections of the people is doubtless the greatest, but
it is precarious and conditional; princes will never be
satisfied with it. The best kings wish to have the power
of being wicked if they please, without ceasing to be
masters. A political preacher will tell them in vain that,
the strength of the people being their own, it is their
greatest interest that the people should be flourishing,
numerous, and formidable; they know very well that that
is not true. Their personal interest is, in the first place,
that the people should be weak and miserable, and
should never be able to resist them. Supposing all the
subjects always perfectly submissive, I admit that it would
then be the prince's interest that the people should be
powerful, in order that this power, being his own, might
render him formidable to his neighbors; but as this
interest is only secondary and subordinate, and as the
two suppositions are incompatible, it is natural that
princes should always give preference to the maxim
which is most immediately useful to them. It is this
that Samuel strongly represented to the Hebrews; it is
this that Machiavelli clearly demonstrated. While pretending to give lessons to kings, he gave great ones to
peoples. The " Prince " of Machiavelli is the book of
republicans.*

We have found, by general considerations, that monarchy is suited only to large States; and we shall find
this again by examining monarchy itself. · The more
numerous the public administrative body is, the more
does the ratio of the Prince to the subjects diminish
and approach equality, so that this ratio is unity or

---

* Machiavelli was an honorable man and a good citizen; but,
attached to the house of the Medici, he was forced, during the oppression of his country, to conceal his love for liberty. The mere choice
of his execrable hero sufficiently manifests his secret intention; and
the opposition between the maxims of his book the "Prince" and
those of his "Discourses on Titus Livius" and his "History of Florence," shows that this profound politician has had hitherto only
superficial or corrupt readers. The court of Rome has strictly prohibited his book; I certainly believe it, for it is that court which he
most clearly depicts.

equality, even in a democracy. This same ratio increases in proportion as the government contracts, and is at its maximum when the government is in the hands of a single person. Then the distance between the Prince and the people is too great, and the State lacks cohesion. In order to unify it, then, intermediate orders, princes, grandees, and nobles, are required to fill them. Now, nothing at all of this kind is proper for a small State, which would be ruined by all these orders.

But if it is difficult for a great State to be well governed, it is much more so for it to be well governed by a single man; and every one knows what happens when the king appoints deputies.

One essential and inevitable defect, which will always render a monarchical government inferior to a republican one, is that in the latter the public voice hardly ever raises to the highest posts any but enlightened and capable men, who fill them honorably; whereas those who succeed in monarchies are most frequently only petty mischief-makers, petty knaves, petty intriguers, whose petty talents, which enable them to attain high posts in courts, only serve to show the public their ineptitude as soon as they have attained them. The people are much less mistaken about their choice than the prince is; and a man of real merit is almost as rare in a royal ministry as a fool at the head of a republican government. Therefore, when by some fortunate chance one of these born rulers takes the helm of affairs in a monarchy almost wrecked by such a fine set of ministers, it is quite astonishing what resources he finds, and his accession to power forms an epoch in a country.

In order that a monarchical State might be well governed, it would be necessary that its greatness or extent should be proportioned to the abilities of him that governs. It is easier to conquer than to rule. With a sufficient lever, the world may be moved by a finger; but to support it the shoulders of Hercules are required. However small a State may be, the prince is almost always too small for it. When, on the contrary, it happens that the State is too small for its chief, which is very rare, it is still badly governed, because the chief, always pursuing his own great designs, forgets the interests of the people, and renders them no less unhappy by the abuse of his transcendent abilities, than an inferior chief by his lack of talent. It would be necessary, so to speak, that a kingdom should be enlarged or contracted in every reign, according to the capacity of the prince; whereas, the talents of a senate having more definite limits, the State may have permanent boundaries, and the administration prosper equally well.

The most obvious inconvenience of the government of a single person is the lack of that uninterrupted succession which forms in the two others a continuous connection. One king being dead, another is necessary; elections leave dangerous intervals; they are stormy; and unless the citizens are of a disinterestedness, an integrity, which this government hardly admits of, intrigue and corruption intermingle with it. It would be hard for a man to whom the State has been sold not to sell it in his turn, and indemnify himself out of the helpless for the money which the powerful have extorted from him. Sooner or later everything becomes venal under such an administration, and the peace which is then enjoyed under a king is worse than the disorder of an interregnum.

What has been done to prevent these evils? Crowns have been made hereditary in certain families; and an order of succession has been established which prevents any dispute on the demise of kings; that is to say, the inconvenience of regencies being substituted for that of elections, an appearance of tranquillity has been preferred to a wise administration, and men have preferred to risk having as their chiefs children, monsters, and imbeciles, rather than have a dispute about the choice of good kings. They have not considered that in thus exposing themselves to the risk of this alternative, they put almost all the chances against themselves. That was a very sensible answer of Dionysius the younger, to whom his father, in reproaching him with a dishonorable action, said: "Have I set you the example in this?" "Ah!" replied the son, "your father was not a king."

All things conspire to deprive of justice and reason a man brought up to govern others. Much trouble is taken, so it is said, to teach young princes the art of reigning; this education does not appear to profit them. It would be better to begin by teaching them the art of obeying. The greatest kings that history has celebrated were not trained to rule; that is a science which men are never less masters of than after excessive study of it, and it is better acquired by obeying than by ruling. *Nam utilissimus idem ac brevissimus bonarum malarumque rerum delectus, cogitare quid aut nolueris sub alio principe, aut volueris.*

A result of this want of cohesion is the instability of royal government, which, being regulated sometimes on one plan, sometimes on another, according to the character of the reigning prince or that of the persons who reign for him, cannot long pursue a fixed aim or a consistent course of conduct, a variableness which always makes the State fluctuate between maxim and maxim, project and project, and which does not exist in other governments, where the Prince is always the same. So we see that, in general, if there is more cunning in a court, there is more wisdom in a senate, and that republics pursue their ends by more steadfast and regular methods; whereas every revolution in a royal ministry produces one in the State, the maxim common to all ministers, and to almost all kings, being to reverse in every respect the acts of their predecessors.

From this same want of cohesion is obtained the solution of a sophism very familiar to royal politicians; this is not only to compare civil government with domestic government, and the prince with the father of a family, an error already refuted, but, further, to ascribe freely to this magistrate all the virtues which he might have occasion for, and always to suppose that the prince is what he ought to be — on which supposition royal government is manifestly preferable to every other, because it is incontestably the strongest, and because it only lacks a corporate will more conformable to the general will to be also the best.

But if, according to Plato, a king by nature is so rare a personage, how many times will nature and fortune conspire to crown him? And if the royal education necessarily corrupts those who receive it, what should be

expected from a succession of men trained to rule? It
is, then, voluntary self-deception to confuse royal government with that of a good king. To see what this government is in itself, we must consider it under incapable
or wicked princes; for such will come to the throne, or
the throne will make them such.

These difficulties have not escaped our authors, but
they have not been embarrassed by them. The remedy,
they say, is to obey without murmuring; God gives bad
kings in his wrath, and we must endure them as chas-
tisements of heaven. Such talk is doubtless edifying,
but I am inclined to think it would be more appropriate
in a pulpit than in a book on politics. What should we
say of a physician who promises miracles, and whose
whole art consists in exhorting the sick man to be
patient? We know well that when we have a bad government it must be endured; the question is to find a
good one.

CHAPTER VII.

MIXED GOVERNMENTS.

PROPERLY speaking, there is no simple government.
A single chief must have subordinate magistrates; a
popular government must have a head. Thus, in the
partition of the executive power, there is always a gradation from the greater number to the less, with this difference, that sometimes the majority depends on the
minority, and sometimes the minority on the majority.

Sometimes there is an equal division, either when the
constituent parts are in mutual dependence, as in the
government of England; or when the authority of each
part is independent, but imperfect, as in Poland. This
latter form is bad, because there is no unity in the government, and the State lacks cohesion.

Is a simple or mixed government the better? A question much debated among publicists, and one to which
the same answer must be made that I have before made
about every form of government.

The simple government is the better in itself, for the reason that it is simple.   But when the executive power is not sufficiently dependent on the legislative, that is, when there is a greater proportion between the Prince and the sovereign than between the people and the Prince, this want of proportion must be remedied by dividing the government; for then all its parts have no less authority over the subjects, and their division renders them all together less strong against the sovereign.

The same inconvenience is also provided against by the establishment of intermediate magistrates, who, leaving the government in its entirety, only serve to balance the two powers and maintain their respective rights. Then the government is not mixed, but temperate.

The opposite inconvenience can be remedied by similar means, and, when the government is too lax, tribunals may be erected to concentrate it.   That is customary in all democracies.   In the first case the government is divided in order to weaken it, and in the second in order to strengthen it; for the maximum of strength and also of weakness is found in simple governments, while the mixed forms give a medium strength.

CHAPTER VIII.

That Every Form of Government is Not Fit for Every Country.

Liberty, not being a fruit of all climates, is not within the reach of all peoples.   The more we consider this principle established by Montesquieu, the more do we perceive its truth; the more it is contested, the greater opportunity is given to establish it by new proofs.

In all the governments of the world, the public person consumes, but produces nothing.   Whence, then, comes the substance it consumes?   From the labor of its members.   It is the superfluity of individuals that supplies the necessaries of the public.   Hence it follows that the civil State can subsist only so long as men's labor produces more than they need.

Now this excess is not the same in all countries of the world. In several it is considerable, in others moderate, in others nothing, in others a minus quantity. This proportion depends on the fertility due to climate, on the kind of labor which the soil requires, on the nature of its products, on the physical strength of its inhabitants, on the greater or less consumption that is necessary to them, and on several other like proportions of which it is composed.

On the other hand, all governments are not of the same nature; there are some more or less wasteful; and the differences are based on this other principle, that the further the public contributions are removed from their source, the more burdensome they are. We must not measure this burden by the amount of the imposts, but by the distance they have to traverse in order to return to the hands from which they have come. When this circulation is prompt and well-established, it matters not whether little or much is paid; the people are always rich, and the finances are always prosperous. On the other hand, however little the people may contribute, if this little does not revert to them, they are soon exhausted by constantly giving; the State is never rich and the people are always in beggary.

It follows from this that the more the distance between the people and the government is increased, the more burdensome do the tributes become; therefore, in a democracy the people are least encumbered, in an aristocracy they are more so, and in a monarchy they bear the greatest weight. Monarchy, then, is suited only to wealthy nations; aristocracy, to States moderate both in wealth and size; democracy, to small and poor States.

Indeed, the more we reflect on it, the more do we find in this the difference between free and monarchical States. In the first, everything is used for the common advantage; in the others, public and private resources are reciprocal, and the former are increased by the diminution of the latter; lastly, instead of governing subjects in order to make them happy, despotism renders them miserable in order to govern them.

There are, then, in every climate natural causes by which we can assign the form of government which is adapted to the nature of the climate, and even say what kind of inhabitants the country should have.

Unfruitful and barren places, where the produce does not repay the labor, ought to remain uncultivated and deserted, or should only be peopled by savages; places where men's toil yields only bare necessaries ought to be inhabited by barbarous nations; in them any polity would be an impossibility. Places where the excess of the produce over the labor is moderate are suitable for free nations; those in which abundant and fertile soil yields much produce for little labor are willing to be governed monarchically, in order that the superfluity of the subjects may be consumed by the luxuries of the Prince; for it is better that this excess should be absorbed by the government than squandered by private persons. There are exceptions, I know; but these exceptions themselves confirm the rule, in that, sooner or later, they produce revolutions which restore things to their natural order.

We should always distinguish general laws from the particular causes which may modify their effects. If the whole south should be covered with republics, and the whole north with despotic States, it would not be less true that, through the influence of climate, despotism is suitable to warm countries, barbarism to cold countries, and a good polity to intermediate regions. I see, however, that while the principle is admitted, its application may be disputed; it will be said that some cold countries are very fertile, and some southern ones very unfruitful. But this is a difficulty only for those who do not examine the matter in all its relations. It is necessary, as I have already said, to reckon those connected with labor, resources, consumption, etc.

Let us suppose that the produce of two districts equal in area is in the ratio of five to ten. If the inhabitants of the former consume four and those of the latter nine parts, the surplus produce of the first will be one-fifth, and that of the second one-tenth. The ratio between these two surpluses being then inversely as that of the produce of each, the district which yields only five will give a surplus double that of the district which produces ten.

But it is not a question of double produce, and I do not think that any one dare, in general, place the fertility of cold countries even on an equality with that of warm countries. Let us, however, assume this equality; let us, if you will, put England in the scales with Sicily, and Poland with Egypt; more to the south we shall have Africa and India; more to the north we shall have nothing. For this equality in produce what a difference in the cultivation! In Sicily it is only necessary to scratch the soil; in England what care is needed to till it! But where more exertion is required to yield the same produce, the surplus must necessarily be very small.

Consider, besides this, that the same number of men consume much less in warm countries. The climate demands that people should be temperate in order to be healthy; Europeans who want to live as at home all die of dysentery and dyspepsia. "We are," says Chardin, "carnivorous beasts, wolves, in comparison with Asiatics. Some attribute the temperance of the Persians to the fact that their country is scantily cultivated; I believe, on the contrary, that their country is not very abundant in provisions because the inhabitants need very little. If their frugality," he continues, "resulted from the poverty of the country, it would be only the poor who would eat little, whereas it is the people generally; and more or less would be consumed in each province, according to the fertility of the country, whereas the same abstemiousness is found throughout the kingdom. They pride themselves greatly on their mode of living, saying that it is only necessary to look at their complexions, to see how much superior they are to those of Christians. Indeed, the complexions of the Persians are smooth; they have beautiful skins, delicate and clear: while the complexions of their subjects, the Armenians, who live in European fashion, are rough and blotched, and their bodies are coarse and heavy."

The nearer we approach the Equator, the less do the people live upon. They eat scarcely any meat; rice, maize, *cuzcuz*, millet, cassava, are their ordinary foods. There are in India millions of men whose diet does not cost a half-penny a day. We see even in Europe palpable differences in appetite between northern and southern nations. A Spaniard will live for eight days on a German's dinner. In countries where men are most voracious luxury is directed to matters of consumption; in England it is displayed in a table loaded with meats; in Italy you are regaled with sugar and flowers.

Again, luxury in dress presents similar differences. In climates where the changes of the seasons are sudden and violent, garments are better and simpler; in those where people dress only for ornament, splendor is more sought after than utility, for clothes themselves are a luxury. At Naples you will see men every day walking to Posilippo with gold-embroidered coats, and no stockings. It is the same with regard to buildings; everything is sacrificed to magnificence when there is nothing to fear from injury by the atmosphere. In Paris and in London people must be warmly and comfortably housed; in Madrid they have superb drawing-rooms, but no windows that shut, while they sleep in mere closets.

The foods are much more substantial and nutritious in warm countries; this is a third difference which cannot fail to influence the second. Why do people eat so many vegetables in Italy? Because they are good, nourishing, and of excellent flavor. In France, where they are grown only on water, they are not nourishing and count almost for nothing on the table; they do not, however, occupy less ground, and they cost at least as much labor to cultivate. It is found by experience that the wheats of Barbary, inferior in other respects to those of France, yield much more flour, and that those of France, in their turn, yield more than the wheats of the north. Whence we may infer that a similar gradation is observable generally, in the same direction, from the Equator to the Pole. Now is it not a manifest disadvantage to have in an equal quantity of produce a smaller quantity of nutriment ?

To all these different considerations I may add one which springs from, and strengthens, them; it is that warm countries have less need of inhabitants than cold countries, but would be able to maintain a greater number; hence a double surplus is produced, always to the advantage of despotism. The greater the surface occupied by the same number of inhabitants, the more difficult do rebellions become, because measures cannot be concerted promptly and secretly, and because it is always easy for the government to discover the plans and cut off communications. But the more closely packed a numerous population is, the less power has a government to usurp the sovereignty; the chiefs deliberate as securely in their cabinets as the prince in his council, and the multitude assemble in the squares as quickly as the troops in their quarters. The advantage, then, of a tyrannical government lies in this, that it acts at great distances. By help of the points of support which it procures, its power increases with the distance, like that of levers.* That of the people, on the other hand, acts only when concentrated; it evaporates and disappears as it extends, like the effect of powder scattered on the ground, which takes fire only grain by grain. The least populous countries are thus the best adapted for tyranny; wild beasts reign only in deserts.

CHAPTER IX.

The Marks of a Good Government.

WHEN, then, it is asked absolutely which is the best government, an insoluble and likewise indeterminate question is propounded; or, if you will, it has as many correct solutions as there are possible combinations in the absolute and relative positions of the nations.

---

* This does not contradict what I said before (Book II. chapter ix.) on the inconveniences of large States; for there it was a question of the authority of the government over its members, and here it is a question of its power against its subjects. Its scattered members serve as points of support to it for operating at a distance upon the people, but it has no point of support for acting on its members themselves. Thus, the length of the lever is the cause of its weakness in the one case, and of its strength in the other.

But if it were asked by what sign it can be known whether a given people is well or ill governed, that would be a different matter, and the question of fact might be determined.

It is however, not settled, because every one wishes to decide it in his own way. Subjects extol the public tranquillity, citizens the liberty of individuals; the former prefer security of possessions, the latter, that of persons; the former are of opinion that the best government is the most severe, the latter maintain that it is the mildest; the one party wish that crimes should be punished and the other that they should be prevented; the one party think it well to be feared by their neighbors, the other party prefer to be unacquainted with them; the one party are satisfied when money circulates, the other party demand that the people should have bread. Even though there should be agreement on these and other similar points, would further progress be made ? Since moral quantities lack a precise mode of measurement, even if people were in accord about the sign, how could they be so about the valuation of it ?

For my part, I am always astonished that people fail to recognize a sign so simple, or that they should have the insincerity not to agree about it. What is the object of political association ? It is the preservation and prosperity of its members. And what is the surest sign that they are preserved and prosperous ? It is their number and population. Do not, then, go and seek elsewhere for this sign so much discussed. All other things being equal, the government under which, without external aids, without naturalizations, and without colonies, the citizens increase and multiply most, is infallibly the best. That under which a people diminishes and decays is the worst. Statisticians, it is now your business; reckon, measure, compare. *

* On the same principle must be judged the centuries which deserve preference in respect of the prosperity of the human race. Those in which literature and art were seen to flourish have been too much admired without the secret object of their cultivation being penetrated, without their fatal consequences being considered: *Idque apud imperitos humanitas vocabatur, quum pars servitutis esset.* Shall we never detect in the maxims of books the gross self-interest which

CHAPTER X.

The Abuse of the Government and Its Tendency to Degenerate.

As THE particular will acts incessantly against the general will, so the government makes a continual effort against the sovereignty. The more this effort is increased, the more is the constitution altered; and as there is here no other corporate will which, by resisting that of the Prince, may produce equilibrium with it, it must happen sooner or later that the Prince at length oppresses the sovereign and violates the social treaty. Therein is the inherent and inevitable vice, which, from the birth of the body politic, tends without intermission to destroy it, just as old age and death at length destroy the human body.

There are two general ways by which a government degenerates, viz, when it contracts, or when the State is dissolved.

makes the authors speak? No, whatever they may say, when, notwithstanding its brilliancy, a country is being depopulated, it is untrue that all goes well, and it is not enough that a poet should have an income of 100,000 livres for his epoch to be the best of all. The apparent repose and tranquillity of the chief men must be regarded less than the welfare of nations as a whole, and especially that of the most populous States. Hail lays waste a few cantons, but it rarely causes scarcity. Riots and civil wars greatly startle the chief men; but they do not produce the real misfortunes of nations, which may even be abated, while it is being disputed who shall tyrannize over them. It is from their permanent condition that their real prosperity or calamities spring; when all is left crushed under the yoke, it is then that everything perishes; it is then that the chief men, destroying them at their leisure, *ubi solitudinem faciunt, pacem appellant.* When the broils of the great agitated the kingdom of France, and the coadjutor of Paris carried a poniard in his pocket to the *Parlement*, that did not prevent the French nation from living happily and harmoniously in free and honorable ease. Greece of old flourished in the midst of the most cruel wars; blood flowed there in streams and the whole country was covered with men. It seemed, said Machiavelli, that amid murders, proscriptions and civil wars, our republic became more powerful; the virtues of its citizens, their manners, their independence, were more effectual in strengthening it than all its dissensions had been in weakening it. A little agitation gives energy to men's minds, and what makes the race truly prosperous is not so much peace as liberty.

(76)

The government contracts when it passes from the majority to the minority, that is, from democracy to aristocracy, and from aristocracy to royalty. That is its natural tendency. If it retrograded from the minority to the majority, it might be said to relax; but this inverse progress is impossible.

In reality, the government never changes its form except when its exhausted energy leaves it too weak to preserve itself; and if it becomes still more relaxed as it extends, its force will be annihilated, and it will no longer subsist. We must therefore concentrate the energy as it dwindles; otherwise the State which it sustains will fall into ruin.

The dissolution of the State may occur in two ways.

Firstly, when the Prince no longer administers the State in accordance with the laws and effects a usurpation of the sovereign power. Then a remarkable change takes place — the State, and not the government, contracts; I mean that the State dissolves, and that another is formed within it, which is composed only of the members of the government, and which is to the rest of the people nothing more than their master and their tyrant. So that as soon as the government usurps the sovereignty, the social compact is broken, and all the ordinary citizens, rightfully regaining their natural liberty, are forced, but not morally bound, to obey.

The same thing occurs also when the members of the government usurp separately the power which they ought to exercise only collectively; which is no less a violation of the laws, and occasions still greater disorder. Then there are, so to speak, as many Princes as magistrates; and the State, not less divided than the government, perishes or changes its form.

When the State is broken up, the abuse of the government, whatever it may be, takes the common name of ANARCHY. To distinguish, democracy degenerates into OCHLOCRACY, aristocracy into OLIGARCHY; I should add that royalty degenerates into TYRANNY; but this last word is equivocal and requires explanation.

In the vulgar sense a tyrant is a king who governs with violence and without regard to justice and the laws. In the strict sense, a tyrant is a private person who arrogates to himself the royal authority without having a right to it. It is in this sense that the Greeks understood the word tyrant; they bestowed it indifferently on good and bad princes whose authority was not legitimate. Thus TYRANT and USURPER are two words perfectly synonymous.

To give different names to different things, I call the usurper of royal authority a TYRANT, and the usurper of sovereign power a DESPOT. The tyrant is he who, contrary to the laws, takes upon himself to govern according to the laws; the despot is he who sets himself above the laws themselves. Thus the tyrant cannot be a despot, but the despot is always a tyrant.

CHAPTER XI.

THE DISSOLUTION OF THE BODY POLITIC.

SUCH is the natural and inevitable tendency of the best constituted governments. If Sparta and Rome have perished, what State can hope to endure for ever? If we wish to form a durable constitution, let us, then, not dream of making it eternal. In order to succeed we must not attempt the impossible, nor flatter ourselves that we are giving to the work of men a stability which human things do not admit of.

The body politic, as well as the human body, begins to die from its birth, and bears in itself the causes of its own destruction. But both may have a constitution more or less robust, and fitted to preserve them a longer or shorter time. The constitution of man is the work of nature; that of the State is the work of art. It does not rest with men to prolong their lives; it does rest with them to prolong that of the State as far as possible, by giving it the best constitution practicable. The best constituted will come to an end, but not so soon as another, unless some unforeseen accident brings about its premature destruction.

The principle of political life is in the sovereign authority. The legislative power is the heart of the State; the executive power is its brain, giving movement to all the parts. The brain may be paralyzed and yet the individual may live. A man remains an imbecile and lives; but so soon as the heart ceases its functions, the animal dies.

It is not by laws that the State subsists, but by the legislative power. The law of yesterday is not binding to-day; but tacit consent is presumed from silence, and the sovereign is supposed to confirm continually the laws which it does not abrogate when able to do so. Whatever it has once declared that it wills, it wills always, unless the declaration is revoked.

Why, then, do people show so much respect for ancient laws? It is on account of their antiquity. We must believe that it is only the excellence of the ancient laws which has enabled them to be so long preserved; unless the sovereign has recognized them as constantly salutary, it would have revoked them a thousand times. That is why, far from being weakened, the laws are ever acquiring fresh vigor in every well-constituted State; the prejudice in favor of antiquity renders them more venerable every day; while, wherever laws are weakened as they grow old, this fact proves that there is no longer any legislative power, and that the State no longer lives.

CHAPTER XII.

How the Sovereign Authority is Maintained.

THE sovereign, having no other force than the legislative power, acts only through the laws; and the laws being nothing but authentic acts of the general will, the sovereign can act only when the people are assembled. The people assembled, it will be said: what a chimera! It is a chimera to-day; but it was not so two thousand years ago. Have men changed their nature?

The limits of the possible in moral things are less narrow than we think; it is our weaknesses, our vices, our prejudices, that contract them. Sordid souls do not believe in great men; vile slaves smile with a mocking air at the word LIBERTY.

From what has been done let us consider what can be done. I shall not speak of the ancient republics of Greece; but the Roman Republic was, it seems to me, a great State, and the city of Rome a great city. The last census in Rome showed that there were 400,000 citizens bearing arms, and the last enumeration of the Empire showed more than 4,000,000 citizens, without reckoning subjects, foreigners, women, children, and slaves.

What a difficulty, we might suppose, there would be in assembling frequently the enormous population of the capital and its environs. Yet few weeks passed without the Roman people being assembled, even several times. Not only did they exercise the rights of sovereignty, but a part of the functions of government. They discussed certain affairs and judged certain causes, and in the public assembly the whole people were almost as often magistrates as citizens.

By going back to the early times of nations, we should find that the majority of the ancient governments, even monarchical ones, like those of the Macedonians and the Franks, had similar councils. Be that as it may, this single incontestable fact solves all difficulties; inference from the actual to the possible appears to me sound.

CHAPTER XIII.

How the Sovereign Authority is Maintained—
(Continued).

IT is not sufficient that the assembled people should have once fixed the constitution of the State by giving their sanction to a body of laws; it is not sufficient that they should have established a perpetual government, or that they should have once for all provided for the election of magistrates. Besides the extraordinary assemblies which unforeseen events may require, it is necessary that there should be fixed and periodical ones which nothing can abolish or prorogue; so that, on the appointed day, the people are rightfully convoked by the law, without needing for that purpose any formal summons.

But, excepting these assemblies which are lawful by their date alone, every assembly of the people that has not been convoked by the magistrates appointed for that duty and according to the prescribed forms, ought to be regarded as unlawful and all that is done in it as invalid, because even the order to assemble ought to emanate from the law.

As for the more or less frequent meetings of the lawful assemblies, they depend on so many considerations that no precise rules can be given about them. Only it may be said generally that the more force a government has the more frequently should the sovereign display itself.

This, I shall be told, may be good for a single city; but what is to be done when the State comprises many cities? Will the sovereign authority be divided? Or must it be concentrated in a single city and render subject all the rest.

I answer that neither alternative is necessary. In the first place, the sovereign authority is simple and undivided, and we cannot divide it without destroying it. In the second place, a city, no more than a nation, can be lawfully subject to another, because the essence of the body politic consists in the union of obedience and liberty, and these words, SUBJECT and SOVEREIGN, are correlatives, the notion underlying them being expressed in the one word citizen.

I answer, further, that it is always an evil to combine several towns into a single State, and, in desiring to effect such a union, we must not flatter ourselves that we shall avoid the natural inconveniences of it. The abuses of great States cannot be brought as an objection against a man who only desires small ones. But how can small States be endowed with sufficient force to resist great ones? Just in the same way as when the Greek towns of old resisted the Great King, and as more recently Holland and Switzerland have resisted the House of Austria.

6

If, however, the State cannot be reduced to proper limits, one resource still remains; it is not to allow any capital, but to make the government sit alternately in each town, and also to assemble in them by turns the estates of the country.

People the territory uniformly, extend the same rights everywhere, spread everywhere abundance and life; in this way the State will become at once the strongest and the best governed that may be possible. Remember that the walls of the towns are formed solely of the remains of houses in the country. For every palace that I see rising in the capital, I seem to see a whole rural district laid in ruins.

CHAPTER XIV.

How the Sovereign Authority is Maintained— (Continued.)

So soon as the people are lawfully assembled as a sovereign body, the whole jurisdiction of the government ceases, the executive power is suspended, and the person of the meanest citizen is as sacred and inviolable as that of the first magistrate, because where the represented are, there is no longer any representative. Most of the tumults that arose in Rome in the *comitia* proceeded from ignorance or neglect of this rule. The consuls were then only presidents of the people and the tribunes simple orators; the Senate had no power at all.

These intervals of suspension, in which the Prince recognizes or ought to recognize the presence of a superior, have always been dreaded by that power; and these assemblies of the people, which are the shield of the body politic and the curb of the government, have in all ages been the terror of the chief men; hence such men are never wanting in solicitude, objections, obstacles, and promises, in the endeavor to make the citizens disgusted with the assemblies. When the latter are avaricious, cowardly, pusillanimous, and more desirous of repose than of freedom, they do not long hold out against the repeated efforts of the government; and thus, as the resisting force constantly increases, the sovereign authority at last disappears, and most of the States decay and perish before their time.

But between the sovereign authority and the arbitrary government there is sometimes introduced an intermediate power of which I must speak.

CHAPTER XV.

DEPUTIES OR REPRESENTATIVES.

So SOON as the service of the State ceases to be the principal business of the citizens, and they prefer to render aid with their purses rather than their persons, the State is already on the brink of ruin. Is it necessary to march to battle, they pay troops and remain at home; is it necessary to go to the council, they elect deputies and remain at home. As a result of indolence and wealth, they at length have soldiers to enslave their country and representatives to sell it.

It is the bustle of commerce and of the arts, it is the greedy pursuit of gain, it is effeminacy and love of comforts, that commute personal services for money. Men sacrifice a portion of their profit in order to increase it at their ease. Give money and soon you will have chains. That word FINANCE is a slave's word; it is unknown among citizens. In a country that is really free, the citizens do everything with their hands and nothing with money: far from paying for exemption from their duties, they would pay to perform them themselves. I am far removed from ordinary ideas; I believe that statute labor (*les corvées*) is less repugnant to liberty than taxation is.

The better constituted a State is, the more do public affairs outweigh private ones in the minds of the citizens. There is, indeed, a much smaller number of private affairs, because the amount of the general prosperity furnishes a more considerable portion to that of each indi-

vidual, and less remains to be sought by individual
exertions. In a well-conducted city-state everyone hastens
to the assemblies: while under a bad government no one
cares to move a step in order to attend them, because no
one takes an interest in the proceedings, since it is foreseen that the general will will not prevail; and so at last
private concerns become all-absorbing. Good laws pave
the way for better ones; bad laws lead to worse ones.
As soon as any one says of the affairs of the State, "Of
what importance are they to me?" we must consider that
the State is lost.

The decline of patriotism, the active pursuit of private
interests, the vast size of States, conquests, and the
abuses of government, have suggested the plan of deputies or representatives of the people in the assemblies
of the nation. It is this which in certain countries they
dare to call the third estate. Thus the private interest
of two orders is put in the first and second rank, the
public interest only in the third.

Sovereignty cannot be represented for the same reason
that it cannot be alienated; it consists essentially in the
general will, and the will cannot be represented; it is the
same or it is different; there is no medium. The deputies
of the people, then, are not and cannot be its representatives; they are only its commissioners and can conclude
nothing definitely. Every law which the people in person have not ratified is invalid; it is not a law. The Eng-.
lish nation thinks that it is free, but is greatly mistaken,
for it is so only during the election of members of Parliament; as soon as they are elected, it is enslaved and
counts for nothing. The use which it makes of the brief
moments of freedom renders the loss of liberty well-
deserved.

The idea of representatives is modern; it comes to us
from feudal government, that absurd and iniquitous government, under which mankind is degraded and the name
of man dishonored. In the republics, and even in the
monarchies, of antiquity, the people never had representatives; they did not know the word. It is very
singular that in Rome, where the tribunes were so sacred,
it was not even imagined that they could usurp the func-

tions of the people, and in the midst of so great a multitude, they never attempted to pass of their own accord
a single *plebiscitum*. We may judge, however, of the
embarrassment which the crowd sometimes caused from
what occurred in the time of the Gracchi, when a part
of the citizens gave their votes on the house-tops. But
where right and liberty are all in all, inconveniences are
nothing. In that wise nation everything was estimated
at a true value; it allowed the lictors to do what the
tribunes had not dared to do, and was not afraid that
the lictors would want to represent it.

To explain, however, in what manner the tribunes sometimes represented it, it is sufficient to understand how
the government represents the sovereign. The law being
nothing but the declaration of the general will, it is
clear that in their legislative capacity the people cannot
be represented; but they can and should be represented
in the executive power, which is only force applied to
law. This shows that very few nations would, upon careful examination, be found to have laws. Be that as it
may, it is certain that the tribunes, having no share in
the executive power, could never represent the Roman
people by right of their office, but only by encroaching
on the rights of the Senate.

Among the Greeks, whatever the people had to do,
they did themselves; they were constantly assembled in
the public place. They lived in a mild climate and they
were not avaricious; slaves performed the manual labor;
the people's great business was liberty. Not having the
same advantages, how are you to preserve the same
rights? Your more rigorous climates give you more wants;*
for six months in a year the public place is untenable,
and your hoarse voices cannot be heard in the open air.
You care more for gain than for liberty, and you fear
slavery far less than you do misery.

What! is liberty maintained only with the help of
slavery? Perhaps; extremes meet. Everything which is
not according to nature has its inconveniences, and civil

* To adopt in cold countries the effeminacy and luxuriousness of Ori-
entals is to be willing to assume their chains, and to submit to them
even more necessarily than they do.

society more than all the rest. There are circumstances so unfortunate that people can preserve their freedom only at the expense of that of others, and the citizen cannot be completely free except when the slave is enslaved to the utmost. Such was the position of Sparta. As for you, modern nations, you have no slaves, but you are slaves; you pay for their feedom with your own. In vain do you boast of this preference; I find in it more of cowardice than of humanity.

I do not mean by all this that slaves are necessary and that the right of slavery is lawful, since I have proved the contrary; I only mention the reasons why modern nations who believe themselves free have representatives, and why ancient nations had none. Be that as it may, as soon as a nation appoints representatives, it is no longer free; it no longer exists.

After very careful consideration I do not see that it is possible henceforward for the sovereign to preserve among us the exercise of its rights unless the State is very small. But if it is very small, will it not be subjugated? No; I shall show hereafter how the external power of a great nation can be combined with the convenient polity and good order a small State.

CHAPTER XVI.

THAT THE INSTITUTION OF THE GOVERNMENT IS NOT A CONTRACT.

THE legislative power being once well established, the question is to establish also the executive power; for this latter, which operates only by particular acts, not being of the essence of the other, is naturally separated from it. If it were possible that the sovereign, considered as such, should have the executive power, law and fact would be so confounded that it could no longer be known what is law and what is not; and the body politic, thus perverted, would soon become a prey to the violence against which it was instituted.

The citizens being all equal by the social contract, all can prescribe what all ought to do, while no one has a right to demand that another should do what he will not do himself. Now, it is properly this right, indispensable to make the body politic live and move, which the sovereign gives to the Prince in establishing the government.

Several have pretended that the instrument in this establishment is a contract between the people and the chiefs whom they set over themselves—a contract by which it is stipulated between the two parties on what conditions the one binds itself to rule, the other to obey. It will be agreed, I am sure, that this is a strange method of contracting. But let us see whether such a position is tenable.

First, the supreme authority can no more be modified than alienated; to limit it is to destroy it. It is absurd and contradictory that the sovereign should acknowledge a superior; to bind itself to obey a master is to regain full liberty.

Further, it is evident that this contract of the people with such or such persons is a particular act; whence it follows that the contract cannot be a law nor an act of sovereignty, and that consequently it is unlawful.

Moreover, we see that the contracting parties themselves would be under the law of nature alone, and without any security for the performance of their reciprocal engagements, which is in every way repugnant to the civil state. He who possesses the power being always capable of executing it, we might as well give the name contract to the act of a man who should say to another: "I give you all my property, on condition that you restore me what you please."

There is but one contract in the State—that of association; and this of itself excludes any other. No public contract can be conceived which would not be a violation of the first.

CHAPTER XVII.

The Institution of the Government.

UNDER what general notion, then, must be included the act by which the government is instituted? I shall observe first that this act is complex, or composed of two others, viz, the establishment of the law and the execution of the law.

By the first, the sovereign determines that there shall be a governing body established in such or such a form; and it is clear that this act is a law.

By the second, the people nominate the chiefs who will be intrusted with the government when established. Now, this nomination being a particular act, is not a second law, but only a consequence of the first, and a function of the government.

The difficulty is to understand how there can be an act of government before the government exists, and how the people, who are only sovereign or subjects, can, in certain circumstances, become the Prince or the magistrates.

Here, however, is disclosed one of those astonishing properties of the body politic, by which it reconciles operations apparently contradictory; for this is effected by a sudden conversion of sovereignty into democracy in such a manner that, without any perceptible change, and merely by a new relation of all to all, the citizens, having become magistrates, pass from general acts to particular acts, and from the law to the execution of it.

This change of relation is not a subtlety of speculation without example in practice; it occurs every day in the Parliament of England, in which the Lower House on certain occasions resolves itself into Grand Committee in order to discuss business better, and thus becomes a simple commission instead of the sovereign court that it was the moment before. In this way it afterward reports to itself, as the House of Commons, what it has just decided in Grand Committee.

(88)

Such is the advantage peculiar to a democratic government, that it can be established in fact by a simple act of the general will; and after this, the provisional government remains in power, should that be the form adopted, or establishes in the name of the sovereign the government prescribed by the law; and thus everything is according to rule. It is impossible to institute the government in any other way that is legitimate without renouncing the principles heretofore established.

CHAPTER XVIII.

MEANS OF PREVENTING USURPATIONS OF THE GOVERNMENT.

FROM these explanations it follows, in confirmation of chapter XVI., that the act which institutes the government is not a contract, but a law; that the depositaries of the executive power are not the masters of the people, but its officers; that the people can appoint them and dismiss them at pleasure; that for them it is not a question of contracting, but of obeying; and that in undertaking the functions which the State imposes on them, they simply fulfill their duty as citizens, without having in any way a right to discuss the conditions.

When, therefore, it happens that the people institute a hereditary government, whether monarchical in a family or aristocratic in one order of citizens, it is not an engagement that they make, but a provisional form which they give to the administration, until they please to regulate it differently.

It is true that such changes are always dangerous, and that the established government must never be touched except when it becomes incompatible with the public good; but this circumspection is a maxim of policy, not a rule of right; and the State is no more bound to leave the civil authority to its chief men than the military authority to its generals.

Moveover it is true that in such a case all the formalities requisite to distinguish a regular and lawful act from a seditious tumult, and the will of a whole people from the clamors of a faction, cannot be too carefully observed. It is especially in this case that only such concession should be made as cannot in strict justice be refused; and from this obligation also the Prince derives a great advantage in preserving its power in spite of the people, without there being able to say that it has usurped the power; for while appearing to exercise nothing but its rights, it may very easily extend them, and, under pretext of maintaining the public peace, obstruct the assemblies designed to re-establish good order; so that it takes advantage of a silence which it prevents from being broken, or of irregularities which it causes to be committed, so as to assume in its favor the approbation of those whom fear renders silent and punish those that dare to speak. It is in this way that the Decemvirs, having at first been elected for one year, and then kept in office for another year, attempted to retain their power in perpetuity by no longer permitting the *comitia* to assemble; and it is by this easy method that all the governments in the world, when once invested with the public force, usurp sooner or later the sovereign authority.

The periodical assemblies of which I have spoken before are fitted to prevent or postpone this evil, especially when they need no formal convocation; for then the Prince cannot interfere with them, without openly proclaiming itself a violator of the laws and an enemy of the State.

These assemblies, which have as their object the maintenance of the social treaty, ought always to be opened with two propositions, which no one should be able to suppress, and which should pass separately by vote.

The first: "Whether it pleases the sovereign to maintain the present form of government."

The second: "Whether it pleases the people to leave the administration to those at present intrusted with it."

I presuppose here what I believe that I have proved, viz, that there is in the State no fundamental law which cannot be revoked, not even the social compact; for if all the citizens assembled in order to break this compact by a solemn agreement, no one can doubt that it would be quite legitimately broken. Grotius even thinks that each man can renounce the State of which he is a member, and regain his natural freedom and his property by quitting the country.* Now it would be absurd if all the citizens combined should be unable to do what each of them can do separately.

* It must be clearly understood that no one should leave in order to evade his duty and relieve himself from serving his country at a moment when it needs him. Flight in that case would be criminal and punishable; it would no longer be retirement, but desertion.

BOOK IV.

CHAPTER I.

THAT THE GENERAL WILL IS INDESTRUCTIBLE.*

So LONG as a number of men in combination are considered as a single body, they have but one will, which relates to the common preservation and to the general well-being. In such a case all the forces of the State are vigorous and simple, and its principles are clear and luminous; it has no confused and conflicting interests; the common good is everywhere plainly manifest and only good sense is required to perceive it. Peace, union, and equality are foes to political subtleties. Upright and simple-minded men are hard to deceive because of their simplicity; allurements and refined pretexts do not impose upon them; they are not even cunning enough to be dupes. When, in the happiest nation in the world, we see troops of peasants regulating the affairs of the State under an oak and always acting wisely, can we refrain from despising the refinements of other nations, who make themselves illustrious and wretched with so much art and mystery?

A State thus governed needs very few laws; and in so far as it becomes necessary to promulgate new ones, this necessity is universally recognized. The first man to propose them only gives expression to what all have previously felt, and neither factions nor eloquence will be needed to pass into law what every one has already resolved to do, so soon as he is sure that the rest will act as he does.

What deceives reasoners is that, seeing only States that are ill-constituted from the beginning, they are impressed with the impossibility of maintaining such a

* This chapter appears to belong more properly to Book II.— ED.

policy in those States; they laugh to think of all the follies to which a cunning knave, an insinuating speaker,
can persuade the people of Paris or London.   They know
not that Cromwell would have been put in irons by the
people of Berne, and the Duke of Beaufort imprisoned
by the Genevese.

But when the social bond begins to be relaxed and the
State weakened, when private interests begin to make
themselves felt and small associations to exercise an
influence on the State, the common interest is injuri-
ously affected and finds adversaries; unanimity no longer
reigns in the voting; the general will is no longer the
will of all; opposition and disputes arise, and the best
counsel does not pass uncontested.

Lastly, when the State, on the verge of ruin, no longer
subsists except in a vain and illusory form, when the
social bond is broken in all hearts, when the basest interest shelters itself impudently under the sacred name
of the public welfare, the general will becomes dumb;
all, under the guidance of secret motives, no more express their opinions as citizens than if the State had
never existed; and, under the name of laws, they deceit-
fully pass unjust decrees which have only private interest
as their end.

Does it follow from this that the general will is destroyed or corrupted?   No; it is always constant, unalterable, and pure; but it is subordinated to others which get
the better of it.   Each, detaching his own interest from
the common interest, sees clearly that he cannot completely separate it; but his share in the injury done to the
State appears to him as nothing in comparison with the
exclusive advantage which he aims at appropriating to
himself.   This particular advantage being excepted, he
desires the general welfare for his own interests quite
as strongly as any other.   Even in selling his vote for
money, he does not extinguish in himself the general
will, but eludes it.   The fault that he commits is to change
the state of the question, and to answer something
different from what he was asked; so that, instead of saying by a vote: "It is beneficial to the State," he says: "It
is beneficial to a certain man or a certain party that such

or such a motion should pass." Thus the law of public
order in assemblies is not so much to maintain in them
the general will as to insure that it shall always be consulted and always respond.

I might in this place make many reflections on the
simple right of voting in every act of sovereignty — a right
which nothing can take away from the citizens — and on
that of speaking, proposing, dividing, and discussing,
which the government is always very careful to leave to
its members only; but this important matter would require
a separate treatise, and I cannot say everything in
this one.

CHAPTER II.

VOTING.

WE SEE from the previous chapter that the manner in
which public affairs are managed may give a sufficiently
trustworthy indication of the character and health of the
body politic. The more that harmony reigns in the assemblies, that is, the more the voting approaches unanimity, the more also is the general will predominant; but
long discussions, dissensions, and uproar proclaim the as-
cendency of private interests and the decline of the State.

This is not so clearly apparent when two or more orders enter into its constitution, as, in Rome, the patricians and plebeians, whose quarrels often disturbed the
comitia, even in the palmiest days of the Republic; but
this exception is more apparent than real, for, at that
time, by a vice inherent in the body politic, there were,
so to speak, two States in one; what is not true of the
two together is true of each separately. And, indeed,
even in the most stormy times, the *plebiscita* of the people, when the Senate did not interfere with them, always
passed peaceably and by a large majority of votes; the
citizens having but one interest, the people had but
one will.

At the other extremity of the circle unanimity returns; that is, when the citizens, fallen into slavery,
have no longer either liberty or will. Then fear and

flattery change votes into acclamations; men no longer
deliberate, but adore or curse. Such was the disgrace-
ful mode of speaking in the Senate under the Emperors. Sometimes it was done with ridiculous precautions.
Tacitus observes that under Otho the senators, in over-
whelming Vitellius with execrations, affected to make
at the same time a frightful noise, in order that, if
he happened to become master, he might not know
what each of them had said.

From these different considerations are deduced the
principles by which we should regulate the method of
counting votes and of comparing opinions, according
as the general will is more or less easy to ascertain
and the State more or less degenerate.

There is but one law which by its nature requires unanimous consent, that is, the social compact; for civil association is the most voluntary act in the world; every
man being born free and master of himself, no one can,
under any pretext whatever, enslave him without his
assent. To decide that the son of a slave is born a slave
is to decide that he is not born a man.

If, then, at the time of the social compact, there are
opponents of it, their opposition does not invalidate the
contract, but only prevents them from being included in
it; they are foreigners among citizens. When the State
is established, consent lies in residence; to dwell in the
territory is to submit to the sovereignty.*

Excepting this original contract, the vote of the majority always binds all the rest, this being a result of
the contract itself. But it will be asked how a man can
be free and yet forced to conform to wills which are not
his own. How are opponents free and yet subject to
laws they have not consented to?

I reply that the question is wrongly put. The citizen
consents to all the laws, even to those which are passed
in spite of him, and even to those which punish him
when he dares to violate any of them. The unvarying

---

* This must always be understood to relate to a free State; for otherwise family, property, want of an asylum, necessity, or violence, may
detain an inhabitant in a country against his will; and then his residence
alone no longer supposes his consent to the contract or to the violation of it.

will of all the members of the State is the general will; it is through that that they are citizens and free. When a law is proposed in the assembly of the people, what is asked of them is not exactly whether they approve the proposition or reject it, but whether it is conformable or not to the general will, which is their own; each one in giving his vote expresses his opinion thereupon; and from the counting of the votes is obtained the declaration of the general will. When, therefore, the opinion opposed to my own prevails, that simply shows that I was mistaken, and that what I considered to be the general will was not so. Had my private opinion prevailed, I should have done something other than I wished; and in that case I should not have been free.

This supposes, it is true, that all the marks of the general will are still in the majority; when they cease to be so, whatever side we take, there is no longer any liberty.

In showing before how particular wills were substituted for general wills in public resolutions, I have sufficiently indicated the means practicable for preventing this abuse; I will speak of it again hereafter. With regard to the proportional number of votes for declaring this will, I have also laid down the principles according to which it may be determined. The difference of a single vote destroys unanimity; but between unanimity and equality there are many unequal divisions, at each of which this number can be fixed according to the condition and requirements of the body politic.

Two general principles may serve to regulate these proportions: the one, that the more important and weighty the resolutions, the nearer should the opinion which prevails approach unanimity; the other, that the greater the despatch requisite in the matter under discussion, the more should we restrict the prescribed difference in the division of opinions; in resolutions which must be come to immediately the majority of a single vote should suffice. The first of these principles appears more suitable to laws, the second to affairs. Be that as it may, it is by their combination that are established the best proportions which can be assigned for the decision of a majority.

CHAPTER III.

ELECTIONS.

WITH regard to the elections of the Prince and the magistrates, which are, as I have said, complex acts, there are two modes of procedure, viz, choice and lot. Both have been employed in different republics, and a very complicated mixture of the two is seen even now in the election of the Doge of Venice.

"Election by lot," says Montesquieu, "is of the nature of democracy." I agree, but how is it so? "The lot," he continues, "is a mode of election which mortifies no one; it leaves every citizen a reasonable hope of serving his country." But these are not the reasons.

If we are mindful that the election of the chiefs is a function of government and not of sovereignty, we shall see why the method of election by lot is more in the nature of democracy, in which the administration is by so much the better as its acts are less multiplied.

In every true democracy, the magistracy is not a boon but an onerous charge, which cannot fairly be imposed on one individual rather than on another. The law alone can impose this burden on the person upon whom the lot falls. For then, the conditions being equal for all, and the choice not being dependent on any human will, there is no particular application to alter the universality of the law.

In an aristocracy the Prince chooses the Prince, the government is maintained by itself, and voting is rightly established.

The instance of the election of the Doge of Venice, far from destroying this distinction, confirms it; this composite form is suitable in a mixed government. For it is an error to take the government of Venice as a true aristocracy. If the people have no share in the government, the nobles themselves are numerous. A multitude of poor *Barnabotes* never come near any magistracy and have for their nobility only the empty title of Excellency and the right to attend the Great Council. This Great Council being as numerous as our General Council at Geneva, its illustrious members have no more privileges than our simple citizens (*citoyens*). It is certain that, setting aside the extreme disparity of the two Republics, the burgesses (*la bourgeoisie*) of Geneva exactly correspond to the Venetian order of patricians; our natives (*natifs*) and residents (*habitants*) represent the citizens and people of Venice; our peasants (*paysans*) represent the subjects of the mainland; in short, in whatever way we consider this Republic apart from its size, its government is no more aristocratic than ours. The whole difference is that, having no chief for life, we have not the same need for election by lot.

Elections by lot would have few drawbacks in a true democracy, in which, all being equal, as well in character and ability as in sentiments and fortune, the choice would become almost indifferent. But I have already said that there is no true democracy.

When choice and lot are combined, the first should be employed to fill the posts that require peculiar talents, such as military appointments; the other is suitable for those in which good sense, justice and integrity are sufficient, such as judicial offices, because, in a well-constituted State, these qualities are common to all the citizens.

Neither lot nor voting has any place in a monarchical government. The monarch being by right sole Prince and sole magistrate, the choice of his lieutenants belongs to him alone. When the Abbé de Saint-Pierre proposed to multiply the councils of the King of France and to elect the members of them by ballot, he did not see that he was proposing to change the form of government.

It would remain for me to speak of the method for recording and collecting votes in the assembly of the people; but perhaps the history of the Roman policy in that respect will explain more clearly all the principles which I might be able to establish. It is not unworthy of a judicious reader to see in some detail how public and private affairs were dealt with in a council of 200,000 men.

CHAPTER IV.

The Roman Comitia.

WE HAVE no very trustworthy records of the early times of Rome; there is even great probability that most of the things which have been handed down are fables, and in general, the most instructive part of the annals of nations, which is the history of their institution, is the most defective. Experience every day teaches us from what causes spring the revolutions of empires; but, as nations are no longer in process of formation, we have scarcely anything but conjectures to explain how they have been formed.

The customs which are found established at least testify that these customs had a beginning. Of the traditions that go back to these origins, those which the greatest authorities countenance, and which the strongest reasons confirm, ought to pass as the most undoubted. These are the principles which I have tried to follow in inquiring how the freest and most powerful nation in the world exercised its supreme power.

After the foundation of Rome, the growing republic, that is, the army of the founder, composed of Albans, Sabines, and foreigners, was divided into three classes, which, from this division, took the name of TRIBES. Each of these tribes was subdivided into ten *curiæ*, and each *curia* into *decuriæ*, at the head of which were placed *curiones* and *decuriones*.

Besides this, a body of one hundred horsemen or knights, called a *centuria*, was drawn from each tribe, whence we see that these divisions, not very necessary in a town, were at first only military. But it seems that an instinct of greatness induced the little town of Rome from the first to adopt a polity suitable to the capital of the world.

From this first division an inconvenience soon resulted; the tribe of the Albans and that of the Sabines remaining always in the same condition, while that of the

foreigners increased continually through perpetual accessions, the last soon outnumbered the two others. The
remedy which Servius found for this dangerous abuse
was to change the mode of division, and for the division
by races, which he abolished, to substitute another derived from the districts of the city occupied by each tribe.
Instead of three tribes be made four, each of which
occupied one of the hills of Rome and bore its name.
Thus, in remedying the existing inequality, he also prevented it for the future; and in order that this might be
a division, not only of localities, but of men, he prohibited the inhabitants of one quarter from removing into
another, which prevented the races from being mingled.

He also doubled the three old *centuriæ* of cavalry and
added twelve others to them, but still under the old
names — a simple and judicious means by which he
effected a distinction between the body of knights and
that of the people, without making the latter murmur.

To these four urban tribes Servius added fifteen others,
called rural tribes, because they were formed of inhabitants of the country, divided into so many cantons. Afterward as many new ones were formed; and the Roman
people were at length divided into thirty-five tribes, a
number which remained fixed until the close of the
Republic.

From this distinction between the urban and the rural
tribes resulted an effect worthy of notice, because there
is no other instance of it, and because Rome owed to it
both the preservation of her manners and the growth of
her empire. It might be supposed that the urban tribes
soon arrogated to themselves the power and the honors,
and were ready to disparage the rural tribes. It was
quite the reverse. We know the taste of the old Romans
for a country life. This taste they derived from their
wise founder, who united with liberty rural and military
works, and relegated, so to speak, to the towns arts,
trades, intrigue, wealth, and slavery.

Thus every eminent man that Rome had being a dweller
in the fields and a tiller of the soil, it was customary to
seek in the country only for the defenders of the Republic.
This condition, being that of the worthiest patricians,

was honored by every one; the simple and laborious life of villagers was preferred to the lax and indolent life of the burgesses of Rome; and many who would have been only wretched proletarians in the city became as laborers in the fields, respected citizens. It is not without reason, said Varro, that our high-minded ancestors established in the village the nursery of those hardy and valiant men who defended them in time of war and sustained them in time of peace. Pliny says positively that the rural tribes were honored because of the men that composed them, while the worthless whom it was desired to disgrace were transferred as a mark of ignominy into the urban tribes. The Sabine, Appius Claudius, having come to settle in Rome, was there loaded with honors and enrolled in a rural tribe, which afterward took the name of his family. Lastly, all the freedmen entered the urban tribes, never the rural; and during the whole of the Republic there is not a single example of any of these freedmen attaining a magistracy, although they had become citizens.

This maxim was excellent, but was pushed so far that at length a change, and certainly an abuse, in government, resulted from it.

First, the censors, after having long arrogated the right of transferring citizens arbitrarily from one tribe to another, allowed the majority to be enrolled in whichever they pleased — a permission which certainly was in no way advantageous, and took away one of the great resources of the censorship. Further, since the great and powerful all enrolled themselves in the rural tribes, while the freedmen who had become citizens remained with the populace in the urban ones, the tribes in general had no longer any district or territory, but all were so intermingled that it was impossible to distinguish the members of each except by the registers; so that the idea of the word TRIBE passed thus from the real to the personal, or rather became almost a chimera.

Moreover, it came about that the urban tribes, being close at hand, were often the most powerful in the *comitia*, and sold the State to those who stooped to buy the votes of the mob of which they were composed.

With regard to the *curiæ*, the founder having formed
ten in each tribe, the whole Roman people, at that time
inclosed in the walls of the city, consisted of thirty
curiæ, each of which had its temples, its gods, its officers, its priests, and its festivals called *compitalia*,
resembling the *paganalia* which the rural tribes had afterward.

In the new division of Servius, the number thirty being
incapable of equal distribution into four tribes, he was
unwilling to touch them; and the *curiæ*, being independent of the tribes, became another division of the inhabitants of Rome. But there was no question of *curiæ* either
in the rural tribes or in the people composing them,
because the tribes having become a purely civil institution, and another mode of levying troops having been
introduced, the military divisions of Romulus were found
superfluous. Thus, although every citizen was enrolled
in a tribe, it was far from being the case that each was
enrolled in a *curia*.

Servius made yet a third division, which had no
relation to the two preceding, but became by its effects
the most important of all. He distributed the whole
Roman people into six classes, which he distinguished,
not by the place of residence, nor by the men, but by
property; so that the first classes were filled with rich
men, the last with poor men, and the intermediate ones
with those who enjoyed a moderate fortune. These six
classes were subdivided into one hundred and ninety-
three other bodies called *centuriæ*, and these bodies were
so distributed that the first class alone comprised more
than a half, and the last formed only one. It thus happened that the class least numerous in men had most
centuriæ, and that the last entire class was counted as
only one subdivision, although it alone contained more
than a half of the inhabitants of Rome.

In order that the people might not so clearly discern
the consequences of this last form, Servius affected to
give it a military aspect. He introduced in the second
class two *centuriæ* of armorers, and two of makers of
instruments of war in the fourth; in each class, except
the last, he distinguished the young and the old, that is

to say, those who were obliged to bear arms, and those who were exempted by law on account of age — a distinction which, more than that of property, gave rise to the necessity of frequently repeating the CENSUS or enumeration; finally he required that the assembly should be held in the *Campus Martius*, and that all who were qualified for service by age should gather there with their arms.

The reason why he did not follow in the last class this same division into seniors and juniors is, that the honor of bearing arms for their country was not granted to the populace of which it was composed; it was necessary to have homes in order to obtain the right of defending them; and out of those innumerable troops of beggars with which the armies of kings nowadays glitter, there is perhaps not one but would have been driven with scorn from a Roman cohort when soldiers were defenders of liberty.

Yet again, there was in the last class a distinction between the *proletarii* and those who were called *capite censi.* The former not altogether destitute, at least supplied citizens to the State, sometimes even soldiers in pressing need. As for those who had nothing at all and could only be counted by heads, they were regarded as altogether unimportant, and Marius was the first who condescended to enroll them.

Without deciding here whether this third enumeration was good or bad in itself, I think I may affirm that nothing but the simple manners of the early Romans — their disinterestedness, their taste for agriculture, their contempt for commerce and for the ardent pursuit of gain — could have rendered it practicable. In what modern nation would rapacious greed, restlessness of spirit, intrigue, continual changes of residence, and the perpetual revolutions of fortune have allowed such an institution to endure for twenty years without the whole State being subverted? It is, indeed, necessary to observe carefully that morality and the censorship, more powerful than this institution, corrected its imperfections in Rome, and that many a rich man was relegated to the class of the poor for making too much display of his wealth.

From all this we may easily understand why mention
is scarcely ever made of more than five classes, although
there were really six.   The sixth, which furnished neither
soldiers to the army, nor voters to the *Campus Martius**
and which was almost useless in the Republic, rarely
counted as anything.

Such were the different divisions of the Roman people.
Let us see now what effect they produced in the assemblies.   These assemblies, lawfully convened, were
called *comitia;* they were usually held in the Forum of
Rome or in the *Campus Martius*, and were distinguished
as *comitia curiata, comitia centuriata*, and *comitia tributa*,
in accordance with that one of the three forms by
which they were regulated.   The *comitia curiata* were
founded by Romulus, the *comitia centuriata* by Servius,
and the *comitia tributa* by the tribunes of the people.
No law received sanction, no magistrate was elected, except in the *comitia*; and as there was no citizen who was
not enrolled in a *curia*, in a *centuria*, or in a tribe, it
follows that no citizen was excluded from the right of
voting, and that the Roman people were truly sovereign
de jure and *de facto*.

In order that the *comitia* might be lawfully assembled,
and that what was done in them might have the force of
law, three conditions were necessary; the first, that the
body or magistrate which convoked them should be invested with the necessary authority for that purpose; the
second, that the assembly should be held on one of the
days permitted by law; the third, that the auguries
should be favorable.

The reason for the first regulation need not be explained; the second is a matter of police; thus it was not
permitted to hold the *comitia* on feast days and market
days, when the country people, coming to Rome on
business, had no leisure to pass the day in the place of
assembly.   By the third, the Senate kept in check a
proud and turbulent people, and seasonably tempered the

*I say, "to the *Campus Martius*," because it was there that the
comitia centuriata assembled; in the two other forms the people
assembled in the Forum or elsewhere; and then the *capite censi* had
as much influence and authority as the chief citizens.

ardor of seditious tribunes; but the latter found more
than one means of freeing themselves from this constraint.

Laws and the election of chiefs were not the only
points submitted for the decision of the *comitia*; the
Roman people having usurped the most important functions of government, the fate of Europe may be said to
have been determined in their assemblies. This variety
of subjects gave scope for the different forms which
these assemblies took according to the matters which had
to be decided.

To judge of these different forms, it is sufficient to
compare them. Romulus, in instituting the *curiæ*, desired
to restrain the Senate by means of the people, and the
people by means of the Senate, while ruling equally over
all. He therefore gave the people by this form all the
authority of numbers in order to balance that of power
and wealth, which he left to the patricians. But, according to the spirit of a monarchy, he left still more advantage to the patricians through the influence of their clients
in securing a plurality of votes. This admirable institution of patrons and clients was a masterpiece of policy
and humanity, without which the patrician order, so opposed to the spirit of a republic, could not have subsisted. Rome alone has had the honor of giving to the
world such a fine institution, from which there never resulted any abuse, and which, notwithstanding, has never
been followed.

Since the form of the assembly of the *curiæ* subsisted
under the kings down to Servius, and since the reign of
the last Tarquin is not considered legitimate, the royal
laws were on this account generally distinguished by the
name of *leges curiatæ*.

Under the Republic the assembly of the *curiæ*, always
limited to the four urban tribes, and containing only the
Roman populace, did not correspond either with the Senate, which was at the head of the patricians, or with the
tribunes, who, although plebeians, were at the head of
the middle-class citizens. It therefore fell into disrepute;
and its degradation was such that its thirty assembled
lictors did what the *comitia curiata* ought to have done.

The *comitia centuriata* was so favorable to the aristocracy that we do not at first see why the Senate did not
always prevail in the *comitia* which bore that name,
and by which the consuls, censors, and other curule
magistrates were elected. Indeed, of the one hundred
and ninety-three *centuriæ* which formed the six classes
of the whole Roman people, the first class comprising
ninety-eight, and the votes being counted only by *centuriæ*,
this first class alone outnumbered in votes all the others.
When all these *centuriæ* were in agreement, the recording of votes was even discontinued; what the minority
had decided passed for a decision of the multitude; and
we may say that in the *comitia centuriata* affairs were
regulated rather by the majority of crowns (*écus*) than
of votes.

But this excessive power was moderated in two ways:
first, the tribunes usually, and a great number of plebeians
always, being in the class of the rich, balanced the influence of the patricians in this first class. The second
means consisted in this, that instead of making the
centuriæ vote according to their order, which would
have caused the first class to begin always, one of them*
was drawn by lot and proceeded alone to the election;
after which all the *centuriæ*, being summoned on another
day according to their rank, renewed the election and
usually confirmed it. Thus the power of example was
taken away from rank to be given to lot, according to
the principle of democracy.

From this practice resulted yet another advantage; the
citizens from the country had time, between the two
elections, to gain information about the merits of the
candidate provisionally chosen, and so record their votes
with knowledge of the case. But, under pretense of
dispatch, this practice came to be abolished and the two
elections took place on the same day.

The *comitia tributa* were properly the council of the
Roman people. They were convoked only by the tribunes;
in them the tribunes were elected and passed their

---

* This *centuria*, thus chosen by lot, was called *prærogativa*, because its suffrage was demanded first; hence came the word *prerogative.*

plebiscita. Not only had the Senate no status in them —
it had not even a right to attend; and, being compelled
to obey laws on which they could not vote, the senators
were, in this respect, less free than the meanest citizens.
This injustice was altogether impolitic, and alone sufficed
to invalidate the decrees of a body to which all the
citizens were not admitted. If all the patricians had
taken part in these *comitia* according to the rights which
they had as citizens, having become in that case simple
individuals, they would have scarcely influenced a form in
which votes were counted by the head, and in which
the meanest proletarian had as much power as the Chief
of the Senate.

We see, then, that besides the order which resulted
from these different divisions for the collection of the
votes of so great a people, these divisions were not
reduced to forms immaterial in themselves, but that each
had results corresponding with the purposes for which it
was chosen.

Without entering upon this in greater detail, it follows
from the preceding explanations that the *comitia tributa*
were more favorable to popular government, and the
comitia centuriata to aristocracy. With regard to the *comitia curiata*, in which the Roman populace alone formed
the majority, as they served only to favor tyranny and
evil designs, they deserved to fall into discredit, the seditious themselves refraining from a means which would
too plainly reveal their projects. It is certain that the
full majesty of the Roman people was found only in the
comitia centuriata, which were alone complete, seeing
that the rural tribes were absent from the *comitia curiata*
and the Senate and the patricians from the *comitia tributa*.

The mode of collecting the votes among the early Romans was as simple as their manners, although still less
simple than in Sparta. Each gave his vote with a loud
voice, and a recording officer duly registered it; a majority of votes in each tribe determined the suffrage of
the tribe; a majority of votes among the tribes determined the suffrage of the people; and so with the *curiæ
centuriæ*. This was a good practice so long as probity
prevailed among the citizens and every one was ashamed

to record his vote publicly for an unjust measure or an unworthy man; but when the people were corrupted and votes were bought, it was expedient that they should be given secretly in order to restrain purchasers by distrust and give knaves an opportunity of not being traitors.

I know that Cicero blames this change and attributes to it in part the fall of the Republic. But although I feel the weight which Cicero's authority ought to have in this matter, I cannot adopt his opinion; on the contrary, I think that through not making sufficient changes of this kind, the downfall of the State was hastened. As the regimen of healthy persons is unfit for invalids, so we should not desire to govern a corrupt people by the laws which suit a good nation. Nothing supports this maxim better than the duration of the republic of Venice, only the semblance of which now exists, solely because its laws are suitable to none but worthless men.

Tablets, therefore, were distributed to the citizens by means of which each could vote without his decision being known; new formalities were also established for the collection of tablets, the counting of votes, the comparison of numbers, etc.; but this did not prevent suspicions as to the fidelity of the officers charged with these duties. At length edicts were framed, the multitude of which proves their uselessness.

Toward the closing years, they were often compelled to resort to extraordinary expedients in order to supply the defects of the laws. Sometimes prodigies were feigned; but this method, which might impose on the people, did not impose on those who governed them. Sometimes an assembly was hastily summoned before the candidates had had time to canvass. Sometimes a whole sitting was consumed in talking when it was seen that the people having been won over were ready to pass a bad resolution. But at last ambition evaded everything; and it seems incredible that in the midst of so many abuses, this great nation, by favor of its ancient institutions, did not cease to elect magistrates, to pass laws, to judge causes, and to dispatch public and private affairs with almost as much facility as the Senate itself could have done.

CHAPTER V.

THE TRIBUNESHIP.

WHEN an exact relation cannot be established among the constituent parts of the State, or when indestructible causes are incessantly changing their relations, a special magistracy is instituted, which is not incorporated with the others, but which replaces each term in its true relation, forming a connection or middle term either between the Prince and the people, or between the Prince and the sovereign, or if necessary between both at once.

This body, which I shall call the TRIBUNESHIP, is the guardian of the laws and of the legislative power. It sometimes serves to protect the sovereign against the government, as the tribunes of the people did in Rome; sometimes to support the government against the people, as the Council of Ten now does in Venice; and sometimes to maintain an equilibrium among all parts, as the ephors did in Sparta.

The tribuneship is not a constituent part of the State, and should have no share in the legislative or in the executive power; but it is in this very circumstance that its own power is greatest; for, while unable to do anything, it can prevent everything. It is more sacred and more venerated, as defender of the laws, than the Prince that executes them and the sovereign that enacts them. This was very clearly seen in Rome, when those proud patricians, who always despised the people as a whole, were forced to bow before a simple officer of the people, who had neither auspices nor jurisdiction.

The tribuneship, wisely moderated, is the strongest support of a good constitution; but if its power be ever so little in excess, it overthrows everything. Weakness is not natural to it; and provided it has some power, it is never less than it should be.

It degenerates into tyranny when it usurps the executive power, of which it is only the moderator, and when it wishes to make the laws which it should only defend. The enormous power of the ephors, which was without danger so long as Sparta preserved her morality, accelerated the corruption when it had begun. The blood of Agis, slain by these tyrants, was avenged by his successor; but the crime and the punishment of the ephors alike hastened the fall of the republic, and, after Cleomenes, Sparta was no longer of any account. Rome, again, perished in the same way; and the excessive power of the tribunes, usurped by degrees, served at last, with the aid of laws framed on behalf of liberty, as a shield for the emperors who destroyed her. As for the Council of Ten in Venice, it is a tribunal of blood, horrible both to the patricians and to the people; and, far from resolutely defending the laws, it has only served since their degradation for striking secret blows which men dare not remark.

The tribuneship, like the government, is weakened by the multiplication of its members. When the tribunes of the Roman people, at first two in number and afterward five, wished to double this number, the Senate allowed them to do so, being quite sure of controlling some by means of others, which did not fail to happen.

The best means of preventing the usurpations of such a formidable body, a means of which no government has hitherto availed itself, would be, not to make this body permanent, but to fix intervals during which it should remain suspended. These intervals, which should not be long enough to allow abuses time to become established, can be fixed by law in such a manner that it may be easy to shorten them in case of need by means of extraordinary commissions.

This method appears to me free from objection, because, as I have said, the tribuneship, forming no part of the constitution, can be removed without detriment; and it seems to me efficacious, because a magistrate newly established does not start with the power that his predecessor had, but with that which the law gives him.

CHAPTER VI.

THE DICTATORSHIP.

THE inflexibility of the laws, which prevents them from being adapted to emergencies, may in certain cases render them pernicious, and thereby cause the ruin of the State in a time of crisis. The order and tardiness of the forms require a space of time which circumstances sometimes do not allow. A thousand cases may arise for which the legislator has not provided, and to perceive that everything cannot be foreseen is a very needful kind of foresight.

We must therefore not desire to establish political institutions so firmly as to take away the power of suspending their effects. Even Sparta allowed her laws to sleep.

But only the greatest dangers can outweigh that of changing the public order, and the sacred power of the laws should never be interfered with except when the safety of the country is at stake. In these rare and obvious cases, the public security is provided for by a special act, which intrusts the care of it to the most worthy man. This commission can be conferred in two ways, according to the nature of the danger.

If an increase in the activity of the government suffices to remedy this evil, we may concentrate it in one or two of its members; in that case it is not the authority of the laws which is changed but only the form of their administration. But if the danger is such that the formal process of law is an obstacle to our security, a supreme head is nominated, who may silence all the laws and suspend for a moment the sovereign authority. In such a case the general will is not doubtful, and it is clear that the primary intention of the people is that the State should not perish. In this way the suspension of the legislative power does not involve its abolition; the magistrate who silences it can make it speak; he dominates it without having power to represent it; he can do everything but make laws.

The first method was employed by the Roman Senate

when it charged the consuls, by a consecrated formula, to provide for the safety of the Republic. The second was adopted when one of the two consuls nominated a dictator,* a usage of which Alba had furnished the precedent to Rome.

At the beginning of the Republic they very often had recourse to the dictatorship, because the State had not yet a sufficiently firm foundation to be able to maintain itself by the vigor of its constitution alone.

Public morality rendering superfluous at that time many precautions that would have been necessary at another time, there was no fear either that a dictator would abuse his authority or that he would attempt to retain it beyond the term. On the contrary, it seemed that so great a power must be a burden to him who was invested with it, such haste did he make to divest himself of it, as if to take the place of the laws were an office too arduous and too dangerous.

Therefore it is the danger, not its abuse, but of its degradation, that makes me blame the indiscreet use of this supreme magistracy in early times; for while it was freely used at elections, at dedications, and in purely formal matters, there was reason to fear that it would become less .formidable in case of need, and that the people would grow accustomed to regard as an empty title that which was only employed in empty ceremonies.

Toward the close of the Republic, the Romans, having become more circumspect, used the dictatorship sparingly with as little reason as they had formerly been prodigal of it. It was easy to see that their fear was ill-founded; that the weakness of the capital then constituted its security against the magistrates whom it had within it; that a dictator could, in certain cases, defend the public liberty without ever being able to assail it; and that the chains of Rome would not be forged in Rome itself, but in her armies. The slight resistance which Marius made against Sylla, and Pompey against Cæsar, showed clearly what might be looked for from the authority within against the force without.

*This nomination was made by night and in secret as if they were ashamed to set a man above the laws.

This error caused them to commit great mistakes; such, for example, was that of not appointing a dictator in the Catiline affair; for as it was only a question of the interior of the city, or at most of some province of Italy, a dictator, with the unlimited authority that the laws gave him, would have easily broken up the conspiracy, which was suppressed only by a combination of happy accidents such as human prudence could not have foreseen.

Instead of that the Senate was content to intrust all its power to the consuls; whence it happened that Cicero, in order to act effectively, was constrained to exceed his authority in a material point, and that although the first transports of joy caused his conduct to be approved, he was afterward justly called to account for the blood of citizens shed contrary to the laws a reproach which could not have been brought against a dictator. But the consul's eloquence won over everybody; and he himself, although a Roman, preferred his own glory to his country's good, and sought not so much the most certain and legitimate means of saving the State as the way to secure the whole credit of this affair.* Therefore he was justly honored as the liberator of Rome and justly punished as a violator of the laws. However brilliant his recall may have been, it was certainly a pardon.

Moreover, in whatever way this important commission may be conferred, it is important to fix its duration at a very short term which can never be prolonged. In the crises which cause it to be established, the State is soon destroyed or saved; and, the urgent need having passed away, the dictatorship becomes tyrannical or useless. In Rome the dictators held office for six months only, and the majority abdicated before the end of this term. Had the term been longer, they would perhaps have been tempted to prolong it still further, as the Decemvirs did their term of one year. The dictator only had time to provide for the necessity which had led to his election; he had no time to think of other projects.

* He could not be satisfied about this in proposing a dictator; he dared not nominate himself, and could not feel sure that his colleague would nominate him.

8

CHAPTER VII.

THE CENSORSHIP.

JUST as the declaration of the general will is made by the law, the declaration of public opinion is made by the censorship. Public opinion is a kind of law of which the censor is minister, and which he only applies to particular cases in the manner of the Prince.

The censorial tribunal, then, far from being the arbiter of the opinion of the people, only declares it, and so soon as it departs from this position, its decisions are fruitless and ineffectual.

It is useless to distinguish the character of a nation from the objects of its esteem, for all these things depend on the same principle and are necessarily intermixed. In all the nations of the world it is not nature but opinion which decides the choice of their pleasures. Reform men's opinions and their manners will be purified of themselves. People always like what is becoming or what they judge to be so; but it is in this judgment that they make mistakes; the question, then, is to guide their judgment. He who judges of manners judges of honor; and he who judges of honor takes his law from opinion.

The opinions of a nation spring from its constitution. Although the law does not regulate morality, it is legislation that gives it birth, and when legislation becomes impaired, morality degenerates; but then the judgment of the censors will not do what the power of the laws has failed to do.

It follows from this that the censorship may be useful to preserve morality, never to restore it. Institute censors while the laws are vigorous; so soon as they have lost their power all is over. Nothing that is lawful has any force when the laws cease to have any.

The censorship supports morality by preventing opinions from being corrupted, by preserving their integrity through wise applications, sometimes even by fixing them when they are still uncertain. The use of seconds

(114)

in duels, carried to a mad extreme in the kingdom of
France, was abolished by these simple words in an edict
of the king: "As for those who have the cowardice to
appoint seconds." This judgment, anticipating that of
the public, immediately decided it. But when the same
edicts wanted to declare that it was also cowardice to
fight a duel, which is very true, but contrary to common
opinion, the public ridiculed this decision, on which its
judgment was already formed.

I have said elsewhere * that as public opinion is not
subject to constraint, there should be no vestige of this
in the tribunal established to represent it. We cannot
admire too much the art with which this force, wholly
lost among the moderns, was set in operation among
the Romans and still better among the Lacedæmonians.

A man of bad character having brought forward a good
measure in the Council of Sparta, the ephors, without
regarding him, caused the same measure to be proposed
by a virtuous citizen. What an honor for the one, what
a stigma for the other, without praise or blame being
given to either! Certain drunkards from Samos defiled
the tribunal of the ephors; on the morrow a public edict
granted permission to the Samians to be filthy. A real
punishment would have been less severe than such impunity. When Sparta pronounced what was or was not
honorable, Greece made no appeal from her decisions.

CHAPTER VIII.

CIVIL RELIGION.

MEN had at first no kings except the gods and no government but a theocracy. They reasoned like Caligula,
and at that time they reasoned rightly. A long period
is needed to change men's sentiments and ideas in order
that they may resolve to take a fellow-man as a master
and flatter themselves that all will be well.

*I merely indicate in this chapter what I have treated at greater
length in the *Letter to M. d'Alembert.*

From the single circumstance that a god was placed at
the head of every political society, it followed that there
were as many gods as nations. Two nations foreign to
each other, and almost always hostile, could not long
acknowledge the same master; two armies engaged in
battle with each other could not obey the same leader.
Thus from national divisions resulted polytheism, and,
from this, theological and civil intolerance, which are by
nature the same, as will be shown hereafter.

The fancy of the Greeks that they recognized their own
gods among barbarous nations arose from their regarding themselves as the natural sovereigns of those
nations. But in our days that is a very ridiculous kind
of erudition which turns on the identity of the gods of
different nations, as if Moloch, Saturn, and Chronos could
be the same god! As if the Baal of the Phœnicians, the
Zeus of the Greeks, and the Jupiter of the Latins could
be the same! As if there could be anything in
common among imaginary beings bearing different
names!

But if it is asked why under paganism, when every
State had its worship and its gods, there were no wars
of religion, I answer that it was for the same reason that
each State, having its peculiar form of worship as well
as its own government, did not distinguish its gods from
its laws. Political warfare was also religious; the departments of the gods were, so to speak, fixed by the limits
of the nations. The god of one nation had no right over
other nations. The gods of the pagans were not jealous
gods; they shared among them the empire of the world;
even Moses and the Hebrew nation sometimes counte-
nanced this idea by speaking of the god of Israel. It is
true that they regarded as naught the gods of the Canaan-
ites, proscribed nations, devoted to destruction, whose
country they were to occupy; but see how they spoke of
the divinities of the neighboring nations whom they were
forbidden to attack: "The possession of what belongs
to Chamos your god," said Jephthah to the Ammonites,
"is it not lawfully your due? By the same title we possess the lands which our conquering god has acquired."
In this, it seems to me, there was a well-recognized par-

ity between the rights of Chamos and those of the god of Israel.

But when the Jews, subjected to the kings of Babylon, and afterward to the kings of Syria, obstinately refused to acknowledge any other god than their own, this refusal being regarded as a rebellion against the conqueror, drew upon them the persecutions which we read of in their history, and of which no other instance appears before Christianity.

Every religion, then, being exclusively attached to the laws of the State which prescribed it, there was no other way of converting a nation than to subdue it, and no other missionaries than conquerors; and the obligation to change their form of worship being the law imposed on the vanquished, it was necessary to begin by conquering before speaking of conversions. Far from men fighting for the gods, it was, as in Homer, the gods who fought for men; each sued for victory from his own god and paid for it with new altars. The Romans, before attacking a place, summoned its gods to abandon it; and when they left to the Tarentines their exasperated gods, it was because they then regarded these gods as subjected to their own and forced to pay them homage. They left the vanquished their gods as they left them their laws. A crown for the Capitoline Jupiter was often the only tribute that they imposed.

At last, the Romans having extended their worship and their laws with their empire, and having themselves often adopted those of the vanquished, the nations of this vast empire, since the right of citizenship was granted to all, found insensibly that they had multitudes of gods and religions, almost the same everywhere; and this is why paganism was at length known in the world as only a single religion.

It was in these circumstances that Jesus came to establish on earth a spiritual kingdom, which, separating the religious from the political system, destroyed the unity of the State, and caused the intestine divisions which have never ceased to agitate Christian nations. Now this new idea of a kingdom in the other world having never been able to enter the minds of the pagans, they always regarded Christians as actual rebels, who, under cover of a hypocritical submission, only sought an opportunity to make themselves independent and supreme, and to usurp by cunning the authority which, in their weakness, they pretend to respect. This was the cause of persecutions.

What the pagans had feared came to pass. Then everything changed its aspect; the humble Christians altered their tone, and soon this pretended kingdom of the other world became, under a visible chief, the most violent despotism in this world.

As, however, there have always been a Prince and civil laws, a perpetual conflict of jurisdiction has resulted from this double power, which has rendered any good polity impossible in Christian States; and no one has ever succeeded in understanding whether he was bound to obey the ruler or the priest.

Many nations, however, even in Europe or on its outskirts, wished to preserve or to re-establish the ancient system, but without success; the spirit of Christianity prevailed over everything. The sacred worship always retained or regained its independence of the sovereign, and without any necessary connection with the body of the State. Mohammed had very sound views; he thoroughly unified his political system; and so long as his form of government subsisted under his successors, the caliphs, the government was quite undivided and in that respect good. But the Arabs having become flourishing, learned, polished, effeminate, and indolent, were subjugated by the barbarians, and then the division between the two powers began again. Although it may be less apparent among the Mohammedans than among the Christians, the division nevertheless exists, especially in the sect of Ali; and there are States, such as Persia, in which it is still seen.

Among us, the kings of England have established themselves as heads of the church, and the Tsars have done the same; but by means of this title they have made themselves its ministers rather than its rulers; they have acquired not so much the right of changing it as the power of maintaining it; they are not its legislators but only its princes. Wherever the clergy form a corporation,* they are masters and legislators in their own country. There are, then, two powers, two sovereigns, in England and in Russia, just as elsewhere.

Of all Christian authors, the philosopher Hobbes is the only one who has clearly seen the evil and its remedy, and who has dared to propose a reunion of the heads of the eagle and the complete restoration of political unity, without which no State or government will ever be well constituted. But he ought to have seen that the domineering spirit of Christianity was incompatible with his system, and that the interest of the priest would always be stronger than that of the State. It is not so much what is horrible and false in his political theory as what is just and true that has rendered it odious.

I believe that by developing historical facts from this point of view, the opposite opinions of Bayle and Warburton might easily be refuted. The former of these maintains that no religion is useful to the body politic; the latter, on the other hand, asserts that Christianity is its strongest support. To the first it might be proved that no State was ever founded without religion serving as its basis, and to the second, that the Christian law is more injurious than useful to a firm constitution of the State. In order to succeed in making myself understood, I need only give a little more precision to the exceedingly vague ideas about religion in its relation to my subject.

Religion, considered with reference to society, which is either general or particular, may also be divided into two kinds, viz, the religion of the man and that of the citizen. The first, without temples, without altars, without rites, limited to the purely internal worship of the supreme God and to the eternal duties of morality, is the pure and simple religion of the Gospel, the true theism,

* It must, indeed, be remarked that it is not so much the formal assemblies, like those in France, that bind the clergy into one body, as the communion of churches. Communion and excommunication are the social pact of the clergy, a pact by means of which they will always be the masters of nations and kings. All priests who are of the same communion are fellow citizens, though they are as far asunder as the poles. This invention is a master-piece of policy. There was nothing similar among pagan priests; therefore they never formed a body of clergy.

and what may be called the natural divine law. The other, inscribed in a single country, gives to it its gods, its peculiar and tutelary patrons. It has its dogmas, its rites, its external worship prescribed by the laws; outside the single nation which observes it, everything is for it infidel, foreign, and barbarous; it extends the duties and rights of men only as far as its altars. Such were all the religions of early nations, to which may be given the name of the divine law, civil or positive.

There is a third and more extravagant kind of religion, which, giving to men two sets of laws, two chiefs, two countries, imposes on them contradictory duties, and prevents them from being at once devout men and citizens. Such is the religion of the Lamas, such is that of the Japanese, such is Roman Christianity. This may be called the religion of the priest. There results from it a kind of mixed and unsocial law which has no name.

Considered politically, these three kinds of religion all have their defects. The third is so evidently bad that it would be a waste of time to stop and prove this. Whatever destroys social unity is good for nothing; all institutions which put a man in contradiction with himself are worthless.

The second is good so far as it combines divine worship with love for the laws, and, by making their country the object of the citizens' adoration, teaches them that to serve the State is to serve the guardian deity. It is a kind of theocracy, in which there ought to be no pontiff but the Prince, no other priests than the magistrates. Then to die for one's country is to suffer martyrdom, to violate the laws is to be impious, and to subject a guilty man to public execration is to devote him to the wrath of the gods: *Sacer esto.*

But it is evil in so far as being based on error and falsehood, it deceives men, renders them credulous and superstitious, and obscures the true worship of the Deity with vain ceremonial. It is evil, again, when, becoming exclusive and tyrannical, it makes a nation sanguinary and intolerant, so that it thirsts after nothing but murder and massacre, and believes that it is performing a holy action in killing whosoever does not acknowledge its gods. This puts such a nation in a natural state of war with all others, which is very prejudicial to its own safety.

There remains, then, the religion of man or Christianity, not that of to-day, but that of the Gospel, which is quite different. By this holy, sublime, and pure religion, men, children of the same God, all recognize one another as brethren, and the social bond which unites them is not dissolved even at death.

But this religion, having no particular relation with the body politic, leaves to the laws only the force that they derive from themselves, without adding to them any other; and thereby one of the great bonds of the particular society remains ineffective. What is more, far from attaching the hearts of citizens to the State, it detaches them from it and from all earthly things. I know of nothing more contrary to the social spirit.

We are told that a nation of true Christians would form the most perfect society conceivable. In this supposition I see only one great difficulty—that a society of true Christians would be no longer a society of men.

I say even that this supposed society, with all its perfection, would be neither the strongest nor the most durable; by virtue of its perfection it would lack cohesion; its perfection, indeed, would be its destroying vice.

Each man would perform his duty; the people would be obedient to the laws, the chief men would be just and moderate, and the magistrates upright and incorruptible; the soldiers would despise death; there would be neither vanity nor luxury. All this is very good; but let us look further.

Christianity is an entirely spiritual religion, concerned solely with heavenly things; the Christian's country is not of this world. He does his duty, it is true; but he does it with a profound indifference as to the good or ill success of his endeavors. Provided that he has nothing to reproach himself with, it matters little to him whether all goes well or ill here below. If the State is flourishing, he scarcely dares to enjoy the public felicity; he fears to take a pride in the glory of his country. If the

State declines, he blesses the hand of God which lies heavy on his people.

In order that the society might be peaceable and harmony maintained, it would be necessary for all citizens without exception to be equally good Christians; but if unfortunately there happens to be in it a single ambitious man, a single hypocrite, a Catiline or a Cromwell for example, such a man will certainly obtain an advantage over his pious compatriots. Christian charity does not suffer men readily to think ill of their neighbors. As soon as a man has found by cunning the art of imposing on them and securing to himself a share in the public authority, he is invested with dignity; God wills that he should be reverenced. Soon he exercises dominion; God wills that he should be obeyed. The depositary of this power abuses it; this is the rod with which God punishes his children. They would have scruples about driving out the usurper; it would be necessary to disturb the public peace, to employ violence, to shed blood; all this ill accords with the meekness of the Christian, and, after all, does it matter whether they are free or enslaved in this vale of woes? The essential thing is to reach paradise, and resignation is but one means the more toward that.

Some foreign war comes on; the citizens march to battle without anxiety; none of them think of flight. They do their duty, but without an ardent desire for victory; they know better how to die than to conquer. What matters it whether they are the victors or the vanquished? Does not Providence know better than they what is needful for them? Conceive what an advantage a bold, impetuous, enthusiastic enemy can derive from this stoical indifference! Set against them those noble peoples who are consumed with a burning love of glory and of country. Suppose your Christian republic opposed to Sparta or Rome; the pious Christians will be beaten, crushed, destroyed, before they have time to collect themselves, or they will owe their safety only to the contempt which the enemy may conceive for them. To my mind that was a noble oath of the soldiers of Fabius; they did not swear to die or to conquer, they swore to return as conquerors, and kept their oath. Never would Christians have done such a thing; they would have believed that they were tempting God.

But I am mistaken in speaking of a Christian republic; each of these two words excludes the other. Christianity preaches only servitude and dependence. Its spirit is too favorable to tyranny for the latter not to profit by it always. True Christians are made to be slaves; they know it and are hardly aroused by it. This short life has too little value in their eyes.

Christian troops are excellent, we are told. I deny it; let them show me any that are such. For my part, I know of no Christian troops. The crusades will be cited. Without disputing the valor of the crusaders, I shall observe that, far from being Christians, they were soldiers of the priest, citizens of the Church; they fought for their spiritual country, which the Church had somehow rendered temporal. Properly regarded, this brings us back to paganism; as the Gospel does not establish a national religion, any sacred war is impossible among Christians.

Under the pagan emperors Christian soldiers were brave; all Christian authors affirm it, and I believe it. There was a rivalry of honor against the pagan troops. As soon as the emperors became Christians, this rivalry no longer subsisted; and when the cross had driven out the eagle, all the Roman valor disappeared.

But, setting aside political considerations, let us return to the subject of right and determine principles on this important point. The right which the social pact gives to the sovereign over its subjects does not, as I have said, pass the limits of public utility.* Subjects, then, owe no account of their opinions to the sovereign except so far as those opinions are of moment to the community. Now it is very important for the State that every citizen

---

*"In the commonwealth," says the Marquis d'Argenson, "each is perfectly free in what does not injure others." That is the unalterable limit; it cannot be more accurately placed. I could not deny myself the pleasure of sometimes quoting this manuscript, although it is not known to the public, in order to do honor to the memory of an illustrious and honorable man, who preserved even in office the heart of a true citizen, and just and sound opinions about the government of his country.

should have a religion which may make him delight in
his duties; but the dogmas of this religion concern neither
the State nor its members, except so far as they affect
morality and the duties which he who professes it is
bound to perform toward others. Each may have, in addition, such opinions as he pleases, without its being the
business of the sovereign to know them; for, as he has
no jurisdiction in the other world, the destiny of his
subjects in the life to come, whatever it may be, is
not his affair, provided they are good citizens in this
life.

There is, however, a purely civil profession of faith,
the articles of which it is the duty of the sovereign to
determine, not exactly as dogmas of religion, but as
sentiments of sociability, without which it is impossible
to be a good citizen or a faithful subject. Without
having power to compel any one to believe them, the
sovereign may banish from the State whoever does not
believe them; it may banish him not as impious, but as
unsociable, as incapable of sincerely loving law and
justice and of sacrificing at need his life to his duty.
But if any one, after publicly acknowledging these
dogmas, behaves like an unbeliever in them, he should
be punished with death; he has committed the greatest
of crimes, he has lied before the laws.

The dogmas of civil religion ought to be simple, few
in number, stated with precision, and without explanations or commentaries. The existence of the Deity,
powerful, wise, beneficent, prescient, and bountiful, the
life to come, the happiness of the just, the punishment
of the wicked, the sanctity of the social contract and of the
laws; these are the positive dogmas. As for the negative
dogmas, I limit them to one only, that is, intolerance; it
belongs to the creeds which we have excluded.

Those who distinguish civil intolerance from theological
intolerance are in my opinion, mistaken. These two
kinds of intolerance are inseparable. It is impossible to
live at peace with people whom we believe to be damned;
to love them would be to hate God who punishes them.
It is absolutely necessary to reclaim them or to punish
them. Wherever theological intolerance is allowed, it

cannot but have some effect in civil life;* and as soon as
it has any, the sovereign is no longer sovereign even in
secular affairs; from that time the priests are the real
masters; the kings are only their officers.

Now that there is, and can be, no longer any exclusive
national religion, we should tolerate all those which tolerate others, so far as their dogmas have nothing contrary
to the duties of a citizen. But whosoever dares to say:
"Outside the Church no salvation," ought to be driven
from the State, unless the State be the Church and the
Prince be the pontiff. Such a dogma is proper only in a
theocratic government; in any other it is pernicious. The
reason for which Henry IV. is said to have embraced
the Romish religion ought to have made any honorable
man renounce it, and especially any prince who knew
how to reason.

* Marriage, for example, being a civil contract, has civil consequences, without which it is even impossible for society to subsist.
Let us, then, suppose that a clergy should succeed in arrogating to
itself the sole right to perform this act, a right which it must necessarily usurp in every intolerant religion; then, is it not clear that in
taking the opportunity to strengthen the Church's authority, it will
render ineffectual that of the Prince, which will no longer have any
subjects except those which the clergy are pleased to give it? Having the option of marrying or not marrying people, according as they
hold or do not hold such or such a doctrine, according as they admit
or reject such or such a formulary, according as they are more or less
devoted to it, is it not clear that by behaving prudently and keeping
firm, the Church alone will dispose of inheritances, offices, citizens,
and the State itself, which cannot subsist when only composed of
bastards? But, it will be said, men will appeal as against abuses;
they will summon, issue decrees, and seize on the temporalities.
What a pity! The clergy, however little they may have, I do not say
of courage, but of good sense, will let this be done and go their way;
they will quietly permit appealing, adjourning, decreeing, seizing, and
will end by remaining masters. It is not, it seems to me, a great
sacrifice to abandon a part, when one is sure of getting possession of
the whole.

CHAPTER IX.

CONCLUSION.

AFTER laying down the principles of political right and attempting to establish the State on its foundations, it would remain to strengthen it in its external relations; which would comprise the law of nations, commerce, the right of war and conquests, public rights, alliances, negotiations, treaties, etc. But all this forms a new subject too vast for my limited scope. I ought always to have confined myself to a narrower sphere.

SIR THOMAS MORE'S

UTOPIA.

Sʳ THOMAS MORE Kⁿᵗ
Lord Chancellor of England.

UTOPIA.

BOOK I.

HENRY VIII., the unconquered King of England, a prince adorned with all the virtues that become a great monarch, having some differences of no small consequence with Charles, the most serene prince of Castile, sent me into Flanders, as his ambassador, for treating and composing matters between them. I was colleague and companion to that incomparable man Cuthbert Tonstal, whom the king with such universal applause lately made Master of the Rolls; but of whom I will say nothing; not because I fear that the testimony of a friend will be suspected, but rather because his learning and virtues are too great for me to do them justice, and so well known, that they need not my commendations unless I would, according to the proverb, "Show the sun with a lanthorn." Those that were appointed by the prince to treat with us met us at Bruges, according to agreement; they were all worthy men. The Margrave of Bruges was their head, and the chief man among them; but he that was esteemed the wisest, and that spoke for the rest, was George Temse, the Provost of Casselsee; both art and nature had concurred to make him eloquent; he was very learned in the law; and as he had a great capacity, so by a long practice in affairs he was very dextrous at unraveling them. After we had several times met without coming to an agreement, they went to Brussels for some days to know the prince's pleasure. And since our business would admit it, I went to Antwerp. While I was there, among many that visited me, there was one that was more acceptable to me than any other, Peter Giles, born at Antwerp, who is a man of great honor, and of a good rank in his town, though less than he deserves; for I do not know if there be anywhere to be

9   (129)

found a more learned and a better bred young man: for as he is both a very worthy and a very knowing person, so he is so civil to all men, so particularly kind to his friends, and so full of candor and affection, that there is not perhaps above one or two anywhere to be found that is in all respects so perfect a friend. He is extraordi‹ narily modest, there is no artifice in him; and yet no man has more of a prudent simplicity; his conversation was so pleasant and so innocently cheerful, that his company in a great measure lessened any longings to go back to my country, and to my wife and children, which an absence of four months had quickened very much. One day as I was returning home from Mass at St. Mary's, which is the chief church, and the most frequented of any in Antwerp, I saw him by accident talking with a stranger, who seemed past the flower of his age; his face was tanned, he had a long beard, and his cloak was hanging carelessly about him, so that by his looks and habit I concluded he was a seaman. As soon as Peter saw me, he came and saluted me; and as I was returning his civility, he took me aside, and pointing to him with whom he had been discoursing, he said, "Do you see that man? I was just thinking to bring him to you." I answered, "He should have been very welcome on your account." "And on his own too," replied he, "if you knew the man, for there is none alive that can give so copious an account of unknown nations and countries as he can do; which I know you very much desire." Then said I, "I did not guess amiss, for at first sight I took him for a seaman." "But you are much mistaken," said he, "for he has not sailed as a seaman, but as a traveler, or rather a philosopher. This Raphael, who from his family carries the name of Hythloday, is not ignorant of the Latin tongue, but is eminently learned in the Greek, having applied himself more particularly to that than to the former, because he had given himself much to philosophy, in which he knew that the Romans have left us nothing that is valuable, except what is to be found in Seneca and Cicero. He is a Portuguese by birth, and was so desirous of seeing the world, that he divided his estate among his brothers, run the same hazard

as Americus Vespucius, and bore a share in three of his
four voyages, that are now published; only he did not
return with him in his last, but obtained leave of him
almost by force, that he might be one of those twenty-
four who were left at the farthest place at which they
touched, in their last voyage to New Castile. The leaving him thus did not a little gratify one that was more
fond of traveling than of returning home, to be buried
in his own country; for he used often to say, that the
way to heaven was the same from all places; and he
that had no grave, had the heaven still over him. Yet
this disposition of mind had cost him dear, if God
had not been very gracious to him; for after he, with
five Castilians, had traveled over many countries, at
last, by strange good fortune, he got to Ceylon, and from
thence to Calicut, where he very happily found some
Portuguese ships; and, beyond all men's expectations,
returned to his native country." When Peter had said
this to me, I thanked him for his kindness, in intending
to give me the acquaintance of a man whose conversation he knew would be so acceptable; and upon that
Raphael and I embraced each other. After those civili-
ties were past which are usual with strangers upon their
first meeting, we all went to my house, and entering
into the garden, sat down on a green bank, and entertained one another in discourse. He told us, that when
Vespucius had sailed away, he and his companions that
stayed behind in New Castile, by degrees insinuated
themselves into the affections of the people of the
country, meeting often with them, and treating them
gently; and at last they not only lived among them without danger, but conversed familiarly with them; and got
so far into the heart of a prince, whose name and
country I have forgot, that he both furnished them plentifully with all things necessary, and also with the conveniences of traveling; both boats when they went by water,
and wagons when they traveled over land: he sent with
them a very faithful guide, who was to introduce and
recommend them to such other princes as they had a
mind to see; and after many days' journey, they came
to towns, and cities, and to commonwealths, that were

both happily governed and well peopled. Under the equator, and as far on both sides of it as the sun moves,
there lay vast deserts that were parched with the perpetual heat of the sun; the soil was withered, all things
looked dismally, and all places were either quite unin-
habited, or abounded with wild beasts and serpents, and
some few men, that were neither less wild nor less cruel
than the beasts themselves. But as they went farther
a new scene opened, all things grew milder, the air
less burning, the soil more verdant, and even the beasts
were less wild; and at last there were nations, towns, and
cities, that had not only mutual commerce among themselves, and with their neighbors, but traded both by
sea and land, to very remote countries. There they
found the conveniences of seeing many countries on all
hands, for no ship went any voyage into which he and
his companions were not very welcome. The first vessels
that they saw were flat-bottomed, their sails were made
of reeds and wicker woven close together, only some
were of leather; but afterward they found ships made
with round keels, and canvas sails, and in all respects like
our ships; and the seamen understood both astronomy
and navigation. He got wonderfully into their favor
by showing them the use of the needle, of which till
then they were utterly ignorant. They sailed before with
great caution, and only in summer time, but now they
count all seasons alike, trusting wholly to the loadstone
in which they are perhaps more secure than safe; so that
there is reason to fear that this discovery, which was
thought would prove so much to their advantage, may
by their imprudence become an occasion of much mischief to them. But it were too long to dwell on all that
he told us he had observed in every place; it would be
too great a digression from our present purpose; whatever is necessary to be told, concerning those wise and
prudent institutions which he observed among civilized
nations, may perhaps be related by us on a more proper
occasion. We asked him many questions concerning all
these things, to which he answered very willingly; only
we made no inquiries after monsters, than which nothing
is more common; for everywhere one may hear of rav-

enous dogs and wolves, and cruel man-eaters; but it is
not so easy to find states that are well and wisely governed.

As he told us of many things that were amiss in those
new-discovered countries, so he reckoned up not a few
things from which patterns might be taken for correcting the errors of these nations among whom we live; of
which an account may be given, as I have already
promised, at some other time; for at present I intend
only to relate those particulars that he told us of the
manners and laws of the Utopians; but I will begin
with the occasion that led us to speak of that commonwealth. After Raphael had discoursed with great judgment on the many errors that were both among us and
these nations; had treated of the wise institutions both
here and there, and had spoken as distinctly of the customs and government of every nation through which he
had passed, as if he had spent his whole life in it; Peter
being struck with admiration, said, "I wonder, Raphael,
how it comes that you enter into no king's service, for I
am sure there are none to whom you would not be very
acceptable: for your learning and knowledge, both of
men and things, is such, that you would not only entertain them very pleasantly, but be of great use to them,
by the examples you could set before them, and the
advices you could give them; and by this means you
would both serve your own interest, and be of great use
to all your friends." "As for my friends," answered he,
"I need not be much concerned, having already done for
them all that was incumbent on me; for when I was not
only in good health, but fresh and young, I distributed
that among my kindred and friends which other people
do not part with till they are old and sick; when they
then unwillingly give that which they can enjoy no longer
themselves. I think my friends ought to rest contented
with this, and not to expect that for their sakes I should
enslave myself to any king whatsoever." "Soft and fair,"
said Peter, "I do not mean that you should be a slave to
any king, but only that you should assist them, and be
useful to them." "The change of the word," said he, "does
not alter the matter." "But term it as you will," replied

Peter, "I do not see any other way in which you can be
so useful, both in private to your friends, and to the
public, and by which you can make your own condition
happier." "Happier!" answered Raphael, "is that to be
compassed in a way so abhorrent to my genius? Now
I live as I will, to which I believe few courtiers
can pretend. And there are so many that court the
favor of great men, that there will be no great loss
if they are not troubled either with me or with others
of my temper." Upon this, said I, "I perceive, Raphael,
that you neither desire wealth nor greatness; and indeed
I value and admire such a man much more than I
do any of the great men in the world. Yet I think
you would do what would well become so generous
and philosophical a soul as yours is, if you would apply
your time and thoughts to public affairs, even though
you may happen to find it a little uneasy to yourself:
and this you can never do with so much advantage, as
by being taken into the counsel of some great prince,
and putting him on noble and worthy actions, which I
know you would do if you were in such a post; for the
springs both of good and evil flow from the prince, over
a whole nation, as from a lasting fountain. So much
learning as you have, even without practice in affairs,
or so great a practice as you have had, without any
other learning, would render you a very fit counselor to
any king whatsoever." "You are doubly mistaken," said
he, "Mr. More, both in your opinion of me, and in the
judgment you make of things: for as I have not that
capacity that you fancy I have; so, if I had it, the public
would not be one jot the better, when I had sacrificed
my quiet to it. For most princes apply themselves
more to affairs of war than to the useful arts of peace;
and in these I neither have any knowledge, nor do I
much desire it: they are generally more set on acquiring
new kingdoms, right or wrong, than on governing well
those they possess. And among the ministers of princes,
there are none that are not so wise as to need no assistance, or at least that do not think themselves so wise,
that they imagine they need none; and if they court any,
it is only those for whom the prince has much personal

favor, whom by their fawnings and flatteries they endeavor to fix to their own interests; and indeed Nature has
so made us, that we all love to be flattered, and to please
ourselves with our own notions. The old crow loves his
young, and the ape her cubs. Now if in such a court,
made up of persons who envy all others, and only admire
themselves, a person should but propose anything that he
had either read in history, or observed in his travels, the
rest would think that the reputation of their wisdom
would sink, and that their interest would be much depressed, if they could not run it down: and if all other
things failed, then they would fly to this, that such or
such things pleased our ancestors, and it were well for
us if we could but match them. They would set up their
rest on such an answer, as a sufficient confutation of all
that could be said; as if it were a great misfortune, that
any should be found wiser than his ancestors; but though
they willingly let go all the good things that were among
those of former ages, yet if better things are proposed
they cover themselves obstinately with this excuse of
reverence to past times. I have met with these proud,
morose, and absurd judgments of things in many places,
particularly once in England." "Was you ever there?"
said I. "Yes, I was," answered he, "and stayed some
months there, not long after the rebellion in the west
was suppressed with a great slaughter of the poor people
that were engaged in it.

"I was then much obliged to that reverend prelate,
John Morton, Archbishop of Canterbury, Cardinal, and
Chancellor of England; a man," said he, "Peter (for Mr.
More knows well what he was), that was not less venerable for his wisdom and virtues, than for the high
character he bore. He was of a middle stature, not broken
with age; his looks begot reverence rather than fear; his
conversation was easy, but serious and grave; he sometimes took pleasure to try the force of those that came
as suitors to him upon business, by speaking sharply,
though decently to them, and by that he discovered their
spirit and presence of mind, with which he was much
delighted, when it did not grow up to impudence, as
bearing a great resemblance to his own temper; and he

looked on such persons as the fittest men for affairs. He spoke both gracefully and weightily; he was eminently skilled in the law, had a vast understanding, and a prodigious memory; and those excellent talents with which Nature had furnished him, were improved by study and experience. When I was in England the king depended much on his counsels, and the government seemed to be chiefly supported by him; for from his youth he had been all along practiced in affairs; and having passed through many traverses of fortune, he had with great cost acquired a vast stock of wisdom, which is not soon lost when it is purchased so dear. One day when I was dining with him there happened to be at table one of the English lawyers, who took occasion to run out in a high commendation of the severe execution of justice upon thieves, who, as he said, were then hanged so fast, that there were sometimes twenty on one gibbet; and upon that he said he could not wonder enough how it came to pass, that since so few escaped, there were yet so many thieves left who were still robbing in all places. Upon this, I who took the boldness to speak freely before the Cardinal, said, there was no reason to wonder at the matter, since this way of punishing thieves was neither just in itself nor good for the public; for as the severity was too great, so the remedy was not effectual; simple theft not being so great a crime that it ought to cost a man his life, no punishment how severe soever being able to restrain those from robbing who can find out no other way of livelihood. 'In this,' said I, 'not only you in England, but a great part of the world imitate some ill masters that are readier to chastise their scholars than to teach them. There are dreadful punishments enacted against thieves, but it were much better to make such good provisions by which every man might be put in a method how to live, and so be preserved from the fatal necessity of stealing and of dying for it.' 'There has been care enough taken for that,' said he, 'there are many handicrafts, and there is husbandry, by which they may make a shift to live unless they have a greater mind to follow ill courses.' 'That will not serve your turn,' said I, 'for many lose their limbs in civil or foreign

wars, as lately in the Cornish rebellion, and some time
ago in your wars with France, who being thus mutilated
in the service of their king and country, can no more
follow their old trades, and are too old to learn new ones;
but since wars are only accidental things, and have
intervals, let us consider those things that fall out every
day. There is a great number of noblemen among you,
that are themselves as idle as drones, that subsist on other
men's labor, on the labor of their tenants, whom, to
raise their revenues, they pare to the quick. This indeed
is the only instance of their frugality, for in all other
things they are prodigal, even to the beggaring of
themselves; but besides this, they carry about with
them a great number of idle fellows, who never learned
any art by which they may gain their living; and
these, as soon as either their lord dies, or they themselves fall sick, are turned out of doors; for your lords
are readier to feed idle people, than to take care of
the sick; and often the heir is not able to keep together so great a family as his predecessor did. Now
when the stomachs of those that are thus turned
out of doors, grow keen, they rob no less keenly;
and what else can they do? for when, by wandering
about, they have worn out both their health and their
clothes, and are tattered, and look ghastly, men of quality will not entertain them, and poor men dare not do it;
knowing that one who has been bred up in idleness and
pleasure, and who was used to walk about with his sword
and buckler, despising all the neighborhood with an insolent scorn, as far below him, is not fit for the spade and
mattock: nor will he serve a poor man for so small a
hire, and in so low a diet as he can afford to give him.'
To this he answered, 'This sort of men ought to be
particularly cherished, for in them consists the force of
the armies for which we have occasion; since their birth
inspires them with a nobler sense of honor, than is to
be found among tradesmen or plowmen.' 'You may
as well say,' replied I, 'that you must cherish thieves
on the account of wars, for you will never want the one,
as long as you have the other; and as robbers prove
sometimes gallant soldiers, so soldiers often prove brave

robbers; so near an alliance there is between those
two sorts of life. But this bad custom, so common
among you, of keeping many servants, is not peculiar
to this nation. In France there is yet a more pestifer-
ous sort of people, for the whole country is full of soldiers, still kept up in time of peace; if such a state of a
nation can be called a peace; and these are kept in pay
upon the same account that you plead for those idle
retainers about noblemen; this being a maxim of those
pretended statesmen that it is necessary for the public
safety, to have a good body of veteran soldiers ever
in readiness. They think raw men are not to be depended on, and they sometimes seek occasions for making war, that they may train up their soldiers in the art
of cutting throats; or as Sallust observed, for keeping
their hands in use, that they may not grow dull by too
long an intermission. But France has learned to its cost,
how dangerous it is to feed such beasts. The fate of the
Romans, Carthaginians, and Syrians, and many other
nations and cities, which were both overturned and quite
ruined by those standing armies, should make others
wiser: and the folly of this maxim of the French,
appears plainly even from this, that their trained soldiers
often find your raw men prove too hard for them; of
which I will not say much, lest you may think I flatter
the English. Every day's experience shows, that the
mechanics in the towns, or the clowns in the country, are
not afraid of fighting with those idle gentlemen, if they
are not disabled by some misfortune in their body, or dis-
pirited by extreme want, so that you need not fear that
those well-shaped and strong men (for it is only such that
noblemen love to keep about them, till they spoil them)
who now grow feeble with ease, and are softened with
their effeminate manner of life, would be less fit for
action if they were well bred and well employed. And
it seems very unreasonable, that for the prospect of a war,
which you need never have but when you please, you
should maintain so many idle men, as will always disturb
you in time of peace, which is ever to be more considered
than war. But I do not think that this necessity of stealing arises only from hence; there is another cause of it

more peculiar to England.' 'What is that?' said the Cardinal. 'The increase of pasture,' said I, 'by which your
sheep, which are naturally mild, and easily kept in order,
may be said now to devour men, and unpeople, not only
villages, but towns; for wherever it is found that the sheep
of any soil yield a softer and richer wool than ordinary,
there the nobility and gentry, and even those holy men,
the abbots, not contented with the old rents which their
farms yielded, nor thinking it enough that they, living at
their ease, do no good to the public, resolve to do it hurt
instead of good. They stop the course of agriculture,
destroying houses and towns, reserving only the churches,
and inclose grounds that they may lodge their sheep in
them. As if forests and parks had swallowed up too
little of the land, those worthy countrymen turn the
best inhabited places in solitudes; for when an insatiable
wretch, who is a plague to his country, resolves to inclose many thousand acres of ground, the owners, as well
as tenants, are turned out of their possessions, by tricks,
or by main force, or being wearied out with ill usage,
they are forced to sell them. By which means those
miserable people, both men and women, married and
unmarried, old and young, with their poor but numerous
families (since country business requires many hands),
are all forced to change their seats, not knowing whither
to go; and they must sell almost for nothing their house-
hold stuff, which could not bring them much money,
even though they might stay for a buyer. When that
little money is at an end, for it will be soon spent, what
is left for them to do, but either to steal and so to be
hanged (God knows how justly), or to go about and beg?
And if they do this, they are put in prison as idle vagabonds; while they would willingly work, but can find
none that will hire them; for there is no more occasion
for country labor, to which they have been bred, when
there is no arable ground left. One shepherd can look
after a flock, which will stock an extent of ground that
would require many hands, if it were to be plowed and
reaped. This likewise in many places raises the price
of corn. The price of wool is also so risen, that the poor
people who were wont to make cloth are no more able

to buy it; and this likewise makes many of them idle. For since the increase of pasture, God has punished the avarice of the owners, by a rot among the sheep, which has destroyed vast numbers of them; to us it might have seemed more just had it fell on the owners themselves. But suppose the sheep should increase ever so much, their price is not like to fall; since though they cannot be called a monopoly, because they are not engrossed by one person, yet they are in so few hands, and these are so rich, that as they are not pressed to sell them sooner than they have a mind to, so they never do it till they have raised the price as high as possible. And on the same account it is that the other kinds of cattle are so dear, because many villages being pulled down, and all country labor being much neglected, there are none who make it their business to breed them. The rich do not breed cattle as they do sheep, but buy them lean, and at low prices; and after they have fattened them on their grounds, sell them again at high rates. And I do not think that all the inconveniences this will produce are yet observed; for as they sell the cattle dear, so if they are consumed faster than the breeding countries from which they are brought can afford them, then the stock must decrease, and this must needs end in great scarcity; and by these means this your island, which seemed as to this particular the happiest in the world, will suffer much by the cursed avarice of a few persons; besides this, the rising of corn makes all people lessen their families as much as they can; and what can those who are dismissed by them do, but either beg or rob? And to this last, a man of a great mind is much sooner drawn than to the former. Luxury likewise breaks in apace upon you, to set forward your poverty and misery; there is an excessive vanity in apparel, and great cost in diet; and that not only in noblemen's families, but even among tradesmen, among the farmers themselves, and among all ranks of persons. You have also many infamous houses, and besides those that are known, the taverns and alehouses are no better; add to these, dice, cards, tables, foot-ball, tennis, and quoits, in which money runs fast away; and those that are initiated into them, must in the conclusion betake themselves to robbing for a supply. Banish these plagues, and give orders that those who have dispeopled so much soil, may either rebuild the villages they have pulled down, or let out their grounds to such as will do it; restrain those engrossings of the rich, that are as bad almost as monopolies; leave fewer occasions to idleness; let agriculture be set up again, and the manufacture of the wool be regulated, that so there may be work found for those companies of idle people whom want forces to be thieves, or who now being idle vagabonds, or useless servants, will certainly grow thieves at last. If you do not find a remedy to these evils, it is a vain thing to boast of your severity in punishing theft, which though it may have the appearance of justice, yet in itself is neither just nor convenient. For if you suffer your people to be ill educated, and their manners to be corrupted from their infancy, and then punish them for those crimes to which their first education disposed them, what else is to be concluded from this, but that you first make thieves and then punish them ?'

"While I was talking thus, the counselor who was present had prepared an answer, and had resolved to resume all I had said, according to the formality of a debate, in which things are generally repeated more faithfully than they are answered; as if the chief trial to be made were of men's memories. 'You have talked prettily for a stranger,' said he, 'having heard of many things among us which you have not been able to consider well; but I will make the whole matter plain to you, and will first repeat in order all that you have said, then I will show how much your ignorance of our affairs has misled you, and will in the last place answer all your arguments. And that I may begin where I promised, there were four things——, 'Hold your peace,' said the Cardinal, 'this will take up too much time; therefore we will at present ease you of the trouble of answering, and reserve it to our next meeting, which shall be to-morrow, if Raphael's affairs and yours can admit of it. But, Raphael,' said he to me, 'I would gladly know upon what reason it is that you think theft ought not to be punished by death? Would you give way to it? Or do you propose any other punishment that will be more useful to the public? For since death does not restrain theft, if men thought their lives would be safe, what fear or force could restrain ill men? On the contrary, they would look on the mitigation of the punishment as an invitation to commit more crimes.' I answered, 'It seems to me a very unjust thing to take away a man's life for a little money; for nothing in the world can be of equal value with a man's life; and if it is said, that it is not for the money that one suffers, but for his breaking the law, I must say, extreme justice is an extreme injury; for we ought not to approve of these terrible laws that make the smallest offenses capital, nor of that opinion of the Stoics, that makes all crimes equal, as if there were no difference to be made between the killing a man and the taking his purse, between which, if we examine things impartially, there is no likeness nor proportion. God has commanded us not to kill, and shall we kill so easily for a little money? But if one shall say, that by the law we are only forbid to kill any, except when the laws of the land allow of it; upon the same grounds, laws may be made in some cases to allow of adultery and perjury: for God having taken from us the right of disposing, either of our own or of other people's lives, if it is pretended that the mutual consent of man in making laws can authorize man-slaughter in cases in which God has given us no example, that it frees people from the obligation of the divine law, and so makes murder a lawful action; what is this, but to give a preference to human laws before the divine? And if this is once admitted, by the same rule men may in all other things put what restrictions they please upon the laws of God. If by the Mosaical law, though it was rough and severe, as being a yoke laid on an obstinate and servile nation, men were only fined, and not put to death for theft, we cannot imagine that in this new law of mercy, in which God treats us with the tenderness of a father, he has given us a greater license to cruelty than he did to the Jews. Upon these reasons it is, that I think putting thieves to death is not lawful; and it is plain and obvious that it is absurd, and of ill consequence to the commonwealth, that a thief and a murderer should be equally punished; for if a robber sees that his danger is the same, if he is convicted of theft as if he were guilty of murder, this will naturally incite him to kill the person whom otherwise he would only have robbed, since if the punishment is the same, there is more security, and less danger of discovery, when he that can best make it is put out of the way; so that terrifying thieves too much provokes them to cruelty.

"'But as to the question, what more convenient way of punishment can be found? I think it is much more easy to find out that, than to invent anything that is worse; why should we doubt but the way that was so long in use among the old Romans, who understood so well the arts of government, was very proper for their punishment? They condemned such as they found guilty of great crimes, to work their whole lives in quarries, or to dig in mines with chains about them. But the method that I liked best, was that which I observed in my travels in Persia, among the Polylerits, who are a considerable and well-governed people. They pay a yearly tribute to the King of Persia; but in all other respects they are a free nation, and governed by their own laws. They lie far from the sea, and are environed with hills; and being contented with the productions of their own country, which is very fruitful, they have little commerce with any other nation; and as they, according to the genius of their country, have no inclination to enlarge their borders; so their mountains, and the pension they pay to the Persian, secure them from all invasions. Thus they have no wars among them; they live rather conveniently than with splendor, and may be rather called a happy nation, than either eminent or famous; for I do not think that they are known so much as by name to any but their next neighbors. Those that are found guilty of theft among them, are bound to make restitution to the owner, and not as it is in other places, to the prince, for they reckon that the prince has no more right to the stolen goods than the thief; but if that which was stolen is no more in being, then the goods of the thieves are estimated, and restitution being made out of them; the remainder is given to their wives and children; and they themselves are condemned to serve in the public works, but are neither imprisoned nor chained, unless there happened to be some extraordinary circumstances in their crimes. They go about loose and free, working for the public. If they are idle or backward to work, they are whipped; but if they work hard, they are well used and treated without any mark of reproach, only the lists of them are called always at night, and then they are shut up. They suffer no other uneasiness, but this of constant labor; for as they work for the public, so they are well entertained out of the public stock, which is done differently in different places. In some places, whatever is bestowed on them, is raised by a charitable contribution; and though this way may seem uncertain, yet so merciful are the inclinations of that people, that they are plentifully supplied by it; but in other places, public revenues are set aside for them; or there is a constant tax of a poll-money raised for their maintenance. In some places they are set to no public work, but every private man that has occasion to hire workmen, goes to the market-places and hires them of the public, a little lower than he would do a freeman: if they go lazily about their task, he may quicken them with the whip. By this means there is always some piece of work or other to be done by them; and beside their livelihood, they earn somewhat still to the public. They all wear a peculiar habit, of one certain color, and their hair is cropped a little above their ears, and a piece of one of their ears is cut off. Their friends are allowed to give them either meat, drink, or clothes, so they are of their proper color; but it is death, both to the giver and taker, if they give them money; nor is it less penal for any freeman to take money from them, upon any account whatsoever: and it is also death for any of these slaves (so they are called) to handle arms. Those of every division of the country are distinguished by a peculiar mark; which it is capital for them to lay aside, to go out of their bounds, or to talk with a slave of another jurisdiction; and the very attempt of an escape is no less penal than an escape itself; it is death for any other slave to be accessory to it; and if a

freeman engages in it he is condemned to slavery. Those
that discover it are rewarded; if freemen, in money; and
if slaves, with liberty, together with a pardon for being
accessory to it; that so they might find their account,
rather in repenting of their engaging in such a design,
than in persisting in it.

"These are their laws and rules in relation to robbery;
and it is obvious that they are as advantageous as they
are mild and gentle; since vice is not only destroyed, and
men preserved, but they are treated in such a manner as
to make them see the necessity of being honest, and of
employing the rest of their lives in repairing the injuries
they have formerly done to society. Nor is there any
hazard of their falling back to their old customs: and so
little do travelers apprehend mischief from them, that
they generally make use of them for guides, from one
jurisdiction to another; for there is nothing left them by
which they can rob, or be the better for it, since as they
are disarmed, so the very having of money is a sufficient
conviction: and as they are certainly punished if discovered, so they cannot hope to escape; for their habit being
in all the parts of it different from what is commonly
worn, they cannot fly away, unless they would go naked,
and even then their cropped ear would betray them.
The only danger to be feared from them, is their conspiring against the Government: but those of one division
and neighborhood can do nothing to any purpose, unless
a general conspiracy were laid among all the slaves of
the several jurisdictions, which cannot be done, since
they cannot meet or talk together; nor will any venture
on a design where the concealment would be so dangerous, and the discovery so profitable. None are quite
hopeless of recovering their freedom, since by their
obedience and patience, and by giving good grounds to
believe that they will change their manner of life for
the future, they may expect at last to obtain their liberty;
and some are every year restored to it, upon the good
character that is given of them. When I had related all
this, I added, that I did not see why such a method
might not be followed with more advantage, than could
ever be expected from that severe justice which the

counselor magnified so much. To this he answered, that
it could never take place in England, without endanger-
ing the whole nation. As he said this, he shook his
head, made some grimaces, and held his peace, while all
the company seemed of his opinion, except the Cardinal,
who said that it was not easy to form a judgment of its
success, since it was a method that never yet had been
tried. 'But if,' said he, 'when the sentence of death
was passed upon a thief, the prince would reprieve him
for a while, and make the experiment upon him, denying
him the privilege of a sanctuary; and then if it had a
good effect upon him, it might take place; and if it did
not succeed, the worst would be to execute the sentence
on the condemned persons at last. And I do not see,'
added he, 'why it would be either unjust, inconvenient,
or at all dangerous, to admit of such a delay: in my
opinion, the vagabonds ought to be treated in the same
manner; against whom, though we have made many laws,
yet we have not been able to gain our end.' When the
Cardinal had done, they all commended the motion,
though they had despised it when it came from me; but
more particularly commended what related to the vagabonds, because it was his own observation.

"I do not know whether it be worth while to tell what
followed, for it was very ridiculous; but I shall venture at
it, for as it is not foreign to this matter, so some good
use may be made of it. There was a jester standing by,
that counterfeited the fool so naturally, that he seemed
to be really one. The jests which he offered were so
cold and dull, that we laughed more at him than at them;
yet sometimes he said, as it were by chance, things that
were not unpleasant; so as to justify the old proverb,
'That he who throws the dice often, will sometimes have
a lucky hit.' When one of the company had said, that
I had taken care of the thieves, and the Cardinal had
taken care of the vagabonds, so that there remained
nothing but that some public provision might be made
for the poor, whom sickness or old age had disabled
from labor. 'Leave that to me,' said the fool, 'and I
shall take care of them; for there is no sort of people
whose sight I abhor more, having been so often vexed

with them, and with their sad complaints; but as dole-
fully soever as they have told their tale, they could never
prevail so far as to draw one penny from me: for either
I had no mind to give them anything, or when I had a
mind to do it, I had nothing to give them: and they now
know me so well, that they will not lose their labor, but
let me pass without giving me any trouble, because they
hope for nothing, no more, in faith, than if I were a
priest: but I would have a law made, for sending all
these beggars to monasteries, the men to the Benedictines
to be made lay-brothers, and the women to be nuns.'
The Cardinal smiled, and approved of it in jest; but the
rest liked it in earnest.   There was a divine present, who
though he was a grave, morose man, yet he was so
pleased with this reflection that was made on the priests
and the monks, that he began to play with the fool, and
said to him, 'This will not deliver you from all beggars,
except you take care of us friars.' 'That is done already,'
answered the fool, 'for the Cardinal has provided for you,
by what he proposed for restraining vagabonds, and setting them to work, for I know no vagabonds like you.'
This was well entertained by the whole company, who
looking at the Cardinal, perceived that he was not ill-
pleased at it; only the friar himself was vexed, as may
be easily imagined, and fell into such a passion, that he
could not forbear railing at the fool, and calling him
knave, slanderer, backbiter, and son of perdition, and
then cited some dreadful threatenings out of the Script-
ures against him.   Now the jester thought he was in his
element, and laid about him freely. 'Good friar,' said
he, 'be not angry, for it is written, " In patience possess your soul." ' The friar answered (for I shall give
you his own words), 'I am not angry, you hangman; at
least I do not sin in it, for the Psalmist says, " Be ye
angry, and sin not." ' Upon this the Cardinal admonished
him gently, and wished him to govern his passions. 'No,
my lord,' said he, 'I speak not but from a good zeal,
which I ought to have; for holy men have had a good
zeal, as it is said, " The zeal of thy house hath eaten me
up;" and we sing in our church, that those who mocked
Elisha as he went up to the house of God, felt the effects

of his zeal; which that mocker, that rogue, that scoun-
drel, will perhaps feel.' 'You do this perhaps with a
good intention,' said the Cardinal; 'but in my opinion,
it were wiser in you, and perhaps better for you, not to
engage in so ridiculous a contest with a fool.' 'No, my
lord,' answered he, 'that were not wisely done; for Solomon, the wisest of men, said, "Answer a fool according to his folly;" which I now do, and show him the
ditch into which he will fall, if he is not aware of it;
for if the many mockers of Elisha, who was but one bald
man, felt the effect of his zeal, what will become of one
mocker of so many friars, among whom there are so
many bald men? We have likewise a Bull, by which all
that jeer us are excommunicated.' When the Cardinal
saw that there was no end of this matter, he made a
sign to the fool to withdraw, turned the discourse another
way; and soon after rose from the table, and dismissing
us, went to hear causes.

"Thus, Mr. More, I have run out into a tedious story,
of the length of which I had been ashamed, if, as you
earnestly begged it of me, I had not observed you to
hearken to it, as if you had no mind to lose any part of
it. I might have contracted it, but I resolved to give it
you at large, that you might observe how those that
despised what I had proposed, no sooner perceived that
the Cardinal did not dislike it, but presently approved of
it, fawned so on him, and flattered him to such a degree,
that they in good earnest applauded those things that he
only liked in jest. And from hence you may gather, how
little courtiers would value either me or my counsels."

To this I answered, "You have done me a great kindness in this relation; for as everything has been related
by you, both wisely and pleasantly, so you have made me
imagine that I was in my own country, and grown young
again, by recalling that good Cardinal to my thoughts, in
whose family I was bred from my childhood: and though
you are upon other accounts very dear to me, yet you
are the dearer, because you honor his memory so much;
but after all this I cannot change my opinion; for I still
think that if you could overcome that aversion which you
have to the Courts of Princes, you might, by the advice

which it is in your power to give, do a great deal of good
to mankind; and this is the chief design that every good
man ought to propose to himself in living: for your friend
Plato thinks that nations will be happy, when either philosophers become kings, or kings become philosophers;
it is no wonder if we are so far from that happiness,
while philosophers will not think it their duty to assist
kings with their councils." "They are not so base-
minded," said he, "but that they would willingly do it:
many of them have already done it by their books, if
those that are in power would but hearken to their good
advice. But Plato judged right, that except kings themselves became philosophers, they who from their childhood are corrupted with false notions, would never fall
in entirely with the councils of philosophers, and this he
himself found to be true in the person of Dionysius.

"Do not you think, that if I were about any king, proposing good laws to him, and endeavoring to root out all
the cursed seeds of evil that I found in him, I should
either be turned out of his Court, or at least be laughed at
for my pains? For instance, what could it signify if I
were about the King of France, and were called into his
cabinet-council, where several wise men, in his hearing,
were proposing many expedients; as by what arts and
practices Milan may be kept; and Naples, that had so
oft slipped out of their hands, recovered; how the Venetians, and after them the rest of Italy, may be subdued;
and then how Flanders, Brabant, and all Burgundy, and
some other kingdoms which he has swallowed already in
his designs, may be added to his empire. One proposes
a league with the Venetians, to be kept as long as he
finds his account in it, and that he ought to communicate
councils with them, and give them some share of the spoil,
till his success makes him need or fear them less, and
then it will be easily taken out of their hands. Another
proposes the hiring the Germans, and the securing the
Switzers by pension. Another proposes the gaining the
Emperor by money, which is omnipotent with him. Another proposes a peace with the King of Aragon, and in
order to cement it, the yielding up the King of Navarre's
pretensions. Another thinks the Prince of Castile is to

be wrought on, by the hope of an alliance, and that some
of his courtiers are to be gained to the French faction by
pensions. The hardest point of all is what to do with England: a treaty of peace is to be set on foot, and if their alliance is not to be depended on, yet it is to be made as
firm as possible; and they are to be called friends, but
suspected as enemies; therefore the Scots are to be kept
in readiness, to be let loose upon England on every occasion; and some banished nobleman is to be supported
underhand (for by the league it cannot be done avowedly)
who has a pretension to the crown, by which means that
suspected prince may be kept in awe. Now when things
are in so great a fermentation, and so many gallant men
are joining councils, how to carry on the war, if so mean
a man as I should stand up and wish them to change
all their councils, to let Italy alone, and stay at home,
since the kingdom of France was indeed greater than
could be well governed by one man; that therefore he
ought not to think of adding others to it: and if after
this, I should propose to them the resolutions of the
Achorians, a people that lie on the southeast of Utopia,
who long ago engaged in war, in order to add to the
dominions of their prince another kingdom, to which he
had some pretensions by an ancient alliance. This they
conquered, but found that the trouble of keeping it was
equal to that by which it was gained; that the conquered
people were always either in rebellion or exposed to foreign invasions, while they were obliged to be incessantly
at war, either for or against them, and consequently
could never disband their army; that in the meantime
they were oppressed with taxes, their money went out of
the kingdom, their blood was spilt for the glory of their
king, without procuring the least advantage to the people,
who received not the smallest benefit from it even in
time of peace; and that their manners being corrupted by
a long war, robbery and murders everywhere abounded,
and their laws fell into contempt; while their king, distracted with the care of two kingdoms, was the less able
to apply his mind to the interests of either. When they
saw this, and that there would be no end to these evils,
they by joint councils made an humble address to their

king, desiring him to choose which of the two kingdoms
he had the greatest mind to keep, since he could not
hold both; for they were too great a people to be governed by a divided king, since no man would willingly
have a groom that should be in common between him and
another. Upon which the good prince was forced to quit
his new kingdom to one of his friends (who was not long
after dethroned), and to be contented with his old one.
To this I would add, that after all those warlike attempts,
the vast confusions, and the consumption both of treasure and of people that must follow them; perhaps upon
some misfortune, they might be forced to throw up all
at last; therefore it seemed much more eligible that the
king should improve his ancient kingdom all he could,
and make it flourish as much as possible; that he should
love his people, and be beloved of them; that he should
live among them, govern them gently, and let other
kingdoms alone, since that which had fallen to his share
was big enough, if not too big for him. Pray how do
you think would such a speech as this be heard?" "I
confess," said I, "I think not very well."

"But what," said he, "if I should sort with another
kind of ministers, whose chief contrivances and consultations were, by what art the prince's treasures might be
increased. Where one proposes raising the value of
specie when the king's debts are large, and lowering it
when his revenues were to come in, that so he might
both pay much with a little, and in a little receive a
great deal; another proposes a pretense of a war, that
money might be raised in order to carry it on, and that
a peace be concluded as soon as that was done; and this
with such appearances of religion as might work on the
people, and make them impute it to the piety of their
prince, and to his tenderness for the lives of his subjects. A third offers some old musty laws, that have
been antiquated by a long disuse; and which, as they had
been forgotten by all the subjects, so they had been also
broken by them; and proposes the levying the penalties
of these laws, that as it would bring in a vast treasure,
so there might be a very good pretense for it, since it
would look like the executing a law, and the doing of

justice. A fourth proposes the prohibiting of many things under severe penalties, especially such as were against the interest of the people, and then the dispensing with these prohibitions upon great compositions, to those who might find their advantage in breaking them. This would serve two ends, both of them acceptable to many; for as those whose avarice led them to transgress would be severely fined, so the selling licenses dear would look as if a prince were tender of his people, and would not easily, or at low rates, dispense with anything that might be against the public good. Another proposes that the judges must be made sure, that they may declare always in favor of the prerogative, that they must be often sent for to Court, that the king may hear them argue those points in which he is concerned; since how unjust soever any of his pretensions may be, yet still some one or other of them, either out of contradiction to others, or the pride of singularity, or to make their court, would find out some pretense or other to give the king a fair color to carry the point: for if the judges but differ in opinion, the clearest thing in the world is made by that means disputable, and truth being once brought in question, the king may then take advantage to expound the law for his own profit; while the judges that stand out will be brought over, either out of fear or modesty; and they being thus gained, all of them may be sent to the bench to give sentence boldly, as the king would have it; for fair pretenses will never be wanting when sentence is to be given in the prince's favor. It will either be said that equity lies of his side, or some words in the law will be found sounding that way, or some forced sense will be put on them; and when all other things fail, the king's undoubted prerogative will be pretended, as that which is above all law; and to which a religious judge ought to have a special regard. Thus all consent to that maxim of Crassus, that a prince cannot have treasure enough, since he must maintain his armies out of it: that a king, even though he would, can do nothing unjustly; that all property is in him, not excepting the very persons of his subjects: and that no man has any other property, but that which the king out of his goodness thinks fit to leave him. And they think it is the prince's interest, that there be as little of this left as may be, as if it were his advantage that his people should have neither riches nor liberty; since these things make them less easy and less willing to submit to a cruel and unjust government; whereas necessity and poverty blunts them, makes them patient, beats them down, and breaks that height of spirit, that might otherwise dispose them to rebel. Now what if after all these propositions were made, I should rise up and assert, that such councils were both unbecoming a king, and mischievous to him: and that not only his honor but his safety consisted more in his people's wealth, than in his own; if I should show that they choose a king for their own sake, and not for his; that by his care and endeavors they may be both easy and safe; and that therefore a prince ought to take more care of his people's happiness than of his own, as a shepherd is to take more care of his flock than of himself. It is also certain, that they are much mistaken that think that the poverty of a nation is a means of the public safety. Who quarrel more than beggars? Who does more earnestly long for a change, than he that is uneasy in his present circumstances? And who run to create confusions with so desperate a boldness, as those who have nothing to lose, hope to gain by them? If a king should fall under such contempt or envy, that he could not keep his subjects in their duty, but by oppression and ill usage, and by rendering them poor and miserable, it were certainly better for him to quit his kingdom, than to retain it by such methods, as makes him while he keeps the name of authority, lose the majesty due to it. Nor is it so becoming the dignity of a king to reign over beggars, as over rich and happy subjects. And therefore Fabricius, a man of a noble and exalted temper, said, he would rather govern rich men, than be rich himself; since for one man to abound in wealth and pleasure, when all about him are mourning and groaning, is to be a gaoler and not a king. He is an unskillful physician, that cannot cure one disease without casting his patient into another: so he that can find no other way for correcting the errors of his people, but by taking from them the conveniences of life, shows that he knows not what it is to govern a free nation. He himself ought rather to shake off his sloth, or to lay down his pride; for the contempt or hatred that his people have for him, takes its rise from the vices in himself. Let him live upon what belongs to him, without wronging others, and accommodate his expense to his revenue. Let him punish crimes, and by his wise conduct let him endeavor to prevent them, rather than be severe when he has suffered them to be too common: let him not rashly revive laws that are abrogated by disuse, especially if they have been long forgotten, and never wanted; and let him never take any penalty for the breach of them, to which a judge would not give way in a private man, but would look on him as a crafty and unjust person for pretending to it. To these things I would add, that law among the Macarians, a people that lie not far from Utopia, by which their king, on the day on which he begins to reign, is tied by an oath confirmed by solemn sacrifices, never to have at once above a thousand pounds of gold in his treasures, or so much silver as is equal to that in value. This law, they tell us, was made by an excellent king, who had more regard to the riches of his country than to his own wealth; and therefore provided against the heaping up of so much treasure, as might impoverish the people. He thought that moderate sum might be sufficient for any accident; if either the king had occasion for it against rebels, or the kingdom against the invasion of an enemy; but that it was not enough to encourage a prince to invade other men's rights, a circumstance that was the chief cause of his making that law. He also thought that it was a good provision for that free circulation of money, so necessary for the course of commerce and exchange; and when a king must distribute all those extraordinary accessions that increase treasure beyond the due pitch, it makes him less disposed to oppress his subjects. Such a king as this will be the terror of ill men, and will be beloved by all the good.

"If, I say, I should talk of these or such like things, to men that had taken their bias another way, how deaf would they be to all I could say?" "No doubt, very

deaf," answered I; and no wonder, for one is never to offer
at propositions or advice that we are certain will not be
entertained. Discourses so much out of the road could
not avail anything, nor have any effect on men whose
minds were prepossessed with different sentiments. This
philosophical way of speculation is not unpleasant among
friends in a free conversation, but there is no room for
it in the Courts of Princes where great affairs are carried on by authority." "That is what I was saying,"
replied he, "that there is no room for philosophy in the
Courts of Princes." "Yes, there is," said I, "but not
for this speculative philosophy that makes everything to
be alike fitting at all times: but there is another philosophy that is more pliable, that knows its proper scene,
accommodates itself to it, and teaches a man with pro-
propriety and decency to act that part which has fallen
to his share. If when one of Plautus's comedies is upon
the stage and a company of servants are acting their
parts, you should come out in the garb of a philosopher,
and repeat out of 'Octavia's discourse of Seneca's to Nero,'
would it not be better for you to say nothing than by
mixing things of such different natures to make an im-
pertinent tragi-comedy? For you spoil and corrupt the
play that is in hand when you mix with it things of an
opposite nature, even though they are much better.
Therefore go through with the play that is acting the
best you can, and do not confound it because another
that is pleasanter comes into your thoughts. It is even
so in a commonwealth, and in the councils of princes; if
ill opinions cannot be quite rooted out, and you cannot
cure some received vice according to your wishes, you
must not therefore abandon the commonwealth, for the
same reasons you should not forsake the ship in a storm
because you cannot command the winds. You are
not obliged to assault people with discourses that
are out of their road, when you see that their received
notions must prevent your making an impression upon them.
You ought rather to cast about and to manage things with
all the dexterity in your power, so that if you are not
able to make them go well they may be as little ill as
possible; for except all men were good everything cannot

be right and that is a blessing that I do not at present hope to see. According to your arguments," answered he, "all that I could be able to do would be to preserve myself from being mad while I endeavored to cure the madness of others; for if I speak truth, I must repeat what I have said to you; and as for lying, whether a philosopher can do it or not, I cannot tell, I am sure I cannot do it. But though these discourses may be uneasy and ungrateful to them, I do not see why they should seem foolish or extravagant: indeed if I should either propose such things as Plato has contrived in his commonwealth, or as the Utopians practice in theirs, though they might seem better, as certainly they are, yet they are so different from our establishment, which is founded on property, there being no such thing among them, that I could not expect that it would have any effect on them; but such discourses as mine, which only call past evils to mind and give warning of what may follow, have nothing in them that is so absurd that they may not be used at any time, for they can only be unpleasant to those who are resolved to run headlong the contrary way; and if we must let alone everything as absurd or extravagant which by reason of the wicked lives of many may seem uncouth, we must, even among Christians, give over pressing the greatest part of those things that Christ hath taught us, though he has commanded us not to conceal them, but to proclaim on the house-tops that which he taught in secret. The greatest parts of his precepts are more opposite to the lives of the men of this age than any part of my discourse has been; but the preachers seemed to have learned that craft to which you advise me, for they, observing that the world would not willingly suit their lives to the rules that Christ has given, have fitted his doctrine as if it had been a leaden rule, to their lives, that so some way or other they might agree with one another. But I see no other effect of this compliance except it be that men become more secure in their wickedness by it. And this is all the success that I can have in a Court, for I must always differ from the rest, and then I shall signify nothing; or if I agree with them, I shall then only help

forward their madness. I do not comprehend what you
mean by your casting about, or by the bending and hand-
ling things so dexterously, that if they go not well they
may go as little ill as may be; for in Courts they will
not bear with a man's holding his peace or conniving at
what others do. A man must barefacedly approve of the
worst counsels, and consent to the blackest designs: so
that he would pass for a spy, or possibly for a traitor,
that did but coldly approve of such wicked practices; and
therefore when a man is engaged in such a society, he
will be so far from being able to mend matters by his
casting about, as you call it, that he will find no occasions
of doing any good: the ill company will sooner corrupt
him, than be the better for him: or if notwithstanding
all their ill company, he still remains steady and innocent,
yet their follies and knavery will be imputed to him; and
by mixing counsels with them, he must bear his share
of all the blame that belongs wholly to others.

" It was no ill simile by which Plato set forth the un-
reasonableness of a philosopher's meddling with government. If a man, says he, was to see a great company
run out every day into the rain, and take delight in being
wet; if he knew that it would be to no purpose for him
to go and persuade them to return to their houses, in
order to avoid the storm, and that all that could be expected by his going to speak to them would be that he
himself should be as wet as they, it would be best for
him to keep within doors; and since he had not influence
enough to correct other people's folly, to take care to
preserve himself.

" Though to speak plainly my real sentiments, I must
freely own, that as long as there is any property, and
while money is the standard of all other things, I cannot
think that a nation can be governed either justly or happily: not justly, because the best things will fall to the
share of the worst men; nor happily, because all things
will be divided among a few (and even these are not in
all respects happy), the rest being left to be absolutely
miserable. Therefore, when I reflect on the wise and
good constitution of the Utopians, among whom all things
are so well governed, and with so few laws; where virtue

hath its due reward, and yet there is such an equality, that every man lives in plenty; when I compare with them so many other nations that are still making new laws, and yet can never bring their constitution to a right regulation, where, notwithstanding, every one has his property; yet all the laws that they can invent have not the power either to obtain or preserve it, or even to enable men certainly to distinguish what is their own from what is another's; of which the many lawsuits that every day break out and are eternally depending, give too plain a demonstration; when, I say, I balance all these things in my thoughts, I grow more favorable to Plato, and do not wonder that he resolved not to make any laws for such as would not submit to a community of all things: for so wise a man could not but foresee that the setting all upon a level was the only way to make a nation happy, which cannot be obtained so long as there is property: for when every man draws to himself all that he can compass, by one title or another, it must needs follow, that how plentiful soever a nation may be, yet a few dividing the wealth of it among themselves, the rest must fall into indigence. So that there will be two sorts of people among them, who deserve that their fortunes should be interchanged; the former useless, but wicked and ravenous; and the latter, who by their constant industry serve the public more than themselves, sincere and modest men. From whence I am persuaded, that till property is taken away there can be no equitable or just distribution of things, nor can the world be happily governed: for as long as that is maintained, the greatest and the far best part of mankind will be still oppressed with a load of cares and anxieties. I confess without taking it quite away, those pressures that lie on a great part of mankind may be made lighter; but they can never be quite removed. For if laws were made to determine at how great an extent in soil and at how much money every man must stop, to limit the prince that he might not grow too great, and to restrain the people that they might not become too insolent, and that none might factiously aspire to public employments; which ought neither to be sold, nor made burdensome by a great expense; since otherwise those that serve in them would be

tempted to reimburse themselves by cheats and violence,
and it would become necessary to find out rich men for
undergoing those employments which ought rather to be
trusted to the wise. These laws, I say, might have
such effects, as good diet and care might have on a
sick man, whose recovery is desperate: they might
allay and mitigate the disease, but it could never be
quite healed, nor the body politic be brought again to
a good habit, as long as property remains; and it will
fall out as in a complication of diseases, that by ap-
plying a remedy to one sore, you will provoke another;
and that which removes the one ill symptom produces
others, while the strengthening one part of the body
weakens the rest." "On the contrary," answered I, "it
seems to me that men cannot live conveniently, where all
things are common; how can there be any plenty, where
every man will excuse himself from labor? For as the
hope of gain doth not excite him, so the confidence that he
has in other men's industry may make him slothful; if
people come to be pinched with want, and yet cannot dispose of anything as their own; what can follow upon this
but perpetual sedition and bloodshed, especially when the
reverence and authority due to magistrates falls to the
ground? For I cannot imagine how that can be kept up
among those that are in all things equal to one another."
"I do not wonder," said he, "that it appears so to you,
since you have no notion, or at least no right one, of
such a constitution; but if you had been in Utopia with
me, and had seen their laws and rules, as I did, for the
space of five years, in which I lived among them; and
during which time I was so delighted with them, that
indeed I should never have left them, if it had not been
to make the discovery of that new world to the Europeans; you would then confess that you had never seen
a people so well constituted as they." "You will not
easily persuade me," said Peter, "that any nation in that
new world is better governed than those among us. For
as our understandings are not worse than theirs, so our
government, if I mistake not, being more ancient, a long
practice has helped us to find out many conveniences of
life; and some happy chances have discovered other

things to us, which no man's understanding could ever have invented." "As for the antiquity, either of their government, or of ours," said he, " you cannot pass a true judgment of it, unless you had read their histories; for if they are to be believed, they had towns among them before these parts were so much as inhabited. And as for those discoveries, that have been either hit on by chance, or made by ingenious men, these might have happened there as well as here. I do not deny but we are more ingenious than they are, but they exceed us much in industry and application. They knew little concerning us before our arrival among them; they call us all by the general name of the nations that lie beyond the Equinoctial Line; for their Chronicle mentions a shipwreck that was made on their coast 1,200 years ago; and that some Romans and Egyptians that were in the ship, getting safe ashore, spent the rest of their days among them; and such was their ingenuity, that from this single opportunity they drew the advantage of learning from those unlooked-for guests, and acquired all the useful arts that were then among the Romans, and which were known to these shipwrecked men; and by the hints that they gave them, they themselves found out even some of those arts which they could not fully explain; so happily did they improve that accident of having some of our people cast upon their shore. But if such an accident has at any time brought any from thence into Europe, we have been so far from improving it, that we do not so much as remember it; as in after-times perhaps it will be forgot by our people that I was ever there. For though they from one such accident made themselves masters of all the good inventions that were among us; yet I believe it would be long before we should learn or put in practice any of the good institutions that are among them. And this is the true cause of their being better governed, and living happier than we, though we come not short of them in point of understanding or outward advantages." Upon this I said to him, " I earnestly beg you would describe that island very particularly to us. Be not too short, but set out in order all things relating to their soil, their rivers, their towns, their people, their manners, constitution, laws, and, in a word, all that you imagine we desire to know. And you may well imagine that we desire to know everything concerning them, of which we are hitherto ignorant.» «I will do it very willingly,» said he, «for I have digested the whole matter carefully; but it will take up some time.» «Let us go then,» said I, «first and dine, and then we shall have leisure enough.» He consented. We went in and dined, and after dinner came back, and sat down in the same place. I ordered my servants to take care that none might come and interrupt us. And both Peter and I desired Raphael to be as good as his word. When he saw that we were very intent upon it, he paused a little to recollect himself, and began in this manner.

11

BOOK II.

THE island of Utopia is in the middle two hundred miles broad, and holds almost at the same breadth over a great part of it; but it grows narrower toward both ends. Its figure is not unlike a crescent: between its horns, the sea comes in eleven miles broad, and spreads itself into a great bay, which is environed with land to the compass of about five hundred miles, and is well secured from winds. In this bay there is no great current, the whole coast is, as it were, one continued harbor, which gives all that live in the island great convenience for mutual commerce; but the entry into the bay, occasioned by rocks on the one hand, and shallows on the other, is very dangerous. In the middle of it there is one single rock which appears above water, and may therefore be easily avoided, and on the top of it there is a tower in which a garrison is kept, the other rocks lie under water, and are very dangerous. The channel is known only to the natives, so that if any stranger should enter into the bay, without one of their pilots, he would run great danger of shipwreck; for even they themselves could not pass it safe, if some marks that are on the coast did not direct their way; and if these should be but a little shifted, any fleet that might come against them, how great soever it were, would be certainly lost. On the other side of the island there are likewise many harbors; and the coast is so fortified, both by nature and art, that a small number of men can hinder the descent of a great army. But they report (and there remains good marks of it to make it credible) that this was no island at first, but a part of the continent. Utopus that conquered it (whose name it still carries, for Abraxa was its first name) brought the rude and uncivilized inhabitants into such a good government, and to that measure of politeness, that they now far excel all the rest of mankind; having soon subdued them, he designed to separate them from the continent, and to bring the sea quite round them. To accomplish this, he ordered a deep channel to be dug fifteen miles long; and that the natives might not think he treated them like slaves, he not only forced the inhabitants, but also his own soldiers, to labor in carrying it on. As he set a vast number of men to work, he beyond all men's expectations brought it to a speedy conclusion. And his neighbors, who at first laughed at the folly of the undertaking, no sooner saw it brought to perfection, than they were struck with admiration and terror.

There are fifty-four cities in the island, all large and well built: the manners, customs, and laws of which are the same, and they are all contrived as near in the same manner as the ground on which they stand will allow. The nearest lie at least twenty-four miles distant from one another, and the most remote are not so far distant, but that a man can go on foot in one day from it, to that which lies next it. Every city sends three of their wisest senators once a year to Amaurot, to consult about their common concerns; for that is the chief town of the island, being situated near the centre of it, so that it is the most convenient place for their assemblies. The jurisdiction of every city extends at least twenty miles: and where the towns lie wider, they have much more ground: no town desires to enlarge its bounds, for the people consider themselves rather as tenants than landlords. They have built over all the country, farmhouses for husbandmen, which are well contrived, and are furnished with all things necessary for country labor. Inhabitants are sent by turns from the cities to dwell in them; no country family has fewer than forty men and women in it, besides two slaves. There is a master and a mistress set over every family; and over thirty families there is a magistrate. Every year twenty of this family come back to the town, after they have stayed two years in the country; and in their room there are other twenty sent from the town, that they may learn country work from those that have been already one year in the country, as they must teach those that come to them the next from the town. By this means such as dwell in those

country farms are never ignorant of agriculture, and so
commit no errors, which might otherwise be fatal, and
bring them under a scarcity of corn. But though there
is every year such a shifting of the husbandmen, to
prevent any man being forced against his will to follow
that hard course of life too long; yet many among them
take such pleasure in it, that they desire leave to continue in it many years.   These husbandmen till the
ground, breed cattle, hew wood, and convey it to the
towns, either by land or water, as is most convenient.
They breed an infinite multitude of chickens in a very
curious manner; for the hens do not sit and hatch them,
but vast number of eggs are laid in a gentle and equal
heat, in order to be hatched, and they are no sooner out
of the shell, and able to stir about, but they seem to
consider those that feed them as their mothers, and
follow them as other chickens do the hen that hatched
them.   They breed very few horses, but those they have
are full of mettle, and are kept only for exercising their
youth in the art of sitting and riding them; for they do
not put them to any work, either of plowing or carriage,
in which they employ oxen; for though their horses are
stronger, yet they find oxen can hold out longer; and as
they are not subject to so many diseases, so they are
kept upon a less charge, and with less trouble; and even
when they are so worn out, that they are no more fit for
labor, they are good meat at last.   They sow no corn,
but that which is to be their bread; for they drink
either wine, cider, or perry, and often water, sometimes
boiled with honey or licorice, with which they abound;
and though they know exactly how much corn will serve
every town, and all that tract of country which belongs
to it, yet they sow much more, and breed more cattle
than are necessary for their consumption; and they give
that overplus of which they make no use to their neighbors. When they want anything in the country which
it does not produce, they fetch that from the town,
without carrying anything in exchange for it. And the
magistrates of the town take care to see it given them;
for they meet generally in the town once a month, upon
a festival day.   When the time of harvest comes, the

magistrates in the country send to those in the towns, and
let them know how many hands they will need for reaping the harvest; and the number they call for being sent
to them, they commonly dispatch it all in one day.

Of Their Towns, Particularly of Amaurot.

HE THAT knows one of their towns, knows them all,
they are so like one another, except where the situation
makes some difference. I shall therefore describe one of
them; and none is so proper as Amaurot; for as none is
more eminent, all the rest yielding in precedence to this,
because it is the seat of their supreme council; so there
was none of them better known to me, I having lived
five years altogether in it.

It lies upon the side of a hill, or rather a rising ground:
its figure is almost square, for from the one side of it,
which shoots up almost to the top of the hill, it runs
down in a descent for two miles to the river Anider; but
it is a little broader the other way that runs along the
bank of that river. The Anider rises about eighty miles
above Amaurot in a small spring at first; but other
brooks falling into it, of which two are more considerable than the rest. As it runs by Amaurot, it is grown
half a mile broad; but it still grows larger and larger,
till after sixty miles' course below it, it is lost in the
ocean, between the town and the sea, and for some miles
above the town, it ebbs and flows every six hours, with
a strong current. The tide comes up for about thirty
miles so full, that there is nothing but salt water in the
river, the fresh water being driven back with its force;
and above that, for some miles, the water is brackish;
but a little higher, as it runs by the town, it is quite
fresh; and when the tide ebbs, it continues fresh all along
to the sea. There is a bridge cast over the river, not of
timber, but of fair stone, consisting of many stately
arches; it lies at that part of the town which is farthest
from the sea, so that ships without any hindrance lie all
along the side of the town. There is likewise another
river that runs by it, which though it is not great, yet it
runs pleasantly, for it rises out of the same hill on which

the town stands, and so runs down through it, and falls
into the Anider.   The inhabitants have fortified the
fountain head of this river, which springs a little without
the towns; that so if they should happen to be besieged,
the enemy might not be able to stop or divert the course
of the water, nor poison it; from thence it is carried in
earthen pipes to the lower streets; and for those places
of the town to which the water of that small river cannot
be conveyed, they have great cisterns for receiving the
rain water, which supplies the want of the other.   The
town is compassed with a high and thick wall, in which
there are many towers and forts; there is also a broad
and deep dry ditch, set thick with thorns, cast round
three sides of the town, and the river is instead of a
ditch on the fourth side.   The streets are very convenient
for all carriage, and are well sheltered from the winds.
Their buildings are good, and are so uniform, that a whole
side of a street looks like one house.   The streets are
twenty feet broad; there lie gardens behind all their
houses; these are large but inclosed with buildings, that
on all hands face the streets; so that every house has
both a door to the street, and a back door to the garden.
Their doors have all two leaves, which, as they are easily
opened, so they shut of their own accord; and there being
no property among them, every man may freely enter
into any house whatsoever.   At every ten years' end they
shift their houses by lots.   They cultivate their gardens
with great care, so that they have both vines, fruits,
herbs, and flowers in them; and all is so well ordered,
and so finely kept, that I never saw gardens anywhere
that were both so fruitful and so beautiful as theirs.   And
this humor of ordering their gardens so well, is not only
kept up by the pleasure they find in it, but also by an
emulation between the inhabitants of the several streets,
who vie with each other; and there is indeed nothing
belonging to the whole town that is both more useful
and more pleasant.   So that he who founded the town,
seems to have taken care of nothing more than of their
gardens; for they say, the whole scheme of the town was
designed at first by Utopus, but he left all that belonged
to the ornament and improvement of it, to be added by

those that should come after him, that being too much
for one man to bring to perfection. Their records, that
contain the history of their town and state, are preserved
with an exact care, and run back 1,760 years. From
these it appears that their houses were at first low and
mean, like cottages, made of any sort of timber, and were
built with mud walls and thatched with straw. But now
their houses are three stories high; the fronts of them
are faced either with stone, plastering, or brick; and
between the facings of their walls they throw in ·their
rubbish. Their roofs are flat, and on them they lay a
sort of plaster, which costs very little, and yet is so tempered that it is not apt to take fire, and yet resists the
weather more than lead. They have great quantities of
glass among them, with which they glaze their windows.
They use also in their windows a thin linen cloth, that
is so oiled or gummed that it both keeps out the wind
and gives free admission to the light.

Of Their Magistrates.

THIRTY families choose every year a magistrate, who
was anciently called the Syphogrant, but is now called
the Philarch; and over every ten Syphogrants, with the
families subject to them, there is another magistrate, who
was anciently called the Tranibor, but of late the Arch-
philarch. All the Syphogrants, who are in number 200,
choose the Prince out of a list of four, who are named
by the people of the four divisions of the city; but they
take an oath before they proceed to an election, that they
will choose him whom they think most fit for the office.
They give their voices secretly so that it is not known for
whom every one gives his suffrage. The Prince is for
life, unless he is removed upon suspicion of some design
to enslave the people. The Tranibors are new chosen
every year, but yet they are for the most part continued.
All their other magistrates are only annual. The Tranibors meet every third day, and oftener if necessary, and
consult with the Prince, either concerning the affairs of
the state in general, or such private differences as may
arise sometimes among the people; though that falls out

but seldom.   There are always two Syphogrants called
into the council chamber, and these are changed every
day.   It is a fundamental rule of their government, that
no conclusion can be made in anything that relates to the
public, till it has been first debated three several days in
their council.   It is death for any to meet and consult
concerning the state, unless it be either in their ordinary
council, or in the assembly of the whole body of the
people.

These things have been so provided among them, that
the Prince and the Tranibors may not conspire together
to change the government, and enslave the people; and
therefore when anything of great importance is set on
foot, it is sent to the Syphogrants; who after they have
communicated it to the families that belong to their divisions, and have considered it among themselves, make
report to the senate; and upon great occasions, the matter
is referred to the council of the whole island. One rule
observed in their council, is, never to debate a thing on the
same day in which it is first proposed; for that is always
referred to the next meeting, that so men may not rashly,
and in the heat of discourse, engage themselves too soon,
which might bias them so much, that instead of consulting
the good of the public, they might rather study to support
their first opinions, and by a perverse and preposterous
sort of shame, hazard their country rather than endanger
their own reputation, or venture the being suspected to
have wanted foresight in the expedients that they at first
proposed.   And therefore to prevent this, they take care
that they may rather be deliberate than sudden in their
motions.

Of Their Trades, and Manner of Life.

AGRICULTURE is that which is so universally understood
among them, that no person, either man or woman, is
ignorant of it; they are instructed in it from their childhood, partly by what they learn at school, and partly by
practice; they being led out often into the fields, about
the town, where they not only see others at work, but are
likewise exercised in it themselves.   Besides agriculture,

which is so common to them all, every man has some
peculiar trade to which he applies himself, such as the
manufacture of wool, or flax, masonry, smith's work, or
carpenter's work; for there is no sort of trade that is in
great esteem among them. Throughout the island they
wear the same sort of clothes without any other distinction, except what is necessary to distinguish the two
sexes, and the married and unmarried. The fashion
never alters; and as it is neither disagreeable nor uneasy, so it is suited to the climate, and calculated both
for their summers and winters. Every family makes
their own clothes; but all among them, women as well
as men, learn one or other of the trades formerly mentioned. Women, for the most part, deal in wool and flax,
which suit best with their weakness, leaving the ruder
trades to the men. The same trade generally passes
down from father to son, inclinations often following
descent; but if any man's genius lies another way, he is
by adoption translated into a family that deals in the
trade to which he is inclined; and when that is to be
done, care is taken not only by his father, but by the
magistrate, that he may be put to a discreet and good
man. And if after a person has learned one trade, he
desires to acquire another, that is also allowed, and is
managed in the same manner as the former. When he
has learned both, he follows that which he likes best,
unless the public has more occasion for the other.

The chief, and almost the only business of the syphogrants, is to take care that no man may live idle, but
that every one may follow his trade diligently; yet they
do not wear themselves out with perpetual toil, from
morning to night, as if they were beasts of burden, which
as it is indeed a heavy slavery, so it is everywhere the
common course of life among all mechanics except the
Utopians; but they, dividing the day and night into
twenty-four hours, appoint six of these for work; three
of which are before dinner; and three after. They then
sup, and at eight o'clock, counting from noon, go to bed
and sleep eight hours. The rest of their time besides
that taken up in work, eating and sleeping, is left to every
man's discretion; yet they are not to abuse that interval

to luxury and idleness, but must employ it in some proper
exercise according to their various inclinations, which is
for the most part reading. It is ordinary to have public
lectures every morning before daybreak; at which none
are obliged to appear but those who are marked out for
literature; yet a great many, both men and women of
all ranks, go to hear lectures of one sort or other, according to their inclinations. But if others, that are not
made for contemplation, choose rather to employ themselves at that time in their trades, as many of them do,
they are not hindered, but are rather commended, as
men that take care to serve their country. After supper, they spend an hour in some diversion, in summer in their gardens, and in winter in the halls where
they eat; where they entertain each other, either with
music or discourse. They do not so much as know dice,
or any such foolish and mischievous games; they have,
however, two sorts of games not unlike our chess; the
one is between several numbers, in which one number,
as it were, consumes another; the other resembles a battle
between the virtues and the vices, in which the enmity
in the vices among themselves, and their agreement
against virtue is not unpleasantly represented; together
with the special oppositions between the particular virtues and vices; as also the methods by which vice either
openly assaults or secretly undermines virtue; and virtue
on the other hand resists it. But the time appointed for
labor is to be narrowly examined, otherwise you may
imagine, that since there are only six hours appointed
for work, they may fall under a scarcity of necessary
provisions. But it is so far from being true, that this
time is not sufficient for supplying them with plenty of
all things, either necessary or convenient; that it is rather
too much; and this you will easily apprehend, if you
consider how great a part of all other nations is quite
idle. First, women generally do little, who are the half
of mankind; and if some few women are diligent, their
husbands are idle; then consider the great company of
idle priests, and of those that are called religious men;
add to these all rich men, chiefly those that have estates
in land, who are called noblemen and gentlemen,

together with their families, made up of idle persons, that are kept more for show than use; add to these, all those strong and lusty beggars, that go about pretending some disease, in excuse for their begging; and upon the whole account you will find that the number of those by whose labors mankind is supplied, is much less than you perhaps imagined. Then consider how few of those that work are employed in labors that are of real service; for we who measure all things by money, give rise to many trades that are both vain and superfluous, and serve only to support riot and luxury. For if those who work were employed only in such things as the conveniences of life require, there would be such an abundance of them, that the prices of them would so sink, that tradesmen could not be maintained by their gains; if all those who labor about useless things, were set to more profitable employments, and if all they that languish out their lives in sloth and idleness, every one of whom consumes as much as any two of the men that are at work, were forced to labor, you may easily imagine that a small proportion of time would serve for doing all that is either necessary, profitable, or pleasant to mankind, especially while pleasure is kept within its due bounds. This appears very plainly in Utopia, for there, in a great city, and in all the territory that lies round it, you can scarce find five hundred, either men or women, by their age and strength, are capable of labor, that are not engaged in it; even the Syphogrants, though excused by the law, yet do not excuse themselves, but work, that by their examples they may incite the industry of the rest of the people. The like exemption is allowed to those, who being recommended to the people by the priests, are by the secret suffrages of the Syphogrants privileged from labor, that they may apply themselves wholly to study; and if any of these fall short of those hopes that they seemed at first to give, they are obliged to return to work. And sometimes a mechanic, that so employs his leisure hours, as to make a considerable advancement in learning, is eased from being a tradesman, and ranked among their learned men. Out of these they choose their ambassadors, their priests, their Tranibors, and the Prince himself; anciently called their Barzenes, but is called of late their Ademus.

And thus from the great numbers among them that are neither suffered to be idle, nor to be employed in any fruitless labor, you may easily make the estimate how much may be done in those few hours in which they are obliged to labor. But besides all that has been already said, it is to be considered that the needful arts among them are managed with less labor than anywhere else. The building or the repairing of houses among us employ many hands, because often a thriftless heir suffers a house that his father built to fall into decay, so that his successor must, at a great cost, repair that which he might have kept up with a small charge: it frequently happens, that the same house which one person built at a vast expense, is neglected by another, who thinks he has a more delicate sense of the beauties of architecture; and he, suffering it to fall to ruin, builds another at no less charge. But among the Utopians, all things are so regulated that men very seldom build upon a new piece of ground; and are not only very quick in repairing their houses, but show their foresight in preventing their decay: so that their buildings are preserved very long, with but little labor; and thus the builders to whom that care belongs are often without employment, except the hewing of timber, and the squaring of stones, that the materials may be in readiness for raising a building very suddenly, when there is any occasion for it. As to their clothes, observe how little work is spent in them: while they are at labor, they are clothed with leather and skins, cast carelessly about them, which will last seven years; and when they appear in public they put on an upper garment, which hides the other; and these are all of one color, and that is the natural color of the wool. As they need less woolen cloth than is used any-where else, so that which they make use of is much less costly. They use linen cloth more; but that is prepared with less labor, and they value cloth only by the white-ness of the linen, or the cleanness of the wool, without much regard to the fineness of the thread; while in other places, four or five upper garments of woolen cloth, of

different colors, and as many vests of silk, will scarce
serve one man; and while those that are nicer think ten
too few, every man there is content with one, which very
often serves him two years. Nor is there anything that
can tempt a man to desire more; for if he had them, he
would neither be the warmer, nor would he make one
jot the better appearance for it. And thus, since they
are all employed in some useful labor, and since they
content themselves with fewer things, it falls out that
there is a great abundance of all things among them: so
that it frequently happens, that for want of other work,
vast numbers are sent out to mend the highways. But
when no public undertaking is to be performed, the hours
of working are lessened. The magistrates never engage
the people in unnecessary labor, since the chief end of
the constitution is to regulate labor by the necessities of
the public, and to allow all the people as much time as
is necessary for the improvement of their minds, in
which they think the happiness of life consists.

OF THEIR TRAFFIC.

BUT it is now time to explain to you the mutual intercourse of this people, their commerce, and the rules by
which all things are distributed among them.

As their cities are composed of families, so their families are made up of those that are nearly related to one
another. Their women, when they grow up, are married
out; but all the males, both children and grandchildren,
live still in the same house, in great obedience to their
common parent, unless age has weakened his understanding; and in that case, he that is next to him in age
comes in his room. But lest any city should become either
too great, or by any accident be dispeopled, provision is
made that none of their cities may contain above six
thousand families, besides those of the country round it.
No family may have less than ten, and more than sixteen persons in it; but there can be no determined number for the children under age. This rule is easily
observed, by removing some of the children of a more
fruitful couple to any other family that does not abound

so much in them. By the same rule, they supply cities
that do not increase so fast, from others that breed
faster; and if there is any increase over the whole island,
then they draw out a number of their citizens out of the
several towns, and send them over to the neighboring
continent; where, if they find that the inhabitants have
more soil than they can well cultivate, they fix a colony,
taking the inhabitants into their society, if they are willing
to live with them; and where they do that of their own
accord, they quickly enter into their method of life, and
conform to their rules, and this proves a happiness to
both nations; for according to their constitution, such
care is taken of the soil, that it becomes fruitful enough
for both, though it might be otherwise too narrow and
barren for any one of them. But if the natives refuse
to conform themselves to their laws, they drive them
out of those bounds which they mark out for themselves,
and use force if they resist. For they account it a very
just cause of war, for a nation to hinder others from
possessing a part of that soil, of which they make no
use, but which is suffered to lie idle and uncultivated;
since every man has by the law of Nature a right to
such a waste portion of the earth as is necessary for his
subsistence. If an accident has so lessened the number
of the inhabitants of any of their towns, that it cannot
be made up from the other towns of the island without
diminishing them too much, which is said to have fallen
out but twice since they were first a people, when great
numbers were carried off by the plague; the loss is then
supplied by recalling as many as are wanted from their
colonies; for they will abandon these rather than suffer
the towns in the island to sink too low.

But to return to their manner of living in society, the
oldest man of every family, as has been already said, is
its governor. Wives serve their husbands, and children
their parents, and always the younger serves the elder.
Every city is divided into four equal parts, and in the
middle of each there is a market place: what is brought
thither, and manufactured by the several families, is
carried from thence to houses appointed for that purpose,
in which all things of a sort are laid by themselves; and

thither every father goes and takes whatsoever he or his family stand in need of, without either paying for it, or leaving anything in exchange. There is no reason for giving a denial to any person, since there is such plenty of everything among them; and there is no danger of a man's asking for more than he needs; they have no inducements to do this, since they are sure that they shall always be supplied. It is the fear of want that makes any of the whole race of animals either greedy or ravenous; but besides fear, there is in man a pride that makes him fancy it a particular glory to excel others in pomp and excess. But by the laws of the Utopians, there is no room for this. Near these markets there are others for all sorts of provisions, where there are not only herbs, fruits, and bread, but also fish, fowl, and cattle. There are also, without their towns, places appointed near some running water, for killing their beasts, and for washing away their filth; which is done by their slaves: for they suffer none of their citizens to kill their cattle, because they think that pity and good nature, which are among the best of those affections that are born with us, are much impaired by the butchering of animals; nor do they suffer anything that is foul or unclean to be brought within their towns, lest the air should be infected by ill smells which might prejudice their health. In every street there are great halls that lie at an equal distance from each other, distinguished by particular names. The Syphogrants dwell in those that are set over thirty families, fifteen lying on one side of it, and as many on the other. In these halls they all meet and have their repasts. The stewards of every one of them come to the market place at an appointed hour; and according to the number of those that belong to the hall, they carry home provisions. But they take more care of their sick than of any others; these are lodged and provided for in public hospitals; they have belonging to every town four hospitals, that are built without their walls, and are so large that they may pass for little towns; by this means, if they had ever such a number of sick persons, they could lodge them conveniently, and at such a distance, that such of them as are sick of infectious diseases may be kept so far from the rest that there can be no danger of contagion. The hospitals are furnished and stored with all things that are convenient for the ease and recovery of the sick; and those that are put in them are looked after with such tender and watchful care, and are so constantly attended by their skillful physicians, that as none is sent to them against their will, so there is scarce one in a whole town that, if he should fall ill, would not choose rather to go thither than lie sick at home.

After the steward of the hospitals has taken for the sick whatsoever the physician prescribes, then the best things that are left in the market are distributed equally among the halls, in proportion to their numbers, only, in the first place, they serve the Prince, the chief priest, the Tranibors, the ambassadors, and strangers, if there are any, which indeed falls out but seldom, and for whom there are houses well furnished, particularly appointed for their reception when they come among them. At the hours of dinner and supper, the whole Syphogranty being called together by sound of trumpet, they meet and eat together, except only such as are in the hospitals, or lie sick at home. Yet after the halls are served, no man is hindered to carry provisions home from the market place; for they know that none does that but for some good reason; for though any that will may eat at home, yet none does it willingly, since it is both ridiculous and foolish for any to give themselves the trouble to make ready an ill dinner at home, when there is a much more plentiful one made ready for him so near hand. All the uneasy and sordid services about these halls are performed by their slaves; but the dressing and cooking their meat, and the ordering their tables, belong only to the women, all those of every family taking it by turns. They sit at three or more tables, according to their number; the men sit toward the wall, and the women sit on the other side, that if any of them should be taken suddenly ill, which is no uncommon case among women with child, she may, without disturbing the rest, rise and go to the nurses' room, who are there with the sucking children; where there is always clean water at hand,

and cradles in which they may lay the young children,
if there is occasion for it, and a fire that they may shift
and dress them before it. Every child is nursed by its
own mother, if death or sickness does not intervene; and
in that case the Syphogrants' wives find out a nurse
quickly, which is no hard matter; for any one that can
do it, offers herself cheerfully; for as they are much inclined to that piece of mercy, so the child whom they
nurse considers the nurse as its mother. All the children
under five years old sit among the nurses, the rest of the
younger sort of both sexes, till they are fit for marriage,
either serve those that sit at table; or if they are not
strong enough for that, stand by them in great silence,
and eat what is given them; nor have they any other
formality of dining. In the middle of the first table,
which stands across the upper end of the hall, sit the
Syphogrant and his wife; for that is the chief and most
conspicuous place; next to him sit two of the most
ancient, for there go always four to a mess. If there is
a temple within that Syphogranty, the priest and his
wife sit with the Syphogrant above all the rest: next them
there is a mixture of old and young, who are so placed,
that as the young are set near others, so they are mixed
with the more ancient; which they say was appointed on
this account, that the gravity of the old people, and the
reverence that is due to them, might restrain the younger
from all indecent words and gestures. Dishes are not
served up to the whole table at first, but the best are
first set before the old, whose seats are distinguished
from the young, and after them all the rest are served
alike. The old men distribute to the younger any curious
meats that happen to be set before them, if there is not
such an abundance of them that the whole company may
be served alike.

Thus old men are honored with a particular respect;
yet all the rest fare as well as they. Both dinner and
supper are begun with some lecture of morality that is
read to them; but it is so short, that it is not tedious
nor uneasy to them to hear it: from hence the old men
take occasion to entertain those about them, with some
useful and pleasant enlargements; but they do not

12

engross the whole discourse so to themselves, during their meals, that the younger may not put in for a share: on the contrary, they engage them to talk, that so they may in that free way of conversation find out the force of every one's spirit, and observe his temper. They dispatch their dinners quickly, but sit long at supper; because they go to work after the one, and are to sleep after the other, during which they think the stomach carries on the concoction more vigorously. They never sup without music; and there is always fruit served up after meat; while they are at table, some burn perfumes, and sprinkle about fragrant ointments and sweet waters: in short, they want nothing that may cheer up their spirits; they give themselves a large allowance that way, and indulge themselves in all such pleasures as are attended with no inconvenience. Thus do those that are in the towns live together; but in the country, where they live at great distance, every one eats at home, and no family wants any necessary sort of provision, for it is from them that provisions are sent unto those that live in the towns.

OF THE TRAVELING OF THE UTOPIANS.

IF ANY man has a mind to visit his friends that live in some other town, or desires to travel and see the rest of the country, he obtains leave very easily from the Syphogrant and Tranibors, when there is no particular occasion for him at home. Such as travel, carry with them a passport from the Prince, which both certifies the license that is granted for traveling, and limits the time of their return. They are furnished with a wagon and a slave, who drives the oxen and looks after them: but unless there are women in the company, the wagon is sent back at the end of the journey as a needless encumbrance. While they are on the road they carry no provisions with them; yet they want nothing, but are everywhere treated as if they were at home. If they stay in any place longer than a night, every one follows his proper occupation, and is very well used by those of his own trade: but if any man goes out of the city to which he belongs, without leave, and is found rambling without

a passport, he is severely treated, he is punished as a
fugitive, and sent home disgracefully; and if he falls again
into the like fault, is condemned to slavery. If any
man has a mind to travel only over the precinct of his
own city, he may freely do it, with his father's permission and his wife's consent; but when he comes into any
of the country houses, if he expects to be entertained
by them, he must labor with them and conform to their
rules: and if he does this he may freely go over the
whole precinct; being thus as useful to the city to which
he belongs, as if he were still within it. Thus you see
that there are no idle persons among them, nor pretenses
of excusing any from labor. There are no taverns, no
alehouses nor stews among them; nor any other occasions
of corrupting each other, of getting into corners, or forming themselves into parties: all men live in full view,
so that all are obliged, both to perform their ordinary
task and to employ themselves well in their spare hours.
And it is certain that a people thus ordered must live in
great abundance of all things; and these being equally
distributed among them no man can want or be obliged
to beg.

In their great council at Amaurot, to which there are
three sent from every town once a year, they examine
what towns abound in provisions, and what are under
any scarcity, that so the one may be furnished from the
other; and this is done freely, without any sort of exchange; for according to their plenty or scarcity, they
supply, or are supplied from one another; so that indeed
the whole island is, as it were, one family. When they
have thus taken care of their whole country, and laid up
stores for two years, which they do to prevent the ill
consequences of an unfavorable season, they order an exportation of the overplus, both of corn, honey, wool, flax,
wood, wax, tallow, leather, and cattle; which they send
out commonly in great quantities to other nations. They
order a seventh part of all these goods to be freely given
to the poor of the countries to which they send them,
and sell the rest at moderate rates. And by this exchange, they not only bring back those few things that
they need at home (for indeed they scarce need any-

thing but iron), but likewise a great deal of gold and silver; and by their driving this trade so long, it is not to be
imagined how vast a treasure they have got among them:
so that now they do not much care whether they sell off
their merchandise for money in hand, or upon trust. A
great part of their treasure is now in bonds; but in all
their contracts no private man stands bound, but the
writing runs in the name of the town; and the towns
that owe them money, raise it from those private hands
that owe it to them, lay it up in their public chamber,
or enjoy the profit of it till the Utopians call for it; and
they choose rather to let the greatest part of it lie in
their hands who make advantage by it, than to call for it
themselves: but if they see that any of their other neighbors stand more in need of it, then they call it in and
lend it to them: whenever they are engaged in war,
which is the only occasion in which their treasure can be
usefully employed, they make use of it themselves. In
great extremities or sudden accidents they employ it in
hiring foreign troops, whom they more willingly expose
to danger than their own people: they give them great
pay, knowing well that this will work even on their enemies, that it will engage them either to betray their own
side, or at least to desert it, and that it is the best means
of raising mutual jealousies among them: for this end
they have an incredible treasure; but they do not keep
it as a treasure, but in such a manner as I am almost
afraid to tell, lest you think it so extravagant, as to be
hardly credible. This I have the more reason to apprehend, because if I had not seen it myself, I could not
have been easily persuaded to have believed it upon any
man's report.

It is certain that all things appear incredible to us, in
proportion as they differ from our own customs. But one
who can judge aright, will not wonder to find, that since
their constitution differs so much from ours, their value
of gold and silver should be measured by a very different standard; for since they have no use for money among
themselves, but keep it as a provision against events
which seldom happen, and between which there are generally long intervening intervals; they value it no fur-

ther than it deserves, that is, in proportion to its use.
So that it is plain, they must prefer iron either to gold
or silver: for men can no more live without iron, than
without fire or water; but Nature has marked out no use
for the other metals, so essential as not easily to be dispensed with. The folly of men has enhanced the value
of gold and silver, because of their scarcity. Whereas, on
the contrary, it is their opinion that Nature, as an indulgent parent, has freely given us all the best things in
great abundance, such as water and earth, but has laid
up and hid from us the things that are vain and useless.

If these metals were laid up in any tower in the kingdom, it would raise a jealousy of the Prince and Senate,
and give birth to that foolish mistrust into which the
people are apt to fall, a jealousy of their intending to
sacrifice the interest of the public to their own private
advantage. If they should work it into vessels, or any
sort of plate, they fear that the people might grow too
fond of it, and so be unwilling to let the plate be run
down, if a war made it necessary to employ it in paying
their soldiers. To prevent all these inconveniences, they
have fallen upon an expedient, which as it agrees with
their other policy, so is it very different from ours, and
will scarce gain belief among us, who value gold so much,
and lay it up so carefully. They eat and drink out of
vessels of earth, or glass, which make an agreeable appearance though formed of brittle materials: while they
make their chamber-pots and close-stools of gold and silver; and that not only in their public halls, but in their
private houses: of the same metals they likewise make
chains and fetters for their slaves; to some of which, as
a badge of infamy, they hang an earring of gold, and
make others wear a chain or a coronet of the same metal;
and thus they take care, by all possible means, to render
gold and silver of no esteem. And from hence it is, that
while other nations part with their gold and silver, as
unwillingly as if one tore out their bowels, those of Utopia would look on their giving in all they possess of those
(metals, when there were any use for them) but as the
parting with a trifle, or as we would esteem the loss of
a penny. They find pearls on their coast; and diamonds

and carbuncles on their rocks; they do not look after them, but if they find them by chance, they polish them, and with them they adorn their children, who are de- lighted with them, and glory in them during their child- hood; but when they grow to years, and see that none but children use such baubles, they of their own accord, without being bidden by their parents, lay them aside; and would be as much ashamed to use them afterward, as children among us, when they come to years, are of their puppets and other toys.

I never saw a clearer instance of the opposite impres- sions that different customs make on people, than I observed in the ambassadors of the Anemolians, who came to Amaurot when I was there. As they came to treat of affairs of great consequence, the deputies from several towns met together to wait for their coming. The ambassadors of the nations that lie near Utopia, knowing their cus- toms, and that fine clothes are in no esteem among them, that silk is despised, and gold is a badge of infamy, used to come very modestly clothed; but the Anemolians lying more remote, and having had little commerce with them, understanding that they were coarsely clothed, and all in the same manner, took it for granted that they had none of those fine things among them of which they made no use; and they being a vain-glorious rather than a wise people, resolved to set themselves out with so much pomp, that they should look like gods, and strike the eyes of the poor Utopians with their splendor. Thus three ambassadors made their entry with an hun- dred attendants, all clad in garments of different colors, and the greater part in silk; the ambassadors themselves, who were of the nobility of their country, were in cloth of gold, and adorned with massy chains, earrings and rings of gold: their caps were covered with bracelets set full of pearls and other gems: in a word, they were set out with all those things that, among the Utopians, were either the badges of slavery, the marks of infamy, or the playthings of children. It was not unpleasant to see, on the one side, how they looked big, when they compared their rich habits with the plain clothes of the Utopians, who were come out in great numbers to see

them make their entry: and, on the other, to observe
how much they were mistaken in the impression which
they hoped this pomp would have made on them. It
appeared so ridiculous a show to all that had never stirred
out of their country, and had not seen the customs of other
nations, that though they paid some reverence to those
that were the most meanly clad, as if they had been the
ambassadors, yet when they saw the ambassadors themselves, so full of gold and chains, they looked upon them
as slaves, and forbore to treat them with reverence. You
might have seen the children, who were grown big enough
to despise their playthings, and who had thrown away
their jewels, call to their mothers, push them gently, and
cry out, " See that great fool that wears pearls and gems, as
if he were yet a child." While their mothers very innocently replied, " Hold your peace, this I believe is one of
the ambassador's fools." Others censured the fashion of
their chains, and observed that they were of no use; for
they were too slight to bind their slaves, who could easily
break them; and besides hung so loose about them, that
they thought it easy to throw them away, and so get
from them. But after the ambassadors had stayed a day
among them, and saw so vast a quantity of gold in their
houses, which was as much despised by them as it was
esteemed in other nations, and beheld more gold and
silver in the chains and fetters of one slave than all their
ornaments amounted to, their plumes fell, and they were
ashamed of all that glory for which they had formerly
valued themselves, and accordingly laid it aside; a resolution that they immediately took when on their engaging in some free discourse with the Utopians, they
discovered their sense of such things and their other customs. The Utopians wonder how any man should be
so much taken with the glaring, doubtful lustre of a
jewel or a stone, that can look up to a star, or to the sun
himself; or how any should value himself because his cloth
is made of a finer thread: for how fine soever that thread
may be, it was once no better than the fleece of a sheep,
and that sheep was a sheep still for all its wearing it.
They wonder much to hear that gold, which in itself is so
useless a thing, should be everywhere so much esteemed,

that even men for whom it was made, and by whom it has its value, should yet be thought of less value than this metal. That a man of lead, who has no more sense than a log of wood, and is as bad as he is foolish, should have many wise and good men to serve him, only because he has a great heap of that metal; and that if it should happen that by some accident or trick of law (which sometimes produces as great changes as chance itself) all this wealth should pass from the master to the meanest varlet of his whole family, he himself would very soon become one of his servants, as if he were a thing that belonged to his wealth, and so were bound to follow its fortune. But they much more admire and detest the folly of those who when they see a rich man, though they neither owe him anything, nor are in any sort dependent on his bounty, yet merely because he is rich give him little less than divine honors; even though they know him to be so covetous and base-minded, that notwithstanding all his wealth, he will not part with one farthing of it to them as long as he lives.

These and such like notions have that people imbibed, partly from their education, being bred in a country whose customs and laws are opposite to all such foolish maxims, and partly from their learning and studies; for though there are but few in any town that are so wholly excused from labor as to give themselves entirely up to their studies, these being only such persons as discover from their childhood an extraordinary capacity and disposition for letters; yet their children, and a great part of the nation, both men and women, are taught to spend those hours in which they are not obliged to work in reading: and this they do through the whole progress of life. They have all their learning in their own tongue, which is both a copious and pleasant language, and in which a man can fully express his mind. It runs over a great tract of many countries, but it is not equally pure in all places. They had never so much as heard of the names of any of those philosophers that are so famous in these parts of the world, before we went among them; and yet they had made the same discoveries as the Greeks, both in music, logic, arithmetic, and geometry. But as

they are almost in everything equal to the ancient philosophers, so they far exceed our modern logicians; for
they have never yet fallen upon the barbarous niceties
that our youth are forced to learn in those trifling logical
schools that are among us; they are so far from mind-
ing chimeras, and fantastical images made in the mind,
that none of them could comprehend what we meant
when we talked to them of a man in the abstract, as
common to all men in particular (so that though we
spoke of him as a thing that we could point at with
our fingers, yet none of them could perceive him), and
yet distinct from every one, as if he were some mon-
strous Colossus or giant. Yet for all this ignorance of
these empty notions, they knew astronomy, and were
perfectly acquainted with the motions of the heavenly
bodies, and have many instruments, well contrived and
divided, by which they very accurately compute the
course and positions of the sun, moon, and stars. But
for the cheat, of divining by the stars, by their oppositions or conjunctions, it has not so much as entered
into their thoughts. They have a particular sagacity,
founded upon much observation, in judging of the weather,
by which they know when they may look for rain,
wind, or other alterations in the air; but as to the
philosophy of these things, the causes of the saltness
of the sea, of its ebbing and flowing, and of the origin
and nature both of the heavens and the earth; they
dispute of them, partly as our ancient philosophers
have done, and partly upon some new hypothesis, in
which, as they differ from them, so they do not in
all things agree among themselves.

As to moral philosophy, they have the same disputes
among them as we have here: they examine what are
properly good both for the body and the mind, and whether
any outward thing can be called truly good, or if that term
belongs only to the endowments of the soul. They inquire
likewise into the nature of virtue and pleasure; but their
chief dispute is concerning the happiness of a man, and
wherein it consists? Whether in some one thing, or in a
great many? They seem, indeed, more inclinable to that
opinion that places, if not the whole, yet the chief part of

a man's happiness in pleasure; and, what may seem more
strange, they make use of arguments even from religion,
notwithstanding its severity and roughness, for the support of that opinion so indulgent to pleasure; for they
never dispute concerning happiness without fetching some
arguments from the principles of religion, as well as from
natural reason, since without the former they reckon that
all our inquiries after happiness must be but conjectural
and defective.

These are their religious principles, that the soul of
man is immortal, and that God of his goodness has designed that it should be happy; and that he has therefore appointed rewards for good and virtuous actions, and
punishments for vice, to be distributed after this life.
Though these principles of religion are conveyed down
among them by tradition, they think that even reason
itself determines a man to believe and acknowledge them,
and freely confess that if these were taken away no man
would be so insensible as not to seek after pleasure by
all possible means, lawful or unlawful; using only this
caution, that a lesser pleasure might not stand in the way
of a greater, and that no pleasure ought to be pursued
that should draw a great deal of pain after it; for they
think it is the maddest thing in the world to pursue
virtue, that is a sour and difficult thing; and not only to
renounce the pleasures of life, but willingly to undergo
much pain and trouble, if a man has no prospect of a
reward. And what reward can there be for one that has
passed his whole life, not only without pleasure, but in
pain, if there is nothing to be expected after death? Yet
they do not place happiness in all sorts of pleasures, but
only in those that in themselves are good and honest.
There is a party among them who place happiness in bare
virtue; others think that our natures are conducted by
virtue to happiness, as that which is the chief good of
man. They define virtue thus, that it is a living according to Nature, and think that we are made by God for
that end; they believe that a man then follows the dictates
of Nature when he pursues or avoids things according to
the direction of reason; they say that the first dictate of
reason is the kindling in us a love and reverence for the

Divine Majesty, to whom we owe both all that we have, and all that we can ever hope for. In the next place, reason directs us to keep our minds as free from passion and as cheerful as we can, and that we should consider ourselves as bound by the ties of good-nature and humanity to use our utmost endeavors to help forward the happiness of all other persons; for there never was any man such a morose and severe pursuer of virtue, such an enemy to pleasure, that though he set hard rules for men to undergo much pain, many watchings, and other rigors, yet did not at the same time advise them to do all they could, in order to relieve and ease the miserable, and who did not represent gentleness and good nature as amiable dispositions. And from thence they infer that if a man ought to advance the welfare and comfort of the rest of mankind, there being no virtue more proper and peculiar to our nature, than to ease the miseries of others, to free from trouble and anxiety, in furnishing them with the comforts of life, in which pleasure consists, Nature much more vigorously leads them to do all this for himself. A life of pleasure is either a real evil, and in that case we ought not to assist others in their pursuit of it, but on the contrary, to keep them from it all we can, as from that which is most hurtful and deadly; or if it is a good thing, so that we not only may, but ought to help others to it, why then ought not a man to begin with himself? Since no man can be more bound to look after the good of another than after his own; for Nature cannot direct us to be good and kind to others, and yet at the same time to be unmerciful and cruel to ourselves. Thus, as they define virtue to be living according to Nature, so they imagine that Nature prompts all people on to seek after pleasure, as the end of all they do. They also observe that in order to our supporting the pleasures of life, Nature inclines us to enter into society; for there is no man so much raised above the rest of mankind as to be the only favorite of Nature, who, on the contrary, seems to have placed on a level all those that belong to the same species. Upon this they infer that no man ought to seek his own conveniences so eagerly as to prejudice others; and therefore they think that not only

all agreements between private persons ought to be
observed; but likewise that all those laws ought to be
kept, which either a good prince has published in due
form, or to which a people, that is neither oppressed with
tyranny nor circumvented by fraud, has consented, for
distributing those conveniences of life which afford us all
our pleasures.

They think it is an evidence of true wisdom for a man
to pursue his own advantages, as far as the laws allow it.
They account it piety to prefer the public good to one's
private concerns; but they think it unjust for a man to
seek for pleasure, by snatching another man's pleasures
from him. And on the contrary, they think it a sign of
a gentle and good soul, for a man to dispense with his
own advantage for the good of others; and that by this
means a good man finds as much pleasure one way, as
he parts with another; for as he may expect the like
from others when he may come to need it, so if that
should fail him, yet the sense of a good action, and the
reflections that he makes on the love and gratitude of
those whom he has so obliged, gives the mind more
pleasure than the body could have found in that from
which it had restrained itself. They are also persuaded
that God will make up the loss of those small pleasures,
with a vast and endless joy, of which religion easily con-
vinces a good soul.

Thus upon an inquiry into the whole matter, they
reckon that all our actions, and even all our virtues,
terminate in pleasure, as in our chief end and greatest
happiness; and they call every motion or state, either of
body or mind, in which Nature teaches us to delight, a
pleasure. Thus they cautiously limit pleasure only to
those appetites to which Nature leads us; for they say
that Nature leads us only to those delights to which reason as well as sense carries us, and by which we neither
injure any other person, nor lose the possession of greater
pleasures, and of such as draw no troubles after them;
but they look upon those delights which men by a foolish, though common, mistake call pleasure, as if they
could change as easily the nature of things as the use of
words; as things that greatly obstruct their real happi-

ness, instead of advancing it, because they so entirely possess the minds of those that are once captivated by them with a false notion of pleasure, that there is no room left for pleasures of a truer or purer kind.

There are many things that in themselves have nothing that is truly delightful; on the contrary, they have a good deal of bitterness in them: and yet from our perverse appetites after forbidden objects, are not only ranked among the pleasures, but are made even the greatest designs of life. Among those who pursue these sophisticated pleasures, they reckon such as I mentioned before, who think themselves really the better for having fine clothes; in which they think they are doubly mistaken, both in the opinion they have of their clothes, and in that they have of themselves: for if you consider the use of clothes, why should a fine thread be thought better than a coarse one? And yet these men, as if they had some real advantages beyond others, and did not owe them wholly to their mistakes, look big, seem to fancy themselves to be more valuable, and imagine that a respect is due to them for the sake of a rich garment, to which they would not have pretended if they had been more meanly clothed; and even resent it as an affront, if that respect is not paid them. It is also a great folly to be taken with outward marks of respect, which signify nothing: for what true or real pleasure can one man find in another's standing bare, or making legs to him? Will the bending of another man's knees give ease to yours? And will the head's being bare cure the madness of yours? And yet it is wonderful to see how this false notion of pleasure bewitches many who delight themselves with the fancy of their nobility, and are pleased with this conceit, that they are descended from ancestors, who have been held for some successions rich, and who have had great possessions; for this is all that makes nobility at present; yet they do not think themselves a whit the less noble, though their immediate parents have left none of this wealth to them, or though they themselves have squandered it away. The Utopians have no better opinion of those who are much taken with gems and precious stones, and who account it a degree of hap-

piness, next to a divine one, if they can purchase one
that is very extraordinary, especially if it be of that sort
of stones that is then in greatest request; for the same
sort is not at all times universally of the same value;
nor will men buy it unless it be dismounted and taken
out of the gold; the jeweler is then made to give good
security, and required solemnly to swear that the stone
is true, that by such an exact caution a false one might
not be bought instead of a true: though if you were to
examine it, your eye could find no difference between
the counterfeit and that which is true; so that they are
all one to you as much as if you were blind. Or can it
be thought that they who heap up an useless mass of
wealth, not for any use that it is to bring them, but
merely to please themselves with the contemplation of
it, enjoy any true pleasure in it? The delight they find
is only a false shadow of joy. Those are no better whose
error is somewhat different from the former, and who
hide it, out of their fear of losing it; for what other
name can fit the hiding it in the earth, or rather the
restoring it to it again, it being thus cut off from being
useful, either to its owner or the rest of mankind? And
yet the owner having hid 'it carefully, is glad, because
he thinks he is now sure of it. If it should be stolen,
the owner, though he might live perhaps ten years after
the theft, of which he knew nothing, would find no difference between his having or losing it; for both ways it
was equally useless to him.

Among those foolish pursuers of pleasure, they reckon
all that delight in hunting, in fowling, or gaming: of
whose madness they have only heard, for they have no
such things among them. But they have asked us, what
sort of pleasure is it that men can find in throwing the
dice? For if there were any pleasure in it, they think the
doing of it so often should give one a surfeit of it: and
what pleasure can one find in hearing the barking and howl-
ing of dogs, which seem rather odious than pleasant
sounds? Nor can they comprehend the pleasure of seeing dogs run after a hare, more than of seeing one dog run
after another; for if the seeing them run is that which
gives the pleasure, you have the same entertainment to

the eye on both these occasions, since that is the same
in both cases; but if the pleasure lies in seeing the hare
killed and torn by the dogs, this ought rather to stir
pity, that a weak, harmless and fearful hare should be
devoured by strong, fierce, and cruel dogs. Therefore
all this business of hunting is, among the Utopians,
turned over to their butchers; and those, as has been
already said, are all slaves, and they look on hunting as
one of the basest parts of a butcher's work: for they account it both more profitable and more decent to kill
those beasts that are more necessary and useful to mankind; whereas the killing and tearing of so small and
miserable an animal can only attract the huntsman with
a false show of pleasure, from which he can reap but
small advantage. They look on the desire of the bloodshed, even of beasts, as a mark of a mind that is already
corrupted with cruelty, or that at least by the frequent
returns of so brutal a pleasure must degenerate into it.

Thus, though the rabble of mankind look upon these,
and on innumerable other things of the same nature, as
pleasures, the Utopians, on the contrary, observing that
there is nothing in them truly pleasant, conclude that
they are not to be reckoned among pleasures: for though
these things may create some tickling in the senses
(which seems to be a true notion of pleasure), yet they
imagine that this does not arise from the thing itself, but
from a depraved custom, which may so vitiate a man's
taste, that bitter things may pass for sweet; as women
with child think pitch or tallow tastes sweeter than honey;
but as a man's sense when corrupted, either by a disease
or some ill habit, does not change the nature of other
things, so neither can it change the nature of pleasure.

They reckon up several sorts of pleasures, which they
call true ones: some belong to the body and others to
the mind. The pleasures of the mind lie in knowledge,
and in that delight which the contemplation of truth
carries with it; to which they add the joyful reflections
on a well-spent life, and the assured hopes of a future
happiness. They divide the pleasures of the body into
two sorts; the one is that which gives our senses some
real delight, and is performed, either by recruiting

nature, and supplying those parts which feed the internal heat of life by eating and drinking; or when nature is eased of any surcharge that oppresses it; when we are relieved from sudden pain, or that which arises from satisfying the appetite which Nature has wisely given to lead us to the propagation of the species. There is another kind of pleasure that arises neither from our receiving what the body requires, nor its being relieved when overcharged, and yet by a secret, unseen virtue affects the senses, raises the passions, and strikes the mind with generous impressions; this is the pleasure that arises from music. Another kind of bodily pleasure is that which results from an undisturbed and vigorous constitution of body, when life and active spirits seem to actuate every part. This lively health, when entirely free from all mixture of pain, of itself gives an inward pleasure, independent of all external objects of delight; and though this pleasure does not so powerfully affect us, nor act so strongly on the senses as some of the others, yet it may be esteemed as the greatest of all pleasures, and almost all the Utopians reckon it the foundation and basis of all the other joys of life; since this alone makes the state of life easy and desirable; and when this is wanting, a man is really capable of no other pleasure. They look upon freedom from pain, if it does not rise from perfect health, to be a state of stupidity rather than of pleasure. This subject has been very narrowly canvassed among them; and it has been debated whether a firm and entire health could be called a pleasure or not? Some have thought that there was no pleasure but what was excited by some sensible motion in the body. But this opinion has been long ago excluded from among them, so that now they almost universally agree that health is the greatest of all bodily pleasures; and that as there is a pain in sickness, which is as opposite in its nature to pleasure as sickness itself is to health, so they hold, that health is accompanied with pleasure; and if any should say that sickness is not really pain, but that it only carries pain along with it, they look upon that as a fetch of subtilty, that does not much alter the matter. It is all one, in their opinion, whether it be said

that health is in itself a pleasure, or that it begets a
pleasure, as fire gives heat; so it be granted, that all
those whose health is entire have a true pleasure in the
enjoyment of it: and they reason thus — what is the
pleasure of eating, but that a man's health which had
been weakened, does, with the assistance of food, drive
away hunger, and so recruiting itself recovers its former
vigor? And being thus refreshed, it finds a pleasure in
that conflict; and if the conflict is pleasure, the victory
must yet breed a greater pleasure, except we fancy that
it becomes stupid as soon as it has obtained that which
it pursued, and so neither knows nor rejoices in its own
welfare. If it is said that health cannot be felt, they
absolutely deny it; for what man is in health that does
not perceive it when he is awake? Is there any man that
is so dull and stupid as not to acknowledge that he feels
a delight in health? And what is delight but another
name for pleasure?

But of all pleasures, they esteem those to be most
valuable that lie in the mind; the chief of which arises
out of true virtue, and the witness of a good conscience.
They account health the chief pleasure that belongs to
the body; for they think that the pleasure of eating and
drinking and all the other delights of sense, are only so
far desirable as they give or maintain health. But they
are not pleasant in themselves, otherwise than as they
resist those impressions that our natural infirmities are
still making upon us: for as a wise man desires rather to
avoid diseases than to take physic; and to be freed from
pain, rather than to find ease by remedies; so it is more
desirable not to need this sort of pleasure than to be
obliged to indulge it. If any man imagines that there
is a real happiness in these enjoyments, he must then confess that he would be the happiest of all men if he
were to lead his life in perpetual hunger, thirst, and
itching, and by consequence in perpetual eating, drinking, and scratching himself; which any one may easily
see would be not only a base, but a miserable state of a
life. These are indeed the lowest of pleasures, and the
least pure; for we can never relish them, but when they
are mixed with the contrary pains. The pain of hunger

13

must give us the pleasure of eating; and here the pain
outbalances the pleasure; and as the pain is more vehe-
ment, so it lasts much longer; for as it begins before
the pleasure, so it does not cease but with the pleasure
that extinguishes it, and both expire together. They
think, therefore, none of those pleasures are to be valued
any further than as they are necessary; yet they rejoice
in them, and with due gratitude acknowledge the tenderness of the great Author of Nature, who has planted
in us appetites, by which those things that are necessary
for our preservation are likewise made pleasant to us.
For how miserable a thing would life be, if those
daily diseases of hunger and thirst were to be carried
off by such bitter drugs as we must use for those diseases that return seldomer upon us? And thus these
pleasant as well as proper gifts of Nature maintain the
strength and sprightliness of our bodies.

They also entertain themselves with the other delights
let in at their eyes, their ears, and their nostrils, as the
pleasant relishes and seasonings of life, which Nature
seems to have marked out peculiarly for man; since no
other sort of animal contemplates the figure and beauty
of the universe; nor is delighted with smells, any farther
than as they distinguish meats by them; nor do they
apprehend the concords or discords of sound: yet in all
pleasures whatsoever they take care that a lesser joy does
not hinder a greater, and that pleasure may never breed
pain, which they think always follows dishonest pleasures.
But they think it madness for a man to wear out the
beauty of his face, or the force of his natural strength;
to corrupt the sprightliness of his body by sloth and
laziness, or to waste it by fasting; that it is madness to
weaken the strength of his constitution, and reject the
other delights of life, unless by renouncing his own satisfaction, he can either serve the public or promote the
happiness of others, for which he expects a greater recompense from God. So that they look on such a course
of life as the mark of a mind that is both cruel to itself,
and ungrateful to the Author of Nature, as if we would
not be beholden to him for his favors, and therefore
reject all his blessings; as one who should afflict him-

self for the empty shadow of virtue; or for no better end to render himself capable of bearing those misfortunes which possibly will never happen.

This is their notion of virtue and of pleasure: they think no man's reason can carry him to a truer idea of them, unless some discovery from Heaven should inspire him with sublimer notions. I have not now the leisure to examine whether they think right or wrong in this matter; nor do I judge it necessary, for I have only undertaken to give you an account of their constitution, but not to defend all their principles. I am sure, that whatsoever may be said of their notions, there is not in the whole world either a better people or a happier government: their bodies are vigorous and lively; and though they are but of a middle stature, and have neither the most fruitful soil nor the purest air in the world, yet they fortify themselves so well by their temperate course of life, against the unhealthiness of their air, and by their industry they so cultivate their soil, that there is nowhere to be seen a greater increase both of corn and cattle, nor are there anywhere healthier men, and freer from diseases: for one may there see reduced to practice, not only all the art that the husbandman employs in manuring and improving an ill soil, but whole woods plucked up by the roots, and in other places new ones planted, where there were none before. Their principal motive for this is the convenience of carriage, that their timber may be either near their towns, or growing on the banks of the sea, or of some rivers, so as to be floated to them; for it is a harder work to carry wood any distance over land than corn. The people are industrious, apt to learn, as well as cheerful and pleasant; and none can endure more labor, when it is necessary; but except in that case they love their ease. They are unwearied pursuers of knowledge; for when we had given them some hints of the learning and discipline of the Greeks, concerning whom we only instructed them (for we know that there was nothing among the Romans, except their historians and their poets, that they would value much), it was strange to see how eagerly they were set on learning that language. We began to read a little of it to them, rather in compliance with their importunity, than out of any hopes of their reaping from it any great advantage. But after a very short trial, we found they made such progress, that we saw our labor was like to be more successful than we could have expected. They learned to write their characters, and to pronounce their language so exactly, had so quick an apprehension, they remembered it so faithfully, and became so ready and correct in the use of it, that it would have looked like a miracle if the greater part of those whom we taught had not been men both of extraordinary capacity and a fit age for instruction. They were for the greatest part chosen from among their learned men, by their chief council, though some studied it of their own accord. In three years' time they became masters of the whole language, so that they read the best of the Greek authors very exactly. I am indeed apt to think that they learned that language the more easily, from its having some relation to their own. I believe that they were a colony of the Greeks; for though their language comes nearer the Persian, yet they retain many names, both for their towns and magistrates, that are of Greek derivation. I happened to carry a great many books with me, instead of merchandise, when I sailed my fourth voyage; for I was so far from thinking of soon coming back, that I rather thought never to have returned at all, and I gave them all my books, among which were many of Plato's and some of Aristotle's works. I had also Theophrastus on Plants, which to my great regret, was imperfect; for having laid it carelessly by, while we were at sea, a monkey had seized upon it, and in many places torn out the leaves. They have no books of grammar but Lascares, for I did not carry Theodorus with me; nor have they any dictionaries but Hesichius and Dioscorides. They esteem Plutarch highly, and were much taken with Lucian's wit, and with his pleasant way of writing. As for the poets, they have Aristophanes, Homer, Euripides, and Sophocles of Aldus's edition; and for historians Thucydides, Herodotus and Herodian. One of my companions, Thricius Apinatus, happened to carry with him some of Hippocrates's works, and Galen's Microtechne,

which they hold in great estimation; for though there is
no nation in the world that needs physic so little as they
do, yet there is not any that honors it so much: they
reckon the knowledge of it one of the pleasantest and most
profitable parts of philosophy, by which, as they search
into the secrets of Nature, so they not only find this study
highly agreeable, but think that such inquiries are very
acceptable to the Author of Nature; and imagine that as
he, like the inventors of curious engines among mankind, has exposed this great machine of the universe to
the view of the only creatures capable of contemplating
it, so an exact and curious observer, who admires his
workmanship, is much more acceptable to him than one
of the herd, who like a beast incapable of reason, looks
on this glorious scene with the eyes of a dull and uncon-
cerned spectator.

The minds of the Utopians when fenced with a love
for learning, are very ingenious in discovering all such
arts as are necessary to carry it to perfection. Two
things they owe to us, the manufacture of paper, and the
art of printing: yet they are not so entirely indebted to
us for these discoveries, but that a great part of the invention was their own. We showed them some books
printed by Aldus, we explained to them the way of making paper, and the mystery of printing; but as we had
never practiced these arts, we described them in a crude
and superficial manner. They seized the hints we gave
them, and though at first they could not arrive at perfection, yet by making many essays they at last found
out and corrected all their errors, and conquered every
difficulty. Before this they only wrote on parchment, on
reeds, or on the barks of trees; but now they have established the manufactures of paper, and set up printing-
presses, so that if they had but a good number of Greek
authors they would be quickly supplied with many cop-
ies of them: at present, though they have no more than
those I have mentioned, yet by several impressions they
have multiplied them into many thousands. If any man
were to go among them that had some extraordinary talent
or that by much traveling had observed the customs of
many nations (which made us to be so well received),

he would receive a hearty welcome; for they are very desirous to know the state of the whole world. Very few go among them on the account of traffic, for what can a man carry to them but iron, or gold, or silver, which merchants desire rather to export than import to a strange country; and as for their exportation, they think it better to manage that themselves than to leave it to foreigners, for by this means, as they understand the state of the neighboring countries better, so they keep up the art of navigation, which cannot be maintained but by much practice.

OF THEIR SLAVES, AND OF THEIR MARRIAGES.

THEY do not make slaves of prisoners of war, except those that are taken in battle; nor of the sons of their slaves, nor of those of other nations: the slaves among them are only such as are condemned to that state of life for the commission of some crime, or, which is more common, such as their merchants find condemned to die in those parts to which they trade, whom they sometimes redeem at low rates; and in other places have them for nothing. They are kept at perpetual labor, and are always chained, but with this difference, that their own natives are treated much worse than others; they are considered as more profligate than the rest, and since they could not be restrained by the advantages of so excellent an education, are judged worthy of harder usage. Another sort of slaves are the poor of neighboring countries, who offer of their own accord to come and serve them; they treat these better, and use them in all other respects as well as their own countrymen, except their imposing more labor upon them, which is no hard task to those who have been accustomed to it; and if any of these have a mind to go back to their own country, which indeed falls out but seldom, as they do not force them to stay, so they do not send them away empty-handed.

I have already told you with what care they look after their sick, so that nothing is left undone that can contribute either to their ease or health; and for those who

are taken with fixed and incurable diseases, they use all
possible ways to cherish them and to make their lives
as comfortable as possible. They visit them often, and
take great pains to make their time pass off easily; but
when any are taken with a torturing and lingering pain,
so that there is no hope, either of recovery or ease, the
priests and magistrates come and exhort them, that since
they are now unable to go on with the business of
life, are become a burden to themselves and to all
about them, and·they have really outlived themselves,
they should no longer nourish such a rooted distemper,
but choose rather to die, since they cannot live but in much
misery: being assured, that if they thus deliver themselves from torture, or are willing that others should do
it, they shall be happy after death. Since by their acting thus, they lose none of the pleasures, but only the
troubles of life; they think they behave not only reason-
ably, but in a manner consistent with religion and piety;
because they follow the advice given them by their priests,
who are the expounders of the will of God. Such as are
wrought on by these persuasions, either starve themselves
of their own accord, or take opium, and by that means
die without pain. But no man is forced on this way of
ending his life; and if they cannot be persuaded to it,
this does not induce them to fail in their attendance and
care of them; but as they believe that a voluntary death,
when it is chosen upon such an authority, is very honorable, so if any man takes away his own life, without the approbation of the priests and the Senate, they
give him none of the honors of a decent funeral, but
throw his body into a ditch.

Their women are not married before eighteen, nor their
men before two-and-twenty, and if any of them run into
forbidden embraces before marriage they are severely
punished, and the privilege of marriage is denied them,
unless they can obtain a special warrant from the Prince.
Such disorders cast a great reproach upon the master
and mistress of the family in which they happen, for it
is supposed they have failed in their duty. The reason
of punishing this so severely is, because they think that
if they were not strictly restrained from all vagrant

appetites, very few would engage in a state in which
they venture the quiet of their whole lives, by being
confined to one person, and are obliged to endure all the
inconveniences with which it is accompanied. In choos-
ing their wives they use a method that would appear to
us very absurd and ridiculous, but it is constantly
observed among them, and is accounted perfectly consistent with wisdom. Before marriage some grave matron
presents the bride naked, whether she is a virgin or a
widow, to the bridegroom, and after that some grave
man presents the bridegroom naked to the bride. We
indeed both laughed at this, and condemned it as very
indecent. But they, on the other hand, wondered at the
folly of the men of all other nations, who, if they are
but to buy a horse of a small value, are so cautious that
they will see every part of him, and take off both his
saddle and all his other tackle, that there may be no
secret ulcer hid under any of them; and that yet in the
choice of a wife, on which depends the happiness or
unhappiness of the rest of his life, a man should venture
upon trust, and only see about a hand's-breadth of the
face, all the rest of the body being covered, under which
there may lie hid what may be contagious, as well as
loathsome. All men are not so wise as to choose a
woman only for her good qualities; and even wise men
consider the body as that which adds not a little to the
mind: and it is certain there may be some such deformity
covered with the clothes as may totally alienate a man
from his wife when it is too late to part with her. If
such a thing is discovered after marriage, a man has no
remedy but patience. They therefore think it is reasonable that there should be good provision made against
such mischievous frauds.

There was so much the more reason for them to make
a regulation in this matter, because they are the only
people of those parts that neither allow of polygamy, nor
of divorces, except in the case of adultery, or insuffer-
able perverseness; for in these cases the Senate dissolves
the marriage, and grants the injured person leave to
marry again; but the guilty are made infamous, and are
never allowed the privilege of a second marriage. None

are suffered to put away their wives against their wills,
from any great calamity that may have fallen on their
persons; for they look on it as the height of cruelty and
treachery to abandon either of the married persons when
they need most the tender care of their comfort, and
that chiefly in the case of old age, which as it carries
many diseases along with it, so it is a disease of itself.
But it frequently falls out that when a married couple
do not well agree, they by mutual consent separate, and
find out other persons with whom they hope they may
live more happily. Yet this is not done without obtaining leave of the Senate, which never admits of a divorce,
but upon a strict inquiry made, both by the senators and
their wives, into the grounds upon which it is desired;
and even when they are satisfied concerning the reasons
of it, they go on but slowly, for they imagine that too
great easiness in granting leave for new marriages would
very much shake the kindness of married people. They
punish severely those that defile the marriage-bed. If
both parties are married they are divorced, and the injured persons may marry one another, or whom they
please; but the adulterer and the adulteress are condemned
to slavery. Yet if either of the injured persons cannot
shake off the love of the married person, they may live
with them still in that state, but they must follow them
to that labor to which the slaves are condemned; and
sometimes the repentance of the condemned, together
with the unshaken kindness of the innocent and injured
person, has prevailed so far with the Prince that he has
taken off the sentence; but those that relapse after they
are once pardoned are punished with death.

Their law does not determine the punishment for
other crimes; but that is left to the Senate, to temper
it according to the circumstances of the fact. Husbands
have power to correct their wives, and parents to chastise their children, unless the fault is so great that a
public punishment is thought necessary for striking terror
into others. For the most part, slavery is the punishment even of the greatest crimes; for as that is no less
terrible to the criminals themselves than death, so they
think the preserving them in a state of servitude is

more for the interest of the commonwealth than killing
them, since as their labor is a greater benefit to the
public than their death could be, so the sight of their
misery is a more lasting terror to other men than that
which would be given by their death. If their slaves
rebel, and will not bear their yoke, and submit to the labor
that is enjoined them, they are treated as wild beasts
that cannot be kept in order, neither by a prison, nor
by their chains; and are at last put to death. But those
who bear their punishment patiently, and are so much
wrought on by that pressure that lies so hard on them
that it appears they are really more troubled for the
crimes they have committed than for the miseries they
suffer, are not out of hope but that at last either the
Prince will, by his prerogative, or the people by their
intercession, restore them again to their liberty, or at
least very much mitigate their slavery. He that tempts
a married woman to adultery, is no less severely punished
than he that commits it; for they believe that a deliberate design to commit a crime, is equal to the fact
itself: since its not taking effect does not make the
person that miscarried in his attempt at all the less
guilty.

They take great pleasure in fools, and as it is thought
a base and unbecoming thing to use them ill, so they
do not think it amiss for people to divert themselves
with their folly: and, in their opinion, this is a great
advantage to the fools themselves: for if men were so
sullen and severe as not at all to please themselves with
their ridiculous behavior and foolish sayings, which is
all they can do to recommend themselves to others, it
could not be expected that they would be so well provided for, nor so tenderly used as they must otherwise
be. If any man should reproach another for his being
misshapen or imperfect in any part of his body, it would
not at all be thought a reflection on the person so
treated, but it would be accounted scandalous in him
that had upbraided another with what he could not help.
It is thought a sign of a sluggish and sordid mind not
to preserve carefully one's natural beauty; but it is likewise infamous among them to use paint. They all see

that no beauty recommends a wife so much to her husband as the probity of her life, and her obedience: for
as some few are caught and held only by beauty, so all
are attracted by the other excellences which charm all
the world.

As they fright men from committing crimes by punishments, so they invite them to the love of virtue by
public honors; therefore they erect statues to the memories of such worthy men as have deserved well of their
country, and set these in their market places, both to
perpetuate the remembrance of their actions, and to be
an incitement to their posterity to follow their example.

If any man aspires to any office, he is sure never to
compass it; they all live easily together, for none of the
magistrates are either insolent or cruel to the people:
they affect rather to be called fathers, and by being
really so, they well deserve the name; and the people
pay them all the marks of honor the more freely, because none are exacted from them. The Prince himself
has no distinction, either of garments, or of a crown;
but is only distinguished by a sheaf of corn carried before him; as the high priest is also known by his being
preceded by a person carrying a wax light.

They have but few laws, and such is their constitution
that they need not many. They very much condemn
other nations, whose laws, together with the commentaries
on them, swell up to so many volumes; for they think it an
unreasonable thing to oblige men to obey a body of laws
that are both of such a bulk, and so dark as not to be
read and understood by every one of the subjects.

They have no lawyers among them, for they consider
them as a sort of people whose profession it is to disguise matters, and to wrest the laws; and therefore they
think it is much better that every man should plead his
own cause, and trust it to the judge, as in other places
the client trusts it to a counselor. By this means they
both cut off many delays, and find out truth more certainly: for after the parties have laid open the merits of
the cause, without those artifices which lawyers are apt
to suggest, the judge examines the whole matter, and supports the simplicity of such well-meaning persons, whom

otherwise crafty men would be sure to run down: and thus they avoid those evils which appear very remarkably among all those nations that labor under a vast load of laws. Every one of them is skilled in their law, for as it is a very short study, so the plainest meaning of which words are capable is always the sense of their laws. And they argue thus: all laws are promulgated for this end, that every man may know his duty; and therefore the plainest and most obvious sense of the words is that which ought to be put upon them; since a more refined exposition cannot be easily comprehended, and would only serve to make the laws become useless to the greater part of mankind, and especially to those who need most the direction of them: for it is all one, not to make a law at all, or to couch it in such terms that without a quick apprehension, and much study, a man cannot find out the true meaning of it; since the generality of mankind are both so dull, and so much employed in their several trades, that they have neither the leisure nor the capacity requisite for such an inquiry.

Some of their neighbors, who are masters of their own liberties, having long ago, by the assistance of the Utopians, shaken off the yoke of tyranny, and being much taken with those virtues which they observe among them, have come to desire that they would send magistrates to govern them; some changing them every year, and others every five years. At the end of their government they bring them back to Utopia, with great expressions of honor and esteem, and carry away others to govern in their stead. In this they seem to have fallen upon a very good expedient for their own happiness and safety; for since the good or ill condition of a nation depends so much upon its magistrates, they could not have made a better choice than by pitching on men whom no advantages can bias; for wealth is of no use to them, since they must so soon go back to their own country; and they being strangers among them, are not engaged in any of their heats or animosities; and it is certain that when public judicatories are swayed, either by avarice or partial affections, there must follow a dissolution of justice, the chief sinew of society.

The Utopians call those nations that come and ask magistrates from them, neighbors; but those to whom they have been of more particular service, friends. And as all other nations are perpetually either making leagues or breaking them, they never enter into an alliance with any state. They think leagues are useless things, and believe that if the common ties of humanity do not knit men together, the faith of promises will have no great effect; and they are the more confirmed in this by what they see among the nations round about them, who are no strict observers of leagues and treaties. We know how religiously they are observed in Europe, more particularly where the Christian doctrine is received, among whom they are sacred and inviolable. Which is partly owing to the justice and goodness of the princes them-selves, and partly to the reverence they pay to the popes; who as they are most religious observers of their own promises, so they exhort all other princes to perform theirs; and when fainter methods do not prevail, they compel them to it by the severity of the pastoral censure, and think that it would be the most indecent thing possible if men who are particularly distinguished by the title of the faithful, should not religiously keep the faith of their treaties. But in that new-found world, which is not more distant from us in situation than the people are in their manners and course of life, there is no trusting to leagues, even though they were made with all the pomp of the most sacred ceremonies; on the contrary, they are on this account sooner broken, some slight pretence being found in the words of the treaties, which are purposely couched in such ambiguous terms that they can never be so strictly bound but they will always find some loophole to escape at; and thus they break both their leagues and their faith. And this is done with such impudence, that those very men who value themselves on having suggested these expedients to their princes, would with a haughty scorn declaim against such craft, or to speak plainer, such fraud and deceit, if they found private men make use of it in their bargains, and would readily say that they deserved to be hanged.

By this means it is, that all sort of justice passes in the

world for a low-spirited and vulgar virtue, far below the
dignity of royal greatness. Or at least, there are set up
two sorts of justice; the one is mean, and creeps on the
ground, and therefore becomes none but the lower part of
mankind, and so must be kept in severely by many re-
straints that it may not break out beyond the bounds that
are set to it. The other is the peculiar virtue of princes,
which as it is more majestic than that which becomes the
rabble, so takes a freer compass; and thus lawful and
unlawful are only measured by pleasure and interest.
These practices of the princes that lie about Utopia,
who make so little account of their faith, seem to be the
reasons that determine them to engage in no confeder-
acies, perhaps they would change their mind if they lived
among us; but yet though treaties were more religiously
observed, they would still dislike the custom of making
them; since the world has taken up a false maxim upon
it, as if there were no tie of Nature uniting one nation
to another, only separated perhaps by a mountain or a
river, and that all were born in a state of hostility, and
so might lawfully do all that mischief to their neighbors
against which there is no provision made by treaties; and
that when treaties are made, they do not cut off the enmity, or restrain the license of preying upon each other,
if by the unskillfulness of wording them there are not
effectual provisos made against them. They, on the
other hand, judge that no man is to be esteemed our enemy
that has never injured us; and that the partnership of
the human nature is instead of a league. And that kindness and good-nature unite men more effectually and with
greater strength than any agreements whatsoever; since
thereby the engagements of men's hearts become stronger
than the bond and obligation of words.

Of Their Military Discipline.

THEY detest war as a very brutal thing; and which,
to the reproach of human nature, is more practised by
men than by any sort of beasts. They, in opposition to
the sentiments of almost all other nations, think that there
is nothing more inglorious than that glory that is gained by

war. And therefore though they accustom themselves daily to military exercises and the discipline of war, in which not only their men but their women likewise are trained up, that in cases of necessity they may not be quite useless; yet they do not rashly engage in war, unless it be either to defend themselves, or their friends, from any unjust aggressors; or out of good nature or in compassion assist an oppressed nation in shaking off the yoke of tyranny. They indeed help their friends, not only in defensive, but also in offensive wars; but they never do that unless they have been consulted before the breach was made, and being satisfied with the grounds on which they went, they had found that all demands of reparation were rejected, so that a war was unavoidable. This they think to be not only just, when one neighbor makes an inroad on another, by public order, and carry away the spoils; but when the merchants of one country are oppressed in another, either under pretense of some unjust laws or by the perverse wresting of good ones. This they count a more just cause of war than the other, because those injuries are done under some color of laws. This was the only ground of that war in which they engaged with the Nephelogetes against the Aleopolitanes, a little before our time; for the merchants of the former having, as they thought, met with great injustice among the latter, which, whether it was in itself right or wrong, drew on a terrible war, in which many of their neighbors were engaged; and their keenness in carrying it on being supported by their strength in maintaining it, it not only shook some very flourishing states, and very much afflicted others, but after a series of much mischief ended in the entire conquest and slavery of the Aleopolitanes, who though before the war they were in all respects much superior to the Nephelogetes, were yet subdued; but though the Utopians had assisted them in the war, yet they pretended to no share of the spoil.

But though they so vigorously assist their friends in obtaining reparation for the injuries they have received in affairs of this nature, yet if any such frauds were committed against themselves, provided no violence was

done to their persons, they would only on their being
refused satisfaction forbear trading with such a people.
This is not because they consider their neighbors more
than their own citizens; but since their neighbors trade
every one upon his own stock, fraud is a more sensible
injury to them than it is to the Utopians, among whom
the public in such a case only suffers. As they expect
nothing in return for the merchandises they export but
that in which they so much abound, and is of little use
to them, the loss does not much affect them; they think
therefore it would be too severe to revenge a loss attended
with so little inconvenience either to their lives, or their
subsistence, with the death of many persons; but if any
of their people is either killed or wounded wrongfully,
whether it be done by public authority or only by private
men, as soon as they hear of it they send ambassadors,
and demand that the guilty persons may be delivered up
to them; and if that is denied, they declare war; but if
it be complied with, the offenders are condemned either
to death or slavery.

They would be both troubled and ashamed of a bloody
victory over their enemies, and think it would be as foolish
a purchase as to buy the most valuable goods at too high
a rate. And in no victory do they glory so much as in
that which is gained by dexterity and good conduct,
without bloodshed. In such cases they appoint public
triumphs, and erect trophies to the honor of those who
have succeeded; for then do they reckon that a man acts
suitably to his nature when he conquers his enemy in
such a way as that no other creature but a man could be
capable of, and that is by the strength of his understanding. Bears, lions, boars, wolves, and dogs, and all
other animals employ their bodily force one against another in which as many of them are superior to men,
both in strength and fierceness, so they are all subdued
by his reason and understanding.

The only design of the Utopians in war is to obtain
that by force, which if it had been granted them in time
would have prevented the war; or if that cannot be done,
to take so severe a revenge on those that have injured
them that they may be terrified from doing the like for

the time to come. By these ends they measure all their designs, and manage them so that it is visible that the appetite of fame or vainglory does not work so much on them as a just care of their own security.

As soon as they declare war, they take care to have a great many schedules, that are sealed with their common seal, affixed in the most conspicuous places of their enemies' country. This is carried secretly, and done in many places all at once. In these they promise great rewards to such as shall kill the prince, and lesser in proportion to such as shall kill any other persons, who are those on whom, next to the prince himself, they cast the chief balance of the war. And they double the sum to him that, instead of killing the person so marked out, shall take him alive and put him in their hands. They offer not only indemnity, but rewards, to such of the persons themselves that are so marked, if they will act against their countrymen: by these means those that are named in the schedules become not only distrustful of their fellow-citizens, but are jealous of one another, and are much distracted by fear and danger; for it has often fallen out that many of them, and even the Prince himself, have been betrayed by those in whom they have trusted most: for the rewards that the Utopians offer are so unmeasurably great, that there is no sort of crime to which men cannot be drawn by them. They consider the risk that those run who undertake such services, and offer a recompense proportioned to the danger; not only a vast deal of gold, but great revenues in lands, that lie among other nations that are their friends, where they may go and enjoy them very securely, and they observe the promises they make of this kind most religiously. They very much approve of this way of corrupting their enemies, though it appears to others to be base and cruel; but they look on it as a wise course, to make an end of what would be otherwise a long war, without so much as hazarding one battle to decide it. They think it likewise an act of mercy and love to mankind to prevent the great slaughter of those that must otherwise be killed in the progress of the war, both on their own side and on that of their enemies, by the death of a few that

14

are most guilty; and that in so doing they are kind even
to their enemies, and pity them no less than their own
people, as knowing that the greater part of them do not
engage in the war of their own accord, but are driven
into it by the passions of their prince.

If this method does not succeed with them, then they
sow seeds of contention among their enemies, and animate
the prince's brother, or some of the nobility, to aspire to
the crown. If they cannot disunite them by domestic
broils, then they engage their neighbors against them,
and make them set on foot some old pretensions, which
are never wanting to princes when they have occasion
for them. These they plentifully supply with money,
though but very sparingly with any auxiliary troops: for
they are so tender of their own people, that they would
not willingly exchange one of them, even with the prince
of their enemies' country.

But as they keep their gold and silver only for such
an occasion, so when that offers itself they easily part
with it, since it would be no inconvenience to them
though they should reserve nothing of it to themselves.
For besides the wealth that they have among them at
home, they have a vast treasure abroad, many nations
round about them being deep in their debt; so that they
hire soldiers from all places for carrying on their wars,
but chiefly from the Zapolets, who live five hundred miles
east of Utopia. They are a rude, wild, and fierce nation,
who delight in the woods and rocks, among which they
were born and bred. They are hardened both against
heat, cold and labor, and know nothing of the delicacies
of life. They do not apply themselves to agriculture,
nor do they care either for their houses or their clothes.
Cattle is all that they look after; and for the greatest
part they live either by hunting, or upon rapine; and are
made, as it were, only for war. They watch all opportunities of engaging in it, and very readily embrace such
as are offered them. Great numbers of them will frequently go out, and offer themselves for a very low pay,
to serve any that will employ them: they know none of
the arts of life, but those that lead to the taking it away;
they serve those that hire them, both with much courage

and great fidelity, but will not engage to serve for any
determined time, and agree upon such terms, that the
next day they may go over to the enemies of those whom
they serve, if they offer them a greater encouragement;
and will perhaps return to them the day after that, upon
a higher advance of their pay. There are few wars in
which they make not a considerable part of the armies
of both sides: so it often falls out that they who are
related, and were hired in the same country, and so have
lived long and familiarly together, forgetting both their
relations and former friendship, kill one another upon
no other consideration than that of being hired to it for
a little money by princes of different interests; and such
a regard have they for money, that they are easily
wrought on by the difference of one penny a day to
change sides. So entirely does their avarice influence them;
and yet this money, which they value so highly, is of
little use to them; for what they purchase thus with their
blood, they quickly waste on luxury, which among them
is but of a poor and miserable form.

This nation serves the Utopians against all people
whatsoever, for they pay higher than any other. The
Utopians hold this for a maxim, that as they seek out
the best sort of men for their own use at home, so they
make use of this worst sort of men for the consumption
of war, and therefore they hire them with the offers of
vast rewards, to expose themselves to all sorts of haz-
ards, out of which the greater part never returns to
claim their promises. Yet they make them good most
religiously to such as escape. This animates them to
adventure again, whenever there is occasion for it; for
the Utopians are not at all troubled how many of these
happen to be killed, and reckon it a service done to
mankind if they could be a means to deliver the world
from such a lewd and vicious sort of people, that seem
to have run together as to the drain of human nature.
Next to these they are served in their wars with those
upon whose account they undertake them, and with the
auxiliary troops of their other friends, to whom they
join a few of their own people, and send some man of
eminent and approved virtue to command in chief.

There are two sent with him, who during his command
are but private men, but the first is to succeed him if
he should happen to be either killed or taken; and in
case of the like misfortune to him, the third comes in
his place; and thus they provide against ill events, that
such accidents as may befall their generals may not
endanger their armies. When they draw out troops of
their own people, they take such out of every city as
freely offer themselves, for none are forced to go against
their wills, since they think that if any man is pressed
that wants courage, he will not only act faintly, but by
his cowardice dishearten others. But if an invasion is
made on their country they make use of such men, if
they have good bodies, though they are not brave; and
either put them aboard their ships or place them on the
walls of their towns, that being so posted they may find
no opportunity of flying away; and thus either shame,
the heat of action, or the impossibility of flying, bears
down their cowardice; they often make a virtue of necessity and behave themselves well, because nothing else is
left them. But as they force no man to go into any
foreign war against his will, so they do not hinder those
women who are willing to go along with their husbands;
on the contrary, they encourage and praise them, and
they stand often next their husbands in the front of the
army. They also place together those who are related,
parents and children, kindred, and those that are mutually
allied, near one another; that those whom Nature has inspired with the greatest zeal for assisting one another, may
be the nearest and readiest to do it; and it is matter of
great reproach if husband or wife survive one another, or if
a child survives his parents, and therefore when they
come to be engaged in action they continue to fight to
the last man, if their enemies stand before them. And
as they use all prudent methods to avoid the endanger-
ing their own men, and if it is possible let all the action
and danger fall upon the troops that they hire, so if it
becomes necessary for themselves to engage, they then
charge with as much courage as they avoided it before
with prudence: nor is it a fierce charge at first, but it
increases by degrees; and as they continue in action,

they grow more obstinate and press harder upon the
enemy, insomuch that they will much sooner die than
give ground; for the certainty that their children will be
well looked after when they are dead, frees them from
all that anxiety concerning them which often masters men
of great courage; and thus they are animated by a noble
and invincible resolution.   Their skill in military affairs
increases their courage; and the wise sentiments which,
according to the laws of their country are instilled into
them in their education, give additional vigor to their
minds: for as they do not undervalue life so as prodi-
gally to throw it away, they are not so indecently fond of
it as to preserve it by base and unbecoming methods.
In the greatest heat of action, the bravest of their youth,
who have devoted themselves to that service, single out
the general of their enemies, set on him either openly or
by ambuscade, pursue him everywhere, and when spent
and wearied out, are relieved by others, who never give
over the pursuit; either attacking him with close weapons when they can get near him, or with those which
wound at a distance, when others get in between them;
so that unless he secures himself by flight, they seldom
fail at last to kill or to take him prisoner.   When they
have obtained a victory, they kill as few as possible, and
are much more bent on taking many prisoners than on
killing those that fly before them; nor do they ever let
their men so loose in the pursuit of their enemies, as not to
retain an entire body still in order; so that if they have
been forced to engage the last of their battalions before
they could gain the day, they will rather let their enemies
all escape than pursue them, when their own army is in
disorder; remembering well what has often fallen out to
themselves, that when the main body of their army has
been quite defeated and broken, when their enemies im-
agining the victory obtained, have let themselves loose
into an irregular pursuit, a few of them that lay for a
reserve, waiting a fit opportunity, have fallen on them
in their chase, and when straggling in disorder and
apprehensive of no danger, but counting the day their
own, have turned the whole action, and wresting
out of their hands a victory that seemed certain and

undoubted, while the vanquished have suddenly become victorious.

It is hard to tell whether they are more dexterous in laying or avoiding ambushes. They sometimes seem to fly when it is far from their thoughts; and when they intend to give ground, they do it so that it is very hard to find out their design. If they see they are ill posted, or are like to be overpowered by numbers, they then either march off in the night with great silence, or by some stratagem delude their enemies: if they retire in the daytime, they do it in such order, that it is no less dangerous to fall upon them in a retreat than in a march. They fortify their camps with a deep and large trench, and throw up the earth that is dug out of it for a wall; nor do they employ only their slaves in this, but the whole army works at it, except those that are then upon the guard; so that when so many hands are at work, a great line and a strong fortification is finished in so short a time that it is scarce credible. Their armor is very strong for defense, and yet is not so heavy as to make them uneasy in their marches; for they can even swim with it. All that are trained up to war practice swimming. Both horse and foot make great use of arrows, and are very expert. They have no swords, but fight with a pole-axe that is both sharp and heavy, by which they thrust or strike down an enemy. They are very good at finding out warlike machines, and disguise them so well, that the enemy does not perceive them till he feels the use of them; so that he cannot prepare such a defense as would render them useless; the chief consideration had in the making them, is that they may be easily carried and managed.

If they agree to a truce, they observe it so religiously that no provocations will make them break it. They never lay their enemies' country waste, nor burn their corn, and even in their marches they take all possible care that neither horse nor foot may tread it down, for they do not know but that they may have use for it themselves. They hurt no man whom they find disarmed, unless he is a spy. When a town is surrendered to them, they take it into their protection: and when they carry a place by storm, they never plunder it, but put those only to the sword that opposed the rendering of it up, and make the rest of the garrison slaves, but for the other inhabitants they do them no hurt; and if any of them had advised a surrender, they give them good rewards out of the estates of those that they condemn, and distribute the rest among their auxiliary troops, but they themselves take no share of the spoil.

When a war is ended, they do not oblige their friends to reimburse their expenses; but they obtain them of the conquered, either in money, which they keep for the next occasion, or in lands, out of which a constant revenue is to be paid them; by many increases, the revenue which they draw out from several countries on such occasions, is now risen to above 700,000 ducats a year. They send some of their own people to receive these revenues, who have orders to live magnificently, and like princes, by which means they consume much of it upon the place; and either bring over the rest to Utopia, or lend it to that nation in which it lies. This they most commonly do, unless some great occasion, which falls out but very seldom, should oblige them to call for it all. It is out of these lands that they assign rewards to such as they encourage to adventure on desperate attempts. If any prince that engages in war with them is making preparations for invading their country, they prevent him, and make his country the seat of the war; for they do not willingly suffer any war to break in upon their island; and if that should happen, they would only defend themselves by their own people, and not call for auxiliary troops to their assistance.

Of the Religions of the Utopians.

THERE are several sorts of religions, not only in different parts of the island, but even in every town; some worshiping the sun, others the moon, or one of the planets: some worship such men as have been eminent in former times for virtue, or glory, not only as ordinary deities, but as the supreme God: yet the greater and wiser sort of them worship none of these, but adore one eternal, invisible, infinite, and incomprehensible Deity; as a being that is far above all our apprehensions, that is spread over the whole universe, not by his bulk, but by his power and virtue; him they call the Father of All, and acknowledge that the beginnings, the increase, the progress, the vicissitudes, and the end of all things come only from him; nor do they offer divine honors to any but to him alone. And indeed, though they differ concerning other things, yet all agree in this, that they think there is one Supreme Being that made and governs the world, whom they call in the language of their country Mithras. They differ in this, that one thinks the God whom he worships is this Supreme Being, and another thinks that his idol is that God; but they all agree in one principle, that whoever is this Supreme Being, he is also that great Essence to whose glory and majesty all honors are ascribed by the consent of all nations.

By degrees, they fall off from the various superstitions that are among them, and grow up to that one religion that is the best and most in request; and there is no doubt to be made but that all the others had vanished long ago, if some of those who advised them to lay aside their superstitions had not met with some unhappy accident, which being considered as inflicted by heaven, made them afraid that the God whose worship had like to have been abandoned, had interposed, and revenged themselves on those who despised their authority.

After they had heard from us an account of the doctrine, the course of life, and the miracles of Christ, and of the wonderful constancy of so many martyrs, whose blood so willingly offered up by them, was the chief occasion of spreading their religion over a vast number of nations; it is not to be imagined how inclined they were to receive it. I shall not determine whether this proceeded from any secret inspiration of God, or whether it was because it seemed so favorable to that community of goods, which is an opinion so particular as well as so dear to them; since they perceived that Christ and his followers lived by that rule, and that it was still kept up in some communities among the sincerest sort of Christians.

From whichsoever of these motives it might be, true it is
that many of them came over to our religion, and were
initiated into it by baptism. But as two of our number
were dead, so none of the four that survived were in
priests' orders; we therefore could only baptize them; so
that to our great regret they could not partake of the
other sacraments that can only be administered by priests;
but they are instructed concerning them, and long most
vehemently for them. They have had great disputes
among themselves, whether one chosen by them to be a
priest would not thereby be qualified to do all the things
that belong to that character, even though he had no
authority derived from the Pope; and they seemed to be
resolved to choose some for that employment, but they
had not done it when I left them.

Those among them that have not received our religion,
do not fright any from it, and use none ill that goes
over to it; so that all the while I was there, one man
only was punished on this occasion. He being newly
baptized, did, notwithstanding all that we could say to
the contrary, dispute publicly concerning the Christian
religion with more zeal than discretion; and with so much
heat, that he not only preferred our worship to theirs,
but condemned all their rites as profane; and cried out
against all that adhered to them, as impious and sacri-
legious persons, that were to be damned to everlasting
burnings. Upon his having frequently preached in this
manner, he was seized, and after trial he was condemned
to banishment, not for having disparaged their religion,
but for his inflaming the people to sedition: for this is
one of their most ancient laws, that no man ought to be
punished for his religion. At the first constitution of
their government, Utopus having understood that before
his coming among them the old inhabitants had been
engaged in great quarrels concerning religion, by which
they were so divided among themselves, that he found it
an easy thing to conquer them, since instead of uniting
their forces against him, every different party in religion
fought by themselves; after he had subdued them, he
made a law that every man might be of what religion
he pleased, and might endeavor to draw others to it by

the force of argument, and by amicable and modest ways,
but without bitterness against those of other opinions;
but that he ought to use no other force but that of
persuasion, and was neither to mix with it reproaches
nor violence; and such as did otherwise were to be condemned to banishment or slavery.

This law was made by Utopus, not only for preserving the public peace, which he saw suffered much by
daily contentions and irreconcilable heats, but because
he thought the interest of religion itself required it. He
judged it not fit to determine anything rashly, and
seemed to doubt whether those different forms of religion might not all come from God, who might inspire
men in a different manner, and be pleased with this variety; he therefore thought it indecent and foolish for
any man to threaten and terrify another to make him
believe what did not appear to him to be true. And
supposing that only one religion was really true, and the
rest false, he imagined that the native force of truth
would at last break forth and shine bright, if supported
only by the strength of argument, and attended to with
a gentle and unprejudiced mind; while on the other
hand, if such debates were carried on with violence and
tumults, as the most wicked are always the most obstinate, so the best and most holy religion might be choked
with superstition, as corn is with briars and thorns; he
therefore left men wholly to their liberty, that they
might be free to believe as they should see cause; only
he made a solemn and severe law against such as should
so far degenerate from the dignity of human nature as
to think that our souls died with our bodies, or that the
world was governed by chance, without a wise overruling
Providence: for they all formerly believed that there was
a state of rewards and punishments to the good and bad
after this life; and they now look on those that think
otherwise as scarce fit to be counted men, since they degrade so noble a being as the soul, and reckon it no better than a beast's: thus they are far from looking on
such men as fit for human society, or to be citizens of
a well-ordered commonwealth; since a man of such
principles must needs, as often as he dares do it,

despise all their laws and customs: for there is no doubt
to be made that a man who is afraid of nothing but
the law, and apprehends nothing after death, will not
scruple to break through all the laws of his country,
either by fraud or force, when by this means he may satisfy his appetites. They never raise any that hold these
maxims, either to honors or offices, nor employ them in
any public trust, but despise them, as men of base and
sordid minds; yet they do not punish them, because they
lay this down as a maxim that a man cannot make himself believe anything he pleases; nor do they drive
any to dissemble their thoughts by threatenings, so
that men are not tempted to lie or disguise their
opinions; which being a sort of fraud, is abhorred
by the Utopians. They take care indeed to prevent their
disputing in defense of these opinions, especially before the
common people; but they suffer, and even encourage them
to dispute concerning them in private with their priests and
other grave men, being confident that they will be cured
of those mad opinions by having reason laid before them.
There are many among them that run far to the other
extreme, though it is neither thought an ill nor unreasonable
opinion, and therefore is not at all discouraged.   They
think that the souls of beasts are immortal; though far
inferior to the dignity of the human soul, and not capable of so great a happiness. They are almost all of them
very firmly persuaded that good men will be infinitely
happy in another state; so that though they are compas-
sionate to all that are sick, yet they lament no man's
death, except they see him loath to depart with life; for
they look on this as a very ill presage, as if the soul,
conscious to itself of guilt, and quite hopeless, was afraid
to leave the body, from some secret hints of approach-
ing misery.   They think that such a man's appearance
before God cannot be acceptable to him, who being called
on does not go out cheerfully but is backward and unwilling, and is, as it were, dragged to it.   They are struck
with horror when they see any die in this manner, and
carry them out in silence and with sorrow, and praying
God that he would be merciful to the errors of the departed soul, they lay the body in the ground; but when

any die cheerfully, and full of hope, they do not mourn
for them, but sing hymns when they carry out their
bodies, and commending their souls very earnestly to
God: their whole behavior is then rather grave than sad,
they burn the body, and set up a pillar where the pile
was made, with an inscription to the honor of the de-
ceased. When they come from the funeral, they discourse
of his good life and worthy actions, but speak of nothing oftener and with more pleasure than of his serenity
at the hour of death. They think such respect paid to
the memory of good men is both the greatest incitement
to engage others to follow their example, and the most
acceptable worship than can be offered them; for they
believe that though by the imperfection of human sight
they are invisible to us, yet they are present among us,
and hear those discourses that pass concerning themselves. They believe it inconsistent with the happiness
of departed souls not to be at liberty to be where they
will, and do not imagine them capable of the ingratitude of not desiring to see those friends with whom they
lived on earth in the strictest bonds of love and kindness: besides they are persuaded that good men after
death have these affections and all other good dispositions increased rather than diminished, and therefore
conclude that they are still among the living, and observe
all they say or do. From hence they engage in all their
affairs with the greater confidence of success, as trusting
to their protection; while this opinion of the presence of
their ancestors is a restraint that prevents their engaging in ill designs.

They despise and laugh at auguries, and the other
vain and superstitious ways of divination, so much observed among other nations; but have great reverence
for such miracles as cannot flow from any of the powers
of Nature, and look on them as effects and indications
of the presence of the supreme Being, of which they
say many instances have occurred among them; and that
sometimes their public prayers, which upon great and
dangerous occasions they have solemnly put up to God,
with assured confidence of being heard, have been
answered in a miraculous manner.

They think the contemplating God in his works, and
the adoring him for them, is a very acceptable piece of
worship to him.

There are many among them, that upon a motive of
religion neglect learning, and apply themselves to no
sort of study; nor do they allow themselves any leisure
time, but are perpetually employed, believing that by
the good things that a man does he secures to himself
that happiness that comes after death. Some of these
visit the sick; others mend highways, cleanse ditches,
repair bridges, or dig turf, gravel or stones. Others fell
and cleave timber, and bring wood, corn, and other
necessaries on carts into their towns. Nor do these only
serve the public, but they serve even private men, more
than the slaves themselves do; for if there is anywhere
a rough, hard, and sordid piece of work to be done,
from which many are frightened by the labor and loath-
someness of it, if not the despair of accomplishing it,
they cheerfully, and of their own accord, take that to
their share; and by that means, as they ease others very
much, so they afflict themselves, and spend their whole
life in hard labor; and yet they do not value themselves
upon this, nor lessen other people's credit to raise their
own; but by their stooping to such servile employments,
they are so far from being despised, that they are so
much the more esteemed by the whole nation.

Of these there are two sorts; some live unmarried and
chaste, and abstain from eating any sort of flesh; and
thus weaning themselves from all the pleasures of the
present life, which they account hurtful, they pursue,
even by the hardest and most painful methods possible,
that blessedness which they hope for hereafter; and the
nearer they approach to it, they are the more cheerful
and earnest in their endeavors after it. Another sort of
them is less willing to put themselves to much toil, and
therefore prefer a married state to a single one, and as
they do not deny themselves the pleasure of it, so they
think the begetting of children is a debt which they owe
to human nature and to their country; nor do they avoid
any pleasure that does not hinder labor, and therefore
eat flesh so much the more willingly, as they find that

by this means they are the more able to work; the
Utopians look upon these as the wiser sect, but they
esteem the others as the most holy.　They would indeed
laugh at any man, who from the principles of reason
would prefer an unmarried state to a married, or a life
of labor to an easy life; but they reverence and admire
such as do it from the motives of religion.　There is
nothing in which they are more cautious than in giving
their opinion positively concerning any sort of religion.
The men that lead those severe lives are called in the
language of their country Brutheskas, which answers to
those we call religious orders.

Their priests are men of eminent piety, and therefore
they are but few, for there are only thirteen in every
town, one for every temple; but when they go to war,
seven of these go out with their forces, and seven others
are chosen to supply their room in their absence; but
these enter again upon their employment when they
return; and those who served in their absence attend
upon the high priest, till vacancies fall by death; for
there is one set over all the rest.　They are chosen by
the people as the other magistrates are, by suffrages
given in secret, for preventing of factions; and when
they are chosen they are consecrated by the college of
priests.　The care of all sacred things, the worship of
God, and an inspection into the manners of the people,
are committed to them.　It is a reproach to a man to be
sent for by any of them, or for them to speak to him in
secret, for that always gives some suspicion.　All that is
incumbent on them is only to exhort and admonish the
people; for the power of correcting and punishing ill
men belongs wholly to the Prince and to the other magistrates.　The severest thing that the priest does, is the
excluding those that are desperately wicked from joining
in their worship.　There is not any sort of punishment
more dreaded by them than this, for as it loads them
with infamy, so it fills them with secret horrors, such is
their reverence to their religion; nor will their bodies be
long exempted from their share of trouble; for if they
do not very quickly satisfy the priests of the truth of
their repentance, they are seized on by the Senate, and

punished for their impiety. The education of youth belongs to the priests, yet they do not take so much care of instructing them in letters as in forming their minds and manners aright; they use all possible methods to infuse very early into the tender and flexible minds of children such opinions as are both good in themselves and will be useful to their country. For when deep impressions of these things are made at that age, they follow men through the whole course of their lives, and conduce much to preserve the peace of the government, which suffers by nothing more than by vices that rise out of ill opinions. The wives of their priests are the most extraordinary women of the whole country; sometimes the women themselves are made priests, though that falls out but seldom, nor are any but ancient widows chosen into that order.

None of the magistrates have greater honor paid them than is paid the priests; and if they should happen to commit any crime, they would not be questioned for it. Their punishment is left to God, and to their own consciences; for they do not think it lawful to lay hands on any man, how wicked soever he is, that has been in a peculiar manner dedicated to God; nor do they find any great inconvenience in this, both because they have so few priests, and because they are chosen with much caution, so that it must be a very unusual thing to find one who merely out of regard to his virtue, and for his being esteemed a singularly good man, was raised up to so great a dignity, degenerate into corruption and vice. And if such a thing should fall out, for man is a changeable creature, yet there being few priests, and these having no authority but what rises out of the respect that is paid them, nothing of great consequence to the public can proceed from the indemnity that the priests enjoy.

They have indeed, very few of them, lest greater numbers sharing in the same honor might make the dignity of that order which they esteem so highly to sink in its reputation. They also think it difficult to find out many of such an exalted pitch of goodness, as to be equal to that dignity which demands the exercise of more than

ordinary virtues. Nor are the priests in greater venera-
tion among them than they are among their neighboring nations, as you may imagine by that which I think
gives occasion for it.

When the Utopians engage in battle, the priests who
accompany them to the war, appareled in their sacred
vestments, kneel down during the action, in a place not
far from the field, and lifting up their hands to heaven,
pray, first for peace, and then for victory to their own
side, and particularly that it may be gained without the
effusion of much blood on either side; and when the victory turns to their side, they run in among their own
men to restrain their fury; and if any of their enemies
see them, or call to them, they are preserved by that
means; and such as can come so near them as to touch
their garments, have not only their lives but their fortunes secured to them; it is upon this account that all
the nations round about consider them so much, and
treat them with such reverence, that they have been often
no less able to preserve their own people from the fury
of their enemies, than to save their enemies from their
rage; for it has sometimes fallen out, that when their
armies have been in disorder, and forced to fly, so that
their enemies were running upon the slaughter and spoil,
the priests, by interposing have separated them from one
another, and stopped the effusion of more blood; so that
by their mediation a peace has been concluded on very
reasonable terms; nor is there any nation about them so
fierce, cruel, or barbarous as not to look upon their persons as sacred and inviolable.

The first and the last day of the month, and of the
year, is a festival. They measure their months by the
course of the moon, and their years by the course of
the sun. The first days are called in their language the
Cynemernes, and the last the Trapemernes; which answers
in our language to the festival that begins, or ends the
season.

They have magnificent temples, that are not only nobly
built, but extremely spacious; which is the more necessary, as they have so few of them; they are a little dark
within, which proceeds not from any error in the archi-

tecture, but is done with design; for their priests think
that too much light dissipates the thoughts, and that a
more moderate degree of it both recollects the mind and
raises devotion. Though there are many different forms
of religion among them, yet all these, how various soever,
agree in the main point, which is the worshiping the
Divine Essence; and therefore there is nothing to be seen
or heard in their temples in which the several persuasions
among them may not agree, for every sect performs those
rites that are peculiar to it, in their private houses; nor
is there anything in the public worship that contradicts
the particular ways of those different sects. There are
no images for God in their temples, so that every one
may represent him to his thoughts, according to the way
of his religion; nor do they call this one God by any
other name but that of Mithras, which is the common
name by which they all express the Divine Essence,
whatsoever otherwise they think it to be; nor are there
any prayers among them but such as every one of them
may use without prejudice to his own opinion.

They meet in their temples on the evening of the
festival that concludes a season: and not having yet
broke their fast, they thank God for their good success
during that year or month, which is then at an end, and
the next day being that which begins the new season,
they meet early in their temples, to pray for the happy
progress of all their affairs during that period upon
which they then enter. In the festival which concludes
the period, before they go to the temple, both wives and
children fall on their knees before their husbands or
parents, and confess everything in which they have
either erred or failed in their duty, and beg pardon for
it. Thus all little discontents in families are removed,
that they may offer up their devotions with a pure and
serene mind; for they hold it a great impiety to enter
upon them with disturbed thoughts, or with a conscious-
ness of their bearing hatred or anger in their hearts to
any person whatsoever; and think that they should become liable to severe punishments if they presume to
offer sacrifices without cleansing their hearts, and recon-
ciling all their differences. In the temples, the two

15

sexes are separated, the men go to the right hand, and the women to the left; and the males and females all place themselves before the head and master or mistress of that family to which they belong; so that those who have the government of them at home may see their deportment in public; and they intermingle them so, that the younger and the older may be set by one another; for if the younger sort were all set together, they would perhaps trifle away that time too much in which they ought to beget in themselves that religious dread of the Supreme Being, which is the greatest and almost the only incitement to virtue.

They offer up no living creature in sacrifice, nor do they think it suitable to the Divine Being, from whose bounty it is that these creatures have derived their lives, to take pleasure in their deaths, or the offering up their blood. They burn incense and other sweet odors, and have a great number of wax lights during their worship; not out of any imagination that such oblations can add anything to the divine Nature, which even prayers cannot do; but as it is a harmless and pure way of worshiping God, so they think those sweet savors and lights, together with some other ceremonies, by a secret and unaccountable virtue, elevate men's souls, and inflame them with greater energy and cheerfulness during the divine worship.

All the people appear in the temples in white garments, but the priest's vestments are parti-colored, and both the work and colors are wonderful. They are made of no rich materials, for they are neither embroidered nor set with precious stones, but are composed of the plumes of several birds, laid together with so much art and so neatly, that the true value of them is far beyond the costliest materials. They say that in the ordering and placing those plumes some dark mysteries are represented, which pass down among their priests in a secret tradition concerning them; and that they are as hieroglyphics, putting them in mind of the blessings that they have received from God, and of their duties both to him and to their neighbors. As soon as the priest appears in those ornaments, they all fall prostrate on the ground, with so much reverence and so deep a silence that such

as look on cannot but be struck with it, as if it were the
effect of the appearance of a Deity. After they have
been for some time in this posture, they all stand up,
upon a sign given by the priest, and sing hymns to the
honor of God, some musical instruments playing all the
while. These are quite of another form than those used
among us: but as many of them are much sweeter than
ours, so others are made use of by us. Yet in one thing
they very much exceed us; all their music, both vocal
and instrumental, is adapted to imitate and express the
passions, and is so happily suited to every occasion, that
whether the subject of the hymn be cheerful or formed to
soothe or trouble the mind, or to express grief or re-
morse, the music takes the impression of whatever is
represented, affects and kindles the passions, and works
the sentiments deep into the hearts of the hearers.
When this is done, both priests and people offer up very
solemn prayers to God in a set form of words; and these
are so composed, that whatsoever is pronounced by the
whole assembly may be likewise applied by every man
in particular to his own condition: in these they acknowledge God to be the author and governor of the world,
and the fountain of all the good they receive, and
therefore offer up to him their thanksgiving; and in
particular bless him for his goodness in ordering
it so, that they are born under the happiest government
in the world, and are of a religion which they hope is
the truest of all others: but if they are mistaken, and if
there is either a better government or a religion more
acceptable to God, they implore his goodness to let them
know it, vowing that they resolve to follow him whith-
ersoever he leads them. But if their government is the
best, and their religion the truest, then they pray that
he may fortify them in it, and bring all the world both
to the same rules of life, and to the same opinions concerning himself; unless, according to the unsearchable-
ness of his mind, he is pleased with a variety of
religions. Then they pray that God may give them an
easy passage at last to himself; not presuming to set
limits to him, how early or late it should be; but if it
may be wished for, without derogating from his supreme

authority, they desire to be quickly delivered, and to be
taken to himself, though by the most terrible kind of
death, rather than to be detained long from seeing him
by the most prosperous course of life. When this prayer
is ended, they all fall down again upon the ground, and
after a little while they rise up, go home to dinner, and
spend the rest of the day in diversion or military exercises.

Thus have I described to you, as particularly as I could,
the constitution of that commonwealth, which I do not
only think the best in the world, but indeed the only
commonwealth that truly deserves that name. In all
other places it is visible, that while people talk of a
commonwealth, every man only seeks his own wealth;
but there, where no man has any property, all men zeal-
ously pursue the good of the public; and, indeed, it is no
wonder to see men act so differently; for in other commonwealths, every man knows that unless he provides for
himself, how flourishing soever the commonwealth may
be, he must die of hunger; so that he sees the necessity
of preferring his own concerns to the public; but in
Utopia, where every man has a right to everything, they
all know that if care is taken to keep the public stores
full, no private man can want anything; for among them
there is no unequal distribution, so that no man is poor,
none in necessity; and though no man has anything, yet
they are all rich; for what can make a man so rich as to
lead a serene and cheerful life, free from anxieties;
neither apprehending want himself, nor vexed with the
endless complaints of his wife? He is not afraid of the
misery of his children, nor is he contriving how to raise
a portion for his daughters, but is secure in this, that
both he and his wife, his children and grandchildren, to
as many generations as he can fancy, will all live both
plentifully and happily; since among them there is no less
care taken of those who were once engaged in labor, but
grow afterward unable to follow it, than there is elsewhere of these that continue still employed. I would
gladly hear any man compare the justice that is among
them with that of all other nations; among whom, may I
perish, if I see anything that looks either like justice or
equity: for what justice is there in this, that a nobleman,

a goldsmith, a banker, or any other man, that either does
nothing at all, or at best is employed in things that are
of no use to the public, should live in great luxury and
splendor, upon what is so ill acquired; and a mean man,
a carter, a smith, or a plowman, that works harder even
than the beasts themselves, and is employed in labors so
necessary, that no commonwealth could hold out a year
without them, can only earn so poor a livelihood, and
must lead so miserable a life, that the condition of the
beasts is much better than theirs? For as the beasts do
not work so constantly, so they feed almost as well, and
with more pleasure; and have no anxiety about what is
to come, whilst these men are depressed by a barren and
fruitless employment, and tormented with the apprehensions of want in their old age; since that which they get
by their daily labor does but maintain them at present,
and is consumed as fast as it comes in, there is no overplus left to lay up for old age.

Is not that government both unjust and ungrateful, that
is so prodigal of its favors to those that are called gentlemen, or goldsmiths, or such others who are idle, or live
either by flattery or by contriving the arts of vain pleasure;
and on the other hand, takes no care of those of a meaner
sort, such as plowmen, colliers, and smiths, without
whom it could not subsist? But after the public has
reaped all the advantage of their service, and they come
to be oppressed with age, sickness, and want, all their
labors and the good they have done is forgotten; and all
the recompense given them is that they are left to die in
great misery. The richer sort are often endeavoring to
bring the hire of laborers lower, not only by their fraudu-
lent practices, but by the laws which they procure to be
made to that effect; so that though it is a thing most unjust in itself, to give such small rewards to those who
deserve so well of the public, yet they have given those
hardships the name and color of justice, by procuring laws
to be made for regulating them.

Therefore I must say that, as I hope for mercy, I can
have no other notion of all the other governments that I
see or know, than that they are a conspiracy of the rich,
who on pretense of managing the public only pursue

their private ends, and devise all the ways and arts they
can find out; first, that they may, without danger, preserve
all that they have so ill acquired, and then that they may
engage the poor to toil and labor for them at as low rates
as possible, and oppress them as much as they please.
And if they can but prevail to get these contrivances established by the show of public authority, which is considered as the representative of the whole people, then they
are accounted laws.   Yet these wicked men after they
have, by a most insatiable covetousness, divided that
among themselves with which all the rest might have been
well supplied, are far from that happiness that is enjoyed
among the Utopians: for the use as well as the desire of
money being extinguished, much anxiety and great occasions of mischief are cut off with them   And who does not
see that the frauds, thefts, robberies, quarrels, tumults, contentions, seditions, murders, treacheries, and witchcrafts,
which are indeed rather punished than restrained by the
severities of law, would all fall off, if money were not any
more valued by the world?   Men's fears, solicitudes, cares,
labors, and watchings would all perish in the same moment with the value of money: even poverty itself, for the
relief of which money seems most necessary, would fall.
But, in order to the apprehending this aright, take one
instance.

Consider any year that has been so unfruitful that
many thousands have died of hunger; and yet if at the
end of that year a survey was made of the granaries of
all the rich men that have horded up the corn, it would
be found that there was enough among them to have prevented all that consumption of men that perished in misery; and that if it had been distributed among them,
none would have felt the terrible effects of that scarcity; so easy a thing would it be to supply all the necessities of life, if that blessed thing called money, which
is pretended to be invented for procuring them, was
not really the only thing that obstructed their being pro-
cured!

I do not doubt that rich men are sensible of this, and
that they well know how much a greater happiness it is
to want nothing necessary than to abound in many super-

fluities, and to be rescued out of so much misery than to
abound with so much wealth; and I cannot think but the
sense of every man's interest, added to the authority of
Christ's commands, who as he was infinitely wise, knew
what was best, and was not less good in discovering it to
us, would have drawn all the world over to the laws of
the Utopians, if pride, that plague of human nature, that
source of so much misery, did not hinder it; for this vice
does not measure happiness so much by its own conveniences as by the miseries of others; and would not be
satisfied with being thought a goddess, if none were left
that were miserable, over whom she might exult. Pride
thinks its own happiness shines the brighter by comparing it with the misfortunes of other persons; that by dis-
playing its own wealth, they may feel their poverty the
more sensibly. This is that infernal serpent that creeps
into the breasts of mortals, and possesses them too much
to be easily drawn out; and therefore I am glad that the
Utopians have fallen upon this form of government, in
which I wish that all the world could be so wise as to
imitate them; for they have indeed laid down such a
scheme and foundation of policy, that as men live happily
under it, so it is like to be of great continuance; for they
having rooted out of the minds of their people all the seeds
both of ambition and faction, there is no danger of any
commotion at home; which alone has been the ruin of
many states, that seemed otherwise to be well secured;
but as long as they live in peace at home, and are governed by such good laws, the envy of all their neighboring princes, who have often though in vain attempted
their ruin, will never be able to put their state into any
commotion or disorder.

When Raphael had thus made an end of speaking,
though many things occurred to me, both concerning the
manners and laws of that people, that seemed very absurd, as well as their way of making war, as in their
notions of religion and divine matters; together with several other particulars, but chiefly what seemed the foundation of all the rest, their living in common, without
the use of money, by which all nobility, magnificence,

splendor, and majesty, which, according to the common opinion, are the true ornaments of a nation, would be quite taken away; yet since I perceived that Raphael was weary, and was not sure whether he could easily bear contradiction, remembering that he had taken notice of some who seemed to think they were bound in honor to support the credit of their own wisdom, by finding out something to censure in all other men's inventions, besides their own; I only commended their constitution, and the account he had given of it in general; and so taking him by the hand, carried him to supper, and told him I would find out some other time for examining this subject more particularly, and for discoursing more copiously upon it; and indeed I shall be glad to embrace an opportunity of doing it. In the meanwhile, though it must be confessed that he is both a very learned man, and a person who has obtained a great knowledge of the world, I cannot perfectly agree to everything he has related; however, there are many things in the Commonwealth of Utopia that I rather wish, than hope, to see followed in our governments.

BACON'S

NEW ATLANTIS.

NEW ATLANTIS.

WE SAILED from Peru, where we had continued by the space of one whole year, for China and Japan, by the South Sea, taking with us victuals for twelve months; and had good winds from the east, though soft and weak, for five months' space and more. But then the wind came about, and settled in the west for many days, so as we could make little or no way, and were sometimes in purpose to turn back. But then again there arose strong and great winds from the south, with a point east; which carried us up, for all that we could do, toward the north: by which time our victuals failed us, though we had made good spare of them. So that finding ourselves, in the midst of the greatest wilderness of waters in the world, without victual, we gave ourselves up for lost men, and prepared for death. Yet we did lift up our hearts and voices to God above, who showeth his wonders in the deep; beseeching him of his mercy, that as in the beginning he discovered the face of the deep, and brought forth dry land, so he would now discover land to us, that we might not perish. And it came to pass, that the next day about evening we saw within a kenning before us, toward the north, as it were, thick clouds which did put us in some hope of land: knowing how that part of the South Sea was utterly unknown; and might have islands or continents, that hitherto were not come to light. Wherefore we bent our course thither, where we saw the appearance of land, all that night; and in the dawning of next day, we might plainly discern that it was a land flat to our sight, and full of boscage, which made it show the more dark. And after an hour and a half's sailing we entered into a good haven, being the port of a fair city. Not great indeed, but well built, and that gave a pleasant view from the sea. And we thinking every minute long

till we were on land, came close to the shore and offered
to land. But straightway we saw divers of the people, with
bastons in their hands, as it were, forbidding us to land:
yet without any cries or fierceness, but only as warning us
off, by signs that they made. Whereupon being not a
little discomfited, we were advising with ourselves what
we should do. During which time there made forth to
us a small boat, with about eight persons in it, whereof
one of them had in his hand a tipstaff of a yellow cane,
tipped at both ends with blue, who made aboard our ship,
without any show of distrust at all. And when he saw
one of our number present himself somewhat afore the
rest, he drew forth a little scroll of parchment (somewhat
yellower than our parchment, and shining like the leaves
of writing tables, but otherwise soft and flexible), and
delivered it to our foremost man. In which scroll were
written in ancient Hebrew, and in ancient Greek, and in
good Latin of the school, and in Spanish these words:
" Land ye not, none of you, and provide to be gone from
this coast within sixteen days, except you have further
time given you; meanwhile, if you want fresh water, or
victual, or help for your sick, or that your ship needeth
repair, write down your wants, and you shall have that
which belongeth to mercy." This scroll was signed with
a stamp of cherubim's wings, not spread, but hanging
downward, and by them a cross. This being delivered,
the officer returned, and left only a servant with us to
receive our answer. Consulting hereupon among ourselves, we were much perplexed. The denial of landing,
and hasty warning us away, troubled us much: on the
other side, to find that the people had languages, and
were so full of humanity, did comfort us not a little. And
above all, the sign of the cross to that instrument, was
to us a great rejoicing, and as it were a certain presage
of good. Our answer was in the Spanish tongue, " That
for our ship, it was well; for we had rather met with calms
and contrary winds, than any tempests. For our sick,
they were many, and in very ill case; so that if they were
not permitted to land, they ran in danger of their lives."
Our other wants we set down in particular, adding, " That
we had some little store of merchandise, which if it

pleased them to deal for, it might supply our wants, without being chargeabl^ unto them." We offered some reward in pistolets unto the servant, and a piece of crimson velvet to be presented to the officer; but the servant took them not, nor would scarce look upon them; and so left us, and went back in another little boat which was sent for him.

About three hours after we had dispatched our answer there came toward us a person (as it seemed) of a place. He had on him a gown with wide sleeves, of a kind of water chamolet, of an excellent azure color, far more glossy than ours: his under apparel was green, and so was his hat, being in the form of a turban, daintily made, and not so huge as the Turkish turbans; and the locks of his hair came down below the brims of it. A reverend man was he to behold. He came in a boat, gilt in some part of it, with four persons more only in that boat; and was followed by another boat, wherein were some twenty. When he was come within a flight-shot of our ship, signs were made to us that we should send forth some to meet him upon the water, which we presently did in our ship-boat, sending the principal man among us save one, and four of our number with him. When we were come within six yards of their boat, they called to us to stay, and not to approach further, which we did. And thereupon the man, whom I before described, stood up, and with a loud voice in Spanish, asked, " Are ye Christians ? " We answered, " We were; " fearing the less, because of the cross we had seen in the subscription. At which answer the said person lift up his right hand toward heaven, and drew it softly to his mouth (which is the gesture they use, when they thank God), and then said: " If ye will swear, all of you, by the merits of the Savior, that ye are no pirates; nor have shed blood, lawfully nor unlawfully, within forty days past; you may have license to come on land." We said, " We were all ready to take that oath." Whereupon one of those that were with him, being (as it seemed) a notary, made an entry of this act. Which done, another of the attendants of the great person, which was with him in the same boat, after his lord had spoken a little to him, said aloud: "My lord would have you know, that it is not of pride, or greatness, that he cometh not aboard your ship: but for that, in your answer, you declare that you have many sick among you, he was warned by the conservator of health of the city that he should keep a distance." We bowed ourselves toward him, and answered: "We were his humble servants; and accounted for great honor and singular humanity toward us, that which was already done: but hoped well, that the nature of the sickness of our men was not infectious." So he returned; and a while after came the notary to us aboard our ship; holding in his hand a fruit of that country, like an orange, but of color between orange-tawny and scarlet: which cast a most excellent odor. He used it (as it seemed) for a preservative against infection. He gave us our oath, "By the name of Jesus, and his merits:" and after told us, that the next day by six of the clock in the morning, we should be sent to, and brought to the strangers' house (so he called it), where we should be accommodated of things, both for our whole and for our sick. So he left us; and when we offered him some pistolets, he smiling, said, "He must not be twice paid for one labor:" meaning (as I take it) that he had salary sufficient of the state for his service. For (as I after learned) they call an officer that taketh rewards twice paid.

The next morning early, there came to us the same officer that came to us at first with his cane, and told us: "He came to conduct us to the strangers' house: and that he had prevented the hour, because we might have the whole day before us for our business. For (said he) if you will follow my advice, there shall first go with me some few of you, and see the place, and how it may be made convenient for you: and then you may send for your sick and the rest of your number, which ye will bring on land." We thanked him, and said, "That his care which he took of desolate strangers, God would reward." And so six of us went on land with him; and when we were on land, he went before us, and turned to us and said, "He was but our servant and our guide." He led us through three fair streets; and all the

way we went there were gathered some people on both
sides, standing in a row; but in so civil a fashion, as if
it had been, not to wonder at us, but to welcome us; and
divers of them, as we passed by them, put their arms
a little abroad, which is their gesture when they bid any
welcome. The strangers' house is a fair and spacious
house, built of brick, of somewhat a bluer color than our
brick; and with handsome windows, some of glass, some
of a kind of cambric oiled. He brought us first into
a fair parlor above stairs, and then asked us, "What
number of persons we were? and how many sick?"
We answered, "We were in all (sick and whole) one and
fifty persons, whereof our sick were seventeen." He desired us to have patience a little, and to stay till he came
back to us which was about an hour after; and then he
led us to see the chambers which were provided for us,
being in number nineteen. They having cast it (as it
seemeth) that four of those chambers, which were better
than the rest, might receive four of the principal men of
our company; and lodge them alone by themselves; and
the other fifteen chambers were to lodge us, two and two
together. The chambers were handsome and cheerful
chambers, and furnished civilly. Then he led us to a
long gallery like a dorture, where he showed us all along
the one side (for the other side was but wall and window)
seventeen cells, very neat ones, having partitions of cedar
wood. Which gallery and cells, being in all forty (many
more than we needed), were instituted as an infirmary
for sick persons. And he told us withal, that as any of
our sick waxed well, he might be removed from his cell
to a chamber: for which purpose there were set forth
ten spare chambers, besides the number we spake of before. This done, he brought us back to the parlor, and
lifting up his cane a little (as they do when they give
and charge or command), said to us, "Ye are to know
that the custom of the land requireth, that after this day
and to-morrow (which we give you for removing your
people from your ship), you are to keep within doors for
three days. But let it not trouble you, nor do not think
yourselves restrained, but rather left to your rest and
ease. You shall want nothing; and there are six of our

people appointed to attend you for any business you may
have abroad." We gave him thanks with all affection
and respect, and said, "God surely is manifested in this
land." We offered him also twenty pistolets, but he
smiled and only said: "What? Twice paid!" And so
he left us. Soon after our dinner was served; in which
was right good viands, both for bread and meat; better
than any collegiate diet that I have known in Europe.
We had also drink of three sorts, all wholesome and
good; wine of the grape; a drink of grain, such as
is with us our ale, but more clear; and a kind of cider
made of a fruit of that country; a wonderful pleasing
and refreshing drink. Besides, there were brought in to
us great store of those scarlet oranges for our sick; which
(they said) were an assured remedy for sickness taken
at sea. There was given us also a box of small grey or
whitish pills, which they wished our sick should take,
one of the pills every night before sleep; which (they
said) would hasten their recovery. The next day, after
that our trouble of carriage and removing of our men
and goods out of our ship was somewhat settled and
quiet, I thought good to call our company together, and
when they were assembled, said unto them, "My dear
friends, let us know ourselves, and how it standeth with
us. We are men cast on land, as Jonas was out of the
whale's belly, when we were as buried in the deep; and
now we are on land, we are but between death and life,
for we are beyond both the old world and the new; and
whether ever we shall see Europe, God only knoweth.
It is a kind of miracle hath brought us hither, and it
must be little less that shall bring us hence. Therefore
in regard of our deliverance past, and our danger present and to come, let us look up to God, and every man
reform his own ways. Besides we are come here among
a Christian people, full of piety and humanity. Let us
not bring that confusion of face upon ourselves, as to
show our vices or unworthiness before them. Yet there
is more, for they have by commandment (though in form
of courtesy) cloistered us within these walls for three
days; who knoweth whether it be not to take some taste
of our manners and conditions? And if they find them bad,

to banish us straightway; if good, to give us further time.
For these men that they have given us for attendance,
may withal have an eye upon us. Therefore, for God's
love, and as we love the weal of our souls and bodies,
let us so behave ourselves, as we may be at peace with
God, and may find grace in the eyes of this people."
Our company with one voice thanked me for my good
admonition, and promised me to live soberly and civilly,
and without giving any the least occasion of offense. So
we spent our three days joyfully, and without care, in
expectation what would be done with us when they were
expired. During which time, we had every hour joy of
the amendment of our sick, who thought themselves cast
into some divine pool of healing, they mended so kindly
and so fast.

The morrow after our three days were past, there came
to us a new man, that we had not seen before, clothed
in blue as the former was, save that his turban was
white with a small red cross on the top. He had
also a tippet of fine linen. At his coming in, he did
bend to us a little, and put his arms abroad. We of our
parts saluted him in a very lowly and submissive manner; as looking that from him we should receive sentence
of life or death. He desired to speak with some few of us.
Whereupon six of us only stayed, and the rest avoided
the room. He said, "I am by office governor of this
house of strangers, and by vocation I am a Christian
priest; and therefore am come to you, to offer you my
service, both as strangers, and chiefly as Christians. Some
things I may tell you, which I think you will not be
unwilling to hear. The state hath given you license to
stay on land for the space of six weeks : and let it not
trouble you, if your occasions ask further time, for the
law in this point is not precise; and I do not doubt, but
myself shall be able to obtain for you such further time
as shall be convenient. Ye shall also understand, that
the strangers' house is at this time rich, and much afore-
hand; for it hath laid up revenue these thirty-seven years;
for so long it is since any stranger arrived in this part;
and therefore take ye no care; the state will defray you
all the time you stay. Neither shall you stay one day

16

the less for that. As for any merchandise you have brought, ye shall be well used, and have your return, either in merchandise or in gold and silver; for to us it is all one. And if you have any other request to make, hide it not; for ye shall find we will not make your countenance to fall by the answer ye shall receive. Only this I must tell you, that none of you must go above a karan (that is with them a mile and a half) from the walls of the city, without special leave." We answered, after we had looked a while upon one another, admiring this gracious and parent-like usage, that we could not tell what to say, for we wanted words to express our thanks; and his noble, free offers left us nothing to ask. It seemed to us, that we had before us a picture of our salvation in heaven; for we that were a while since in the jaws of death, were now brought into a place where we found nothing but consolations. For the commandment laid upon us, we would not fail to obey it, though it was impossible but our hearts should be inflamed to tread further upon this happy and holy ground. We added, that our tongues should first cleave to the roofs of our mouths, ere we should forget, either this reverend person, or this whole nation, in our prayers. We also most humbly besought him to accept of us as his true servants, by as just a right as ever men on earth were bounden; laying and presenting both our persons and all we had at his feet. He said, he was a priest and looked for a priest's reward; which was our brotherly love, and the good of our souls and bodies. So he went from us, not without tears of tenderness in his eyes, and left us also confused with joy and kindness, saying among ourselves, that we were come into a land of angels, which did appear to us daily and present us with comforts, which we thought not of, much less expected.

The next day, about ten of the clock, the governor came to us again, and after salutations, said familiarly, that he was come to visit us; and called for a chair, and sat him down; and we being some ten of us (the rest were of the meaner sort, or else gone abroad), sat down with him; and when we were set, he began thus: "We of this island of Bensalem (for so they called it in their language) have this: that by means of our solitary situation, and of the laws of secrecy, which we have for our travelers, and our rare admission of strangers; we know well most part of the habitable world, and are ourselves unknown. Therefore because he that knoweth least is fittest to ask questions, it is more reason, for the entertainment of the time, that ye ask me questions, than that I ask you." We answered, that we humbly thanked him, that he would give us leave so to do. And that we conceived by the taste we had already, that there was no worldly thing on earth more worthy to be known than the state of that happy land. But above all (we said) since that we were met from the several ends of the world, and hoped assuredly that we should meet one day in the kingdom of heaven (for that we were both parts Christians), we desired to know (in respect that land was so remote, and so divided by vast and unknown seas from the land where our Savior walked on earth) who was the apostle of that nation, and how it was converted to the faith? It appeared in his face, that he took great contentment in this our question; he said, "Ye knit my heart to you, by asking this question in the first place: for it showeth that you first seek the kingdom of heaven: and I shall gladly, and briefly, satisfy your demand.

"About twenty years after the ascension of our Savior it came to pass, that there was seen by the people of Renfusa (a city upon the eastern coast of our island, within sight, the night was cloudy and calm), as it might be some mile in the sea, a great pillar of light; not sharp, but in form of a column, or cylinder, rising from the sea, a great way up toward heaven; and on the top of it was seen a large cross of light, more bright and resplendent than the body of the pillar. Upon which so strange a spectacle, the people of the city gathered apace together upon the sands, to wonder; and so after put themselves into a number of small boats to go nearer to this marvelous sight. But when the boats were come within about sixty yards of the pillar, they found themselves all bound, and could go no further, yet so as they might move to go about, but might not approach nearer;

so as the boats stood all as in a theater, beholding this light, as an heavenly sign. It so fell out, that there was in one of the boats one of the wise men of the Society of Salomon's House; which house or college, my good brethren, is the very eye of this kingdom, who having a while attentively and devoutly viewed and contemplated this pillar and cross, fell down upon his face; and then raised himself upon his knees, and lifting up his hands to heaven, made his prayers in this manner:

"'Lord God of heaven and earth; thou hast vouchsafed of thy grace, to those of our order to know thy works of creation, and true secrets of them; and to discern (as far as appertaineth to the generations of men) between divine miracles, works of Nature, works of art and impostures, and illusions of all sorts. I do here acknowledge and testify before this people, that the thing we now see before our eyes, is thy finger, and a true miracle. And forasmuch as we learn in our books, that thou never workest miracles, but to a divine and excellent end (for the laws of Nature are thine own laws, and thou exceedest them not but upon great cause), we most humbly beseech thee to prosper this great sign, and to give us the interpretation and use of it in mercy; which thou dost in some part secretly promise, by sending it unto us.'

"When he had made his prayer, he presently found the boat he was in movable and unbound; whereas all the rest remained still fast; and taking that for an assurance of leave to approach, he caused the boat to be softly and with silence rowed toward the pillar; but ere he came near it, the pillar and cross of light broke up, and cast itself abroad, as it were into a firmament of many stars, which also vanished soon after, and there was nothing left to be seen but a small ark, or chest of cedar, dry and not wet at all with water, though it swam; and in the fore end of it, which was toward him, grew a small green branch of palm; and when the wise man had taken it with all reverence into his boat, it opened of itself, and there were found in it a book and a letter, both written in fine parchment, and wrapped in sindons of linen. The book contained all the canonical books of the Old and

New Testament, according as you have them (for we know well what the churches with you receive), and the Apocalypse itself; and some other books of the New Testament, which were not at that time written, were nevertheless in the book. And for the letter, it was in these words:

" 'I Bartholomew, a servant of the Highest, and apostle of Jesus Christ, was warned by an angel that appeared to me in a vision of glory, that I should commit this ark to the floods of the sea. Therefore I do testify and declare unto that people where God shall ordain this ark to come to land, that in the same day is come unto them salvation and peace, and good will from the Father, and from the Lord Jesus.'

" There was also in both these writings, as well the book as the letter, wrought a great miracle, conform to that of the apostles, in the original gift of tongues. For there being at that time, in this land, Hebrews, Persians, and Indians, besides the natives, every one read upon the book and letter, as if they had been written in his own language. And thus was this land saved from infidelity (as the remain of the old world was from water) by an ark, through the apostolical and miraculous evangelism of St. Bartholomew." And here he paused, and a messenger came, and called him forth from us. So this was all that passed in that conference.

The next day, the same governor came again to us, immediately after dinner, and excused himself, saying, " That the day before he was called from us somewhat abruptly, but now he would make us amends, and spend time with us, if we held his company and conference agreeable." We answered, that we held it so agreeable and pleasing to us, as we forgot both dangers past, and fears to come, for the time we heard him speak; and that we thought an hour spent with him was worth years of our former life. He bowed himself a little to us, and after we were set again, he said, " Well, the questions are on your part." One of our number said, after a little pause, that there was a matter we were no less desirous to know than fearful to ask, lest we might presume too far. But encouraged by his rare humanity toward us (that could

scarce think ourselves strangers, being his vowed and pro-
fessed servants), we would take the hardness to propound
it; humbly beseeching him, if he thought it not fit to be
answered, that he would pardon it, though he rejected it.
We said, we well observed those his words, which he
formerly spake, that this happy island, where we now
stood, was known to few, and yet knew most of the
nations of the world, which we found to be true, consid-
ering they had the languages of Europe, and knew much
of our state and business; and yet we in Europe (notwithstanding all the remote discoveries and navigations
of this last age) never heard any of the least inkling or
glimpse of this island. This we found wonderful strange;
for that all nations have interknowledge one of another,
either by voyage into foreign parts, or by strangers that
come to them; and though the traveler into a foreign
country doth commonly know more by the eye than he
that stayeth at home can by relation of the traveler: yet
both ways suffice to make a mutual knowledge, in some
degree, on both parts. But for this island, we never
heard tell of any ship of theirs, that had been seen to
arrive upon any shore of Europe; no, nor of either the
East or West Indies, nor yet of any ship of any other
part of the world, that had made return for them. And
yet the marvel rested not in this. For the situation of
it (as his lordship said) in the secret conclave of such a
vast sea might cause it. But then, that they should have
knowledge of the languages, books, affairs, of those that
lie such a distance from them, it was a thing we could
not tell what to make of; for that it seemed to us a condition and propriety of divine powers and beings, to be
hidden and unseen to others, and yet to have others
open, and as in a light to them. At this speech the governor gave a gracious smile and said, that we did well
to ask pardon for this question we now asked, for that
it imported, as if we thought this land a land of ma-
gicians, that sent forth spirits of the air into all parts,
to bring them news and intelligence of other countries.
It was answered by us all, in all possible humbleness,
but yet with a countenance taking knowledge, that we
knew that he spake it but merrily. That we were apt

enough to think, there was somewhat supernatural in this island, but yet rather as angelical than magical. But to let his lordship know truly what it was that made us tender and doubtful to ask this question, it was not any such conceit, but because we remembered he had given a touch in his former speech, that this land had laws of secrecy touching strangers. To this he said, "You remember it aright; and therefore in that I shall say to you, I must reserve some particulars, which it is not lawful for me to reveal, but there will be enough left to give you satisfaction.

"You shall understand (that which perhaps you will scarce think credible) that about three thousand years ago, or somewhat more, the navigation of the world (especially for remote voyages) was greater than at this day. Do not think with yourselves, that I know not how much it is increased with you, within these threescore years; I know it well, and yet I say, greater then than now; whether it was, that the example of the ark, that saved the remnant of men from the universal deluge, gave men confidence to adventure upon the waters, or what it was; but such is the truth. The Phœnicians, and especially the Tyrians, had great fleets; so had the Carthaginians their colony, which is yet farther west. Toward the east the shipping of Egypt, and of Palestine, was likewise great. China also, and the great Atlantis (that you call America), which have now but junks and canoes, abounded then in tall ships. This island (as appeareth by faithful registers of those times) had then fifteen hundred strong ships, of great content. Of all this there is with you sparing memory, or none; but we have large knowledge thereof.

"At that time, this land was known and frequented by the ships and vessels of all the nations before named. And (as it cometh to pass) they had many times men of other countries, that were no sailors, that came with them; as Persians, Chaldeans, Arabians, so as almost all nations of might and fame resorted hither; of whom we have some stirps and little tribes with us at this day. And for our own ships, they went sundry voyages, as well to your straits, which you call the Pillars of Hercules, as to other parts in the Atlantic and Mediterranean Seas; as to Paguin (which is the same with Cambalaine) and Quinzy, upon the Oriental Seas, as far as to the borders of the East Tartary.

"At the same time, and an age after or more, the inhabitants of the great Atlantis did flourish. For though the narration and description which is made by a great man with you, that the descendants of Neptune planted there, and of the magnificent temple, palace, city and hill; and the manifold streams of goodly navigable rivers, which as so many chains environed the same site and temple; and the several degrees of ascent, whereby men did climb up to the same, as if it had been a Scala Cœli; be all poetical and fabulous; yet so much is true, that the said country of Atlantis, as well as that of Peru, then called Coya, as that of Mexico, then named Tyrambel, were mighty and proud kingdoms, in arms, shipping, and riches; so mighty, as at one time, or at least within the space of ten years, they both made two great expeditions: they of Tyrambel through the Atlantic to the Mediterranean Sea; and they of Coya, through the South Sea upon this our island; and for the former of these, which was into Europe, the same author among you, as it seemeth, had some relation from the Egyptian priest, whom he citeth. For assuredly, such a thing there was. But whether it were the ancient Athenians that had the glory of the repulse and resistance of those forces, I can say nothing; but certain it is there never came back either ship or man from that voyage. Neither had the other voyage of those of Coya upon us had better fortune, if they had not met with enemies of greater clemency. For the king of this island, by name Altabin, a wise man and a great warrior, knowing well both his own strength and that of his enemies, handled the matter so, as he cut off their land forces from their ships, and entoiled both their navy and their camp with a greater power than theirs, both by sea and land; and compelled them to render themselves without striking a stroke; and after they were at his mercy, contenting himself only with their oath, that they should no more bear arms against him, dismissed them all in safety. But the divine

revenge overtook not long after those proud enterprises.
For within less than the space of one hundred years the
Great Atlantis was utterly lost and destroyed; not by a
great earthquake, as your man saith, for that whole tract
is little subject to earthquakes, but by a particular deluge, or inundation; those countries having at this day
far greater rivers, and far higher mountains, to pour
down waters, than any part of the old world. But it is
true that the same inundation was not deep, not past
forty foot, in most places, from the ground, so that
although it destroyed man and beast generally, yet some
few wild inhabitants of the wood escaped. Birds also
were saved by flying to the high trees and woods. For
as for men, although they had buildings in many places
higher than the depth of the water, yet that inundation,
though it were shallow, had a long continuance, whereby
they of the vale that were not drowned perished for
want of food and other things necessary. So as marvel
you not at the thin population of America, nor at the
rudeness and ignorance of the people; for you must account your inhabitants of America as a young people,
younger a thousand years at the least than the rest of
the world, for that there was so much time between the
universal flood and their particular inundation. For
the poor remnant of human seed which remained in their
mountains, peopled the country again slowly, by little
and little, and being simple and a savage people (not
like Noah and his sons, which was the chief family of
the earth), they were not able to leave letters, arts, and
civility to their posterity; and having likewise in their
mountainous habitations been used, in respect of the extreme cold of those regions, to clothe themselves with
the skins of tigers, bears, and great hairy goats, that
they have in those parts; when after they came down
into the valley, and found' the intolerable heats which
are there, and knew no means of lighter apparel, they
were forced to begin the custom of going naked, which
continueth at this day. Only they take great pride and
delight in the feathers of birds, and this also they took
from those their ancestors of the mountains, who were
invited unto it, by the infinite flight of birds, that came

up to the high grounds, while the waters stood below. So you see, by this main accident of time, we lost our traffic with the Americans, with whom of all others, in regard they lay nearest to us, we had most commerce. As for the other parts of the world, it is most manifest that in the ages following (whether it were in respect of wars, or by a natural revolution of time) navigation did everywhere greatly decay, and specially far voyages (the rather by the use of galleys, and such vessels as could hardly brook the ocean) were altogether left and omitted. So then, that part of intercourse which could be from other nations, to sail to us, you see how it hath long since ceased; except it were by some rare accident, as this of yours. But now of the cessation of that other part of intercourse, which might be by our sailing to other nations, I must yield you some other cause. For I cannot say, if I shall say truly, but our shipping for num-ber, strength, mariners, pilots, and all things that ap-pertain to navigation, is as great as ever; and therefore why we should sit at home, I shall now give you an ac-count by itself; and it will draw nearer, to give you satisfaction, to your principal question.

"There reigned in this island, about 1,900 years ago, a king, whose memory of all others we most adore; not superstitiously, but as a divine instrument, though a mortal man: his name was Salomona; and we esteem him as the lawgiver of our nation. This king had a large heart, inscrutable for good; and was wholly bent to make his kingdom and people happy. He therefore taking into consideration how sufficient and substantive this land was, to maintain itself without any aid at all of the foreigner; being 5,000 miles in circuit, and of rare fertility of soil, in the greatest part thereof; and finding also the shipping of this country might be plentifully set on work, both by fishing and by transportations from port to port, and likewise by sailing unto some small islands that are not far from us, and are under the crown and laws of this state; and recalling into his memory the happy and flourishing estate wherein this land then was, so as it might be a thousand ways altered to the worse, but scarce any one way to the better; though

nothing wanted to his noble and heroical intentions, but
only (as far as human foresight might reach) to give
perpetuity to that which was in his time so happily
established, therefore among his other fundamental
laws of this kingdom he did ordain the interdicts and
prohibitions which we have touching entrance of
strangers; which at that time (though it was after the
calamity of America) was frequent; doubting novelties
and commixture of manners. It is true, the like law
against the admission of strangers without license is an
ancient law in the kingdom of China, and yet continued
in use. But there it is a poor thing; and hath made
them a curious, ignorant, fearful foolish nation. But
our lawgiver made his law of another temper. For first,
he hath preserved all points of humanity, in taking order
and making provision for the relief of strangers distressed; whereof you have tasted." At which speech
(as reason was) we all rose up, and bowed ourselves.
He went on: "That king also still desiring to join
humanity and policy together; and thinking it against
humanity, to detain strangers here against their wills;
and against policy, that they should return, and discover
their knowledge of this estate, he took this course; he
did ordain, that of the strangers that should be permitted
to land, as many at all times might depart as many
as would; but as many as would stay, should have
very good conditions, and means to live from the state.
Wherein he saw so far, that now in so many ages since
the prohibition, we have memory not of one ship that
ever returned, and but of thirteen persons only, at
several times, that chose to return in our bottoms. What
those few that returned may have reported abroad, I
know not. But you must think, whatsoever they have
said, could be taken where they came but for a dream.
Now for our traveling from hence into parts abroad,
our lawgiver thought fit altogether to restrain it. So is
it not in China. For the Chinese sail where they will,
or can; which showeth, that their law of keeping out
strangers is a law of pusillanimity and fear. But this
restraint of ours hath one only exception, which is admirable; preserving the good which cometh by communi-

cating with strangers, and avoiding the hurt: and I will now open it to you. And here I shall seem a little to digress, but you will by-and-by find it pertinent. Ye shall understand, my dear friends, that among the excellent acts of that king, one above all hath the pre-eminence. It was the erection and institution of an order, or society, which we call Salomon's House; the noblest foundation, as we think, that ever was upon the earth, and the lantern of this kingdom. It is dedicated to the study of the works and creatures of God. Some think it beareth the founder's name a little corrupted, as if it should be Solomon's House. But the records write it as it is spoken. So as I take it to be de-nominate of the king of the Hebrews, which is famous with you and no strangers to us; for we have some parts of his works which with you are lost; namely, that natural history which he wrote of all plants, from the cedar of Libanus to the moss that groweth out of the wall; and of all things that have life and motion. This maketh me think that our king finding himself to symbolize, in many things, with that king of the Hebrews, which lived many years before him, honored him with the title of this foun-dation. And I am the rather induced to be of this opinion, for that I find in ancient records, this order or society is sometimes called Solomon's House, and sometimes the College of the Six Days' Works; whereby I am satisfied that our excellent king had learned from the Hebrews that God had created the world, and all that therein is, within six days: and therefore he instituted that house, for the finding out of the true nature of all things, whereby God might have the more glory in the work-manship of them, and men the more fruit in their use of them, did give it also that second name. But now to come to our present purpose. When the king had for-bidden to all his people navigation into any part that was not under his crown, he made, nevertheless, this ordinance; that every twelve years there should be set forth out of this kingdom, two ships, appointed to several voyages; that in either of these ships there should be a mission of three of the fellows or brethren of Salomon's House, whose errand was only to give us knowledge of the affairs

and state of those countries to which they were designed;
and especially of the sciences, arts, manufactures, and
inventions of all the world; and withal to bring unto us
books, instruments, and patterns in every kind: that the
ships, after they had landed the brethren, should return;
and that the brethren should stay abroad till the new
mission, the ships are not otherwise fraught than with
store of victuals, and good quantity of treasure to remain
with the brethren, for the buying of such things, and
rewarding of such persons, as they should think fit. Now
for me to tell you how the vulgar sort of mariners are
contained from being discovered at land, and how they
that must be put on shore for any time, color themselves
under the names of other nations, and to what places
these voyages have been designed; and what places of
rendezvous are appointed for the new missions, and the
like circumstances of the practice, I may not do it, neither
is it much to your desire. But thus you see we maintain a
trade, not for gold, silver, or jewels, nor for silks, nor
for spices, nor any other commodity of matter; but only
for God's first creature, which was light; to have light, I
say, of the growth of all parts of the world." And when
he had said this, he was silent, and so were we all; for
indeed we were all astonished to hear so strange things
so probably told. And he perceiving that we were willing
to say somewhat, but had it not ready, in great courtesy
took us off, and descended to ask us questions of our
voyage and fortunes, and in the end concluded that we
might do well to think with ourselves, what time of stay
we would demand of the state, and bade us not to scant
ourselves; for he would procure such time as we desired.
Whereupon we all rose up and presented ourselves to kiss
the skirt of his tippet, but he would not suffer us, and so
took his leave. But when it came once among our
people, that the state used to offer conditions to strangers
that would stay, we had work enough to get any of our
men to look to our ship, and to keep them from going
presently to the governor, to crave conditions; but with
much ado we restrained them, till we might agree what
course to take.

We took ourselves now for freemen, seeing there was

no danger of our utter perdition, and lived most joyfully,
going abroad and seeing what was to be seen in the city
and places adjacent, within our tedder; and obtaining
acquaintance with many of the city, not of the meanest
quality, at whose hands we found such humanity, and
such a freedom and desire to take strangers, as it were,
into their bosom, as was enough to make us forget all
that was dear to us in our own countries: and continually we met with many things, right worthy of observation and relation; as indeed, if there be a mirror in the
world, worthy to hold men's eyes, it is that country.
One day there were two of our company bidden to a
feast of the family, as they call it; a most natural, pious,
and reverend custom it is, showing that nation to be
compounded of all goodness.   This is the manner of it:
it is granted to any man that shall live to see thirty
persons descended of his body, alive together, and all
above three years old, to make this feast, which is done
at the cost of the state.   The father of the family, whom
they call the Tirsan, two days before the feast, taketh
to him three of such friends as he liketh to choose, and
is assisted also by the governor of the city or place where
the feast is celebrated, and all the persons of the family,
of both sexes, are summoned to attend him.   These two
days the Tirsan sitteth in consultation, concerning the
good estate of the family.   There, if there be any dis-
cord or suits between any of the family, they are compounded and appeased.   There, if any of the family be
distressed or decayed, order is taken for their relief, and
competent means to live.   There, if any be subject to
vice, or take ill courses, they are reproved and censured.
So likewise direction is given touching marriages, and
the courses of life which any of them should take, with
divers other the like orders and advices.   The governor
assisteth to the end, to put into execution, by his public
authority, the decrees and orders of the Tirsan, if they
should be disobeyed, though that seldom needeth; such
reverence and obedience they give to the order of Nature.
The Tirsan doth also then ever choose one man from
among his sons, to live in house with him; who is
called ever after the Son of the Vine.   The reason will

hereafter appear. On the feast day, the father or Tirsan cometh forth after divine service into a large room where the feast is celebrated; which room hath an half-pace at the upper end. Against the wall, in the middle of the half-pace, is a chair placed for him, with a table and carpet before it. Over the chair is a state, made round or oval, and it is of ivy; an ivy somewhat whiter than ours, like the leaf of a silver asp, but more shining; for it is green all winter. And the state is curiously wrought with silver and silk of divers colors, broiding or binding in the ivy; and is ever of the work of some of the daughters of the family; and veiled over at the top, with a fine net of silk and silver. But the substance of it is true ivy; whereof after it is taken down, the friends of the family are desirous to have some leaf or sprig to keep. The Tirsan cometh forth with all his generation or lineage, the males before him, and the females following him; and if there be a mother, from whose body the whole lineage is descended, there is a traverse placed in a loft above on the right hand of the chair, with a privy door, and a carved window of glass, leaded with gold and blue; where she sitteth, but is not seen. When the Tirsan is come forth, he sitteth down in the chair; and all the lineage place themselves against the wall, both at his back, and upon the return of the half-pace, in order of their years, without difference of sex, and stand upon their feet. When he is set, the room being always full of company, but well kept and without disorder, after some pause there cometh in from the lower end of the room a Taratan (which is as much as an herald), and on either side of him two young lads: whereof one carrieth a scroll of their shining yellow parchment, and the other a cluster of grapes of gold, with a long foot or stalk. The herald and children are clothed with mantles of sea-water green satin; but the herald's mantle is streamed with gold, and hath a train. Then the herald with three curtsies, or rather inclinations, cometh up as far as the half-pace, and there first taketh into his hand the scroll. This scroll is the king's charter, containing gift of revenue, and many privileges, exemptions, and points of honor, granted to the father of the family, and it is ever styled and directed, "To such an one, our well-beloved friend and creditor," which is a title proper only to this case. For they say, the king is debtor to no man, but for propagation of his subjects; the seal set to the king's charter is the king's image, embossed or molded in gold; and though such charters be expedited of course, and as of right, yet they are varied by discretion, according to the number and dignity of the family. This charter the herald readeth aloud; and while it is read, the father or Tirsan standeth up, supported by two of his sons, such as he chooseth. Then the herald mounteth the half-pace, and delivereth the charter into his hand: and with that there is an acclamation, by all that are present, in their language, which is thus much, "Happy are the people of Bensalem." Then the herald taketh into his hand from the other child the cluster of grapes, which is of gold; both the stalk, and the grapes. But the grapes are daintily enameled; and if the males of the family be the greater number, the grapes are enameled purple, with a little sun set on the top; if the females, then they are enameled into a greenish yellow, with a crescent on the top. The grapes are in number as many as there are descendants of the family. This golden cluster the herald delivereth also to the Tirsan; who presently delivereth it over to that son that he had formerly chosen, to be in house with him; who beareth it before his father, as an ensign of honor, when he goeth in public ever after; and is thereupon called the Son of the Vine. After this ceremony endeth the father or Tirsan retireth; and after some time cometh forth again to dinner, where he sitteth alone under the state, as before; and none of his descendants sit with him, of what degree or dignity so ever, except he hap to be of Salomon's House. He is served only by his own children, such as are male; who perform unto him all service of the table upon the knee, and the women only stand about him, leaning against the wall. The room below his half-pace hath tables on the sides for the guests that are bidden; who are served with great and comely order; and toward the end of dinner (which in the greatest feasts with them lasteth never above an hour and a half) there

is an hymn sung, varied according to the invention of
him that composeth it (for they have excellent poesy),
but the subject of it is always the praises of Adam, and
Noah, and Abraham; whereof the former two peopled the
world, and the last was the father of the faithful: con-
cluding ever with a thanksgiving for the nativity of our
Savior, in whose birth the births of all are only blessed.
Dinner being done, the Tirsan retireth again; and having
withdrawn himself alone into a place, where he maketh
some private prayers, he cometh forth the third time, to
give the blessing; with all his descendants, who stand
about him as at the first. Then he calleth them forth by
one and by one, by name as he pleaseth, though seldom
the order of age be inverted. The person that is called
(the table being before removed) kneeleth down before the
chair, and the father layeth his hand upon his head, or
her head, and giveth the blessing in these words: "Son
of Bensalem (or daughter of Bensalem), thy father saith
it; the man by whom thou hast breath and life speaketh
the word; the blessing of the everlasting Father, the
Prince of Peace, and the Holy Dove be upon thee, and
make the days of thy pilgrimage good and many." This
he saith to every of them; and that done, if there be
any of his sons of eminent merit and virtue, so they be
not above two, he calleth for them again, and saith,
laying his arm over their shoulders, they standing: "Sons,
it is well you are born, give God the praise, and perse-
vere to the end." And withal delivereth to either of
them a jewel, made in the figure of an ear of wheat,
which they ever after wear in the front of their turban,
or hat; this done, they fall to music and dances, and
other recreations, after their manner, for the rest of the
day. This is the full order of that feast.

By that time six or seven days were spent, I was fallen
into straight acquaintance with a merchant of that city,
whose name was Joabin. He was a Jew and circumcised;
for they have some few stirps of Jews yet remaining
among them, whom they leave to their own religion.
Which they may the better do, because they are of a
far differing disposition from the Jews in other parts.
For whereas they hate the name of Christ, and have a

17

secret inbred rancor against the people among whom
they live; these, contrariwise, give unto our Savior many
high attributes, and love the nation of Bensalem extremely. Surely this man of whom I speak would ever
acknowledge that Christ was born of a Virgin; and that
he was more than a man; and he would tell how God
made him ruler of the seraphims, which guard his
throne; and they call him also the Milken Way, and the
Eliah of the Messiah, and many other high names,
which though they be inferior to his divine majesty, yet
they are far from the language of other Jews. And for
the country of Bensalem, this man would make no end
of commending it, being desirous by tradition among the
Jews there to have it believed that the people thereof
were of the generations of Abraham, by another son,
whom they call Nachoran; and that Moses by a secret
cabala ordained the laws of Bensalem which they now
use; and that when the Messias should come, and sit in
his throne at Hierusalem, the King of Bensalem should
sit at his feet, whereas other kings should keep a great
distance. But yet setting aside these Jewish dreams, the
man was a wise man and learned, and of great policy,
and excellently seen in the laws and customs of that nation. Among other discourses one day I told him, I
was much affected with the relation I had from some of
the company of their custom in holding the feast of the
family, for that, methought, I had never heard of a so-
lemnity wherein Nature did so much preside. And because propagation of families proceedeth from the nuptial
copulation, I desired to know of him what laws and customs they had concerning marriage, and whether they
kept marriage well, and whether they were tied to one
wife? For that where population is so much affected,
and such as with them it seemed to be, there is commonly permission of plurality of wives. To this he said:
" You have reason for to commend that excellent institution of the feast of the family; and indeed we have experience, that those families that are partakers of the
blessings of that feast, do flourish and prosper ever after,
in an extraordinary manner. But hear me now, and I
will tell you what I know. You shall understand that

there is not under the heavens so chaste a nation as this of Bensalem, nor so free from all pollution or foulness. It is the virgin of the world; I remember, I have read in one of your European books, of an holy hermit among you, that desired to see the spirit of fornication, and there appeared to him a little foul ugly Ethiope; but if he had desired to see the spirit of chastity of Bensalem, it would have appeared to him in the likeness of a fair beautiful cherubim. For there is nothing, among mortal men, more fair and admirable than the chaste minds of this people. Know, therefore, that with them there are no stews, no dissolute houses, no courtesans, nor anything of that kind. Nay, they wonder, with detestation, at you in Europe, which permit such things. They say ye have put marriage out of office; for marriage is ordained a remedy for unlawful concupiscence; and natural concupiscence seemeth as a spur to marriage. But when men have at hand a remedy, more agreeable to their corrupt will, marriage is almost expulsed. And therefore there are with you seen infinite men that marry not, but choose rather a libertine and impure single life, than to be yoked in marriage; and many that do marry, marry late, when the prime and strength of their years is past. And when they do marry, what is marriage to them but a very bargain; wherein is sought alliance, or portion, or reputation, with some desire (almost indifferent) of issue; and not the faithful nuptial union of man and wife, that was first instituted. Neither is it possible that those that have cast away so basely so much of their strength, should greatly esteem children (being of the same matter) as chaste men do. So likewise during marriage is the case much amended, as it ought to be if those things were tolerated only for necessity; no, but they remain still as a very affront to marriage. The haunting of those dissolute places, or resort to courtesans, are no more punished in married men than in bachelors. And the depraved custom of change, and the delight in meretricious embracements (where sin is turned into art), maketh marriage a dull thing, and a kind of imposition or tax. They hear you defend these things, as done to avoid greater evils; as advoutries, deflowering of virgins,

unnatural lust, and the like. But they say, this is a preposterous wisdom; and they call it Lot's offer, who to
save his guests from abusing, offered his daughters; nay,
they say further, that there is little gained in this; for
that the same vices and appetites do still remain and
abound, unlawful lust being like a furnace, that if you
stop the flames altogether it will quench, but if you
give it any vent it will rage; as for masculine love, they
have no touch of it; and yet there are not so faithful and
inviolate friendships in the world again as are there, and
to speak generally (as I said before) I have not read of
any such chastity in any people as theirs. And their usual
saying is that whosoever is unchaste cannot reverence himself; and they say that the reverence of a man's self, is,
next religion, the chiefest bridle of all vices." And when
he had said this the good Jew paused a little; whereupon
I, far more willing to hear him speak on than to speak myself; yet thinking it decent that upon his pause of speech
I should not be altogether silent, said only this; that I
would say to him, as the widow of Sarepta said to Elias:
"that he was come to bring to memory our sins"; and
that I confess the righteousness of Bensalem was greater
than the righteousness of Europe. At which speech he
bowed his head and went on in this manner: "They have
also many wise and excellent laws touching marriage.
They allow no polygamy. They have ordained that none
do intermarry, or contract, until a month be passed from
their first interview. Marriage without consent of parents they do not make void, but they mulct it in the in-
heritors; for the children of such marriages are not
admitted to inherit above a third part of their parents'
inheritance. I have read in a book of one of your men, of
a feigned commonwealth, where the married couple are
permitted, before they contract, to see one another naked.
This they dislike; for they think it a scorn to give a
refusal after so familiar knowledge; but because of many
hidden defects in men and women's bodies, they have a more
civil way; for they have near every town a couple of pools
(which they call Adam and Eve's pools), where it is permitted to one of the friends of the man, and another of the
friends of the woman, to see them severally bathe naked."

And as we were thus in conference, there came one
that seemed to be a messenger, in a rich huke, that
spake with the Jew; whereupon he turned to me and
said, "You will pardon me, for I am commanded away
in haste." The next morning he came to me again, joyful as it seemed and said, "There is word come to the
governor of the city, that one of the fathers of Salomon's
House will be here this day seven-night; we have seen
none of them this dozen years. His coming is in state;
but the cause of his coming is secret. I will provide you
and your fellows of a good standing to see his entry."
I thanked him, and told him I was most glad of the
news. The day being come he made his entry. He was
a man of middle stature and age, comely of person, and
had an aspect as if he pitied men. He was clothed in a
robe of fine black cloth with wide sleeves, and a cape;
his under garment was of excellent white linen down
to the foot, girt with a girdle of the same; and a sin-
don or tippet of the same about his neck. He had
gloves that were curious, and set with stone; and shoes
of peach-colored velvet. His neck was bare to the
shoulders. His hat was like a helmet, or Spanish mon-
tero; and his locks curled below it decently; they were of
color brown. His beard was cut round and of the same
color with his hair, somewhat lighter. He was carried in
a rich chariot, without wheels, litter-wise, with two horses
at either end, richly trapped in blue velvet embroidered;
and two footmen on each side in the like attire. The
chariot was all of cedar, gilt, and adorned with crystal;
save that the fore-end had panels of sapphires, set in
borders of gold, and the hinder-end the like of emeralds
of the Peru color. There was also a sun of gold, radiant
upon the top, in the midst; and on the top before a small
cherub of gold, with wings displayed. The chariot was
covered with cloth of gold tissued upon blue. He had
before him fifty attendants, young men all, in white satin
loose coats up to the mid-leg, and stockings of white silk;
and shoes of blue velvet; and hats of blue velvet, with
fine plumes of divers colors, set round like hatbands.
Next before the chariot went two men, bare-headed, in
linen garments down to the foot, girt, and shoes of blue

velvet, who carried the one a crosier, the other a pastoral staff like a sheephook; neither of them of metal, but the crosier of balm-wood, the pastoral staff of cedar. Horsemen he had none, neither before nor behind his chariot; as it seemeth, to avoid all tumult and trouble. Behind his chariot went all the officers and principals of the companies of the city. He sat alone, upon cushions, of a kind of excellent plush, blue; and under his foot curious carpets of silk of divers colors, like the Persian, but far finer. He held up his bare hand, as he went, as blessing the people, but in silence. The street was wonderfully well kept; so that there was never any army had their men stand in better battle-array than the people stood. The windows likewise were not crowded, but everyone stood in them, as if they had been placed. When the show was passed, the Jew said to me, "I shall not be able to attend you as I would, in regard of some charge the city hath laid upon me for the entertaining of this great person." Three days after the Jew came to me again, and said, "Ye are happy men; for the father of Salomon's House taketh knowledge of your being here, and commanded me to tell you, that he will admit all your company to his presence, and have private conference with one of you, that ye shall choose; and for this hath appointed the next day after to-morrow. And because he meaneth to give you his blessing, he hath appointed it in the forenoon." We came at our day and hour, and I was chosen by my fellows for the private access. We found him in a fair chamber, richly hanged, and carpeted under foot, without any degrees to the state; he was set upon a low throne richly adorned, and a rich cloth of state over his head of blue satin embroidered. He was alone, save that he had two pages of honor, on either hand one, finely attired in white. His under garments were the like that we saw him wear in the chariot; but instead of his gown, he had on him a mantle with a cape, of the same fine black, fastened about him. When we came in, as we were taught, we bowed low at our first entrance; and when we were come near his chair, he stood up, holding forth his hand ungloved, and in posture of blessing; and we every one of us stooped down, and kissed the end of his tippet. That done, the rest departed, and I remained. Then he warned the pages forth of the room, and caused me to sit down beside him, and spake to me thus in the Spanish tongue:—

"God bless thee, my son; I will give thee the greatest jewel I have. For I will impart unto thee, for the love of God and men, a relation of the true state of Salomon's House. Son, to make you know the true state of Salomon's House, I will keep this order. First, I will set forth unto you the end of our foundation. Secondly, the preparations and instruments we have for our works. Thirdly, the several employments and functions whereto our fellows are assigned. And fourthly, the ordinances and rites which we observe.

"The end of our foundation is the knowledge of causes, and secret motions of things; and the enlarging of the bounds of human empire, to the effecting of all things possible.

"The preparations and instruments are these. We have large and deep caves of several depths; the deepest are sunk 600 fathoms; and some of them are digged and made under great hills and mountains; so that if you reckon together the depth of the hill, and the depth of the cave, they are, some of them, above three miles deep. For we find that the depth of an hill, and the depth of a cave from the flat, is the same thing; both remote alike from the sun and heaven's beams, and from the open air. These caves we call the lower region. And we use them for all coagulations, indurations, refrigerations, and conservations of bodies. We use them likewise for the imitation of natural mines and the producing also of new artificial metals, by compositions and materials which we use and lay there for many years. We use them also sometimes (which may seem strange) for curing of some diseases, and for prolongation of life, in some hermits that choose to live there, well accommodated of all things necessary, and indeed live very long; by whom also we learn many things.

"We have burials in several earths, where we put divers cements, as the Chinese do their porcelain. But we have them in greater variety, and some of them more fine. We also have great variety of composts and soils, for the making of the earth fruitful.

"We have high towers, the highest about half a mile in height, and some of them likewise set upon high mountains, so that the vantage of the hill with the tower, is in the highest of them three miles at least. And these places we call the upper region, account the air between the high places and the low, as a middle region. We use these towers, according to their several heights and situations, for insulation, refrigeration, conservation, and for the view of divers meteors — as winds, rain, snow, hail; and some of the fiery meteors also. And upon them, in some places, are dwellings of hermits, whom we visit sometimes, and instruct what to observe.

"We have great lakes, both salt and fresh, whereof we have use for the fish and fowl. We use them also for burials of some natural bodies, for we find a difference in things buried in earth, or in air below the earth, and things buried in water. We have also pools, of which some do strain fresh water out of salt, and others by art do turn fresh water into salt. We have also some rocks in the midst of the sea, and some bays upon the shore for some works, wherein is required the air and vapor of the sea. We have likewise violent streams and cataracts, which serve us for many motions; and likewise engines for multiplying and enforcing of winds to set also on divers motions.

"We have also a number of artificial wells and fountains, made in imitation of the natural sources and baths, as tincted upon vitriol, sulphur, steel, brass, lead, niter, and other minerals; and again, we have little wells for infusions of many things; where the waters take the virtue quicker and better than in vessels or basins. And among them we have a water, which we call water of Paradise, being by that we do it made very sovereign for health and prolongation of life.

"We have also great and spacious houses, where we imitate and demonstrate meteors — as snow, hail, rain, some artificial rains of bodies, and not of water, thunders, lightnings; also generations of bodies in air — as frogs flies, and divers others.

"We have also certain chambers, which we call chambers of health, where we qualify the air as we think good and proper for the cure of divers diseases, and preservation of health.

"We have also fair and large baths, of several mixtures, for the cure of diseases, and the restoring of man's body from arefaction; and others for the confirming of it in strength of sinews, vital parts, and the very juice and substance of the body.

"We have also large and various orchards and gardens, wherein we do not so much respect beauty as variety of ground and soil, proper for divers trees and herbs, and some very spacious, where trees and berries are set, whereof we make divers kinds of drinks, besides the vineyards. In these we practice likewise all conclusions of grafting, and inoculating, as well of wild trees as fruit trees, which produceth many effects. And we make by art, in the same orchards and gardens, trees and flowers, to come earlier or later than their seasons, and to come up and bear more speedily than by their natural course they do. We make them also by art greater much than their nature; and their fruit greater and sweeter, and of different taste, smell, color, and figure, from their nature. And many of them we so order, as that they become of medicinal use.

"We have also means to make divers plants rise by mixtures of earths without seeds, and likewise to make divers new plants, differing from the vulgar, and to make one tree or plant turn into another.

"We have also parks, and inclosures of all sorts, of beasts and birds; which we use not only for view or rareness, but likewise for dissections and trials, that thereby may take light what may be wrought upon the body of man. Wherein we find many strange effects: as continuing life in them, though divers parts, which you account vital, be perished and taken forth; resuscitating of some that seem dead in appearance, and the like. We try also all poisons, and other medicines upon them, as well of chirurgery as physic. By art likewise we make them greater or smaller than their kind is, and contrariwise dwarf them and stay their growth; we make them more fruitful and bearing than their kind is, and contrariwise barren and not generative. Also we make them differ in color, shape, activity, many ways. We find means to make commixtures and copulations of divers kinds, which have produced many new kinds, and them not barren, as the general opinion is. We make a number of kinds of serpents, worms, flies, fishes of putrefaction, whereof some are advanced (in effect) to be perfect creatures, like beasts or birds, and have sexes, and do propagate. Neither do we this by chance, but we know beforehand of what matter and commixture, what kind of those creatures will arise.

"We have also particular pools where we make trials upon fishes, as we have said before of beasts and birds.

"We have also places for breed and generation of those kinds of worms and flies which are of special use; such as are with you your silkworms and bees.

"I will not hold you long with recounting of our brew-houses, bake-houses, and kitchens, where are made divers drinks, breads, and meats, rare and of special effects. Wines we have of grapes, and drinks of other juice, of fruits, of grains, and of roots, and of mixtures with honey, sugar, manna, and fruits dried and decocted; also of the tears or wounding of trees, and of the pulp of canes. And these drinks are of several ages, some to the age or last of forty years. We have drinks also brewed with several herbs, and roots, and spices; yea, with several fleshes, and white meats; whereof some of the drinks are such as they are in effect meat and drink both, so that divers, especially in age, do desire to live with them with little or no meat or bread. And above all we strive to have drinks of extreme thin parts, to insinuate into the body, and yet without all biting, sharpness, or fretting; insomuch as some of them put upon the back of your hand, will with a little stay pass through to the palm, and yet taste mild to the mouth. We have also waters, which we ripen in that fashion, as they become nourishing, so that they are indeed excellent drinks, and many will use no other. Bread we have of several grains, roots, and kernels; yea, and some of flesh, and fish, dried, with divers kinds of leavings and seasonings; so that some do extremely move appetites, some do nourish so, as divers do live of them, without any other meat, who live very long. So for meats, we have some of them so beaten and made tender, and mortified, yet without all corrupting, as a weak heat of the stomach will turn them into good chilus, as well as a strong heat would meat otherwise prepared. We have some meats also and bread, and drinks, which taken by men, enable them to fast long after; and some other, that used make the very flesh of men's bodies sensibly more hard and tough, and their strength far greater than otherwise it would be.

"We have dispensatories or shops of medicines; wherein you may easily think, if we have such variety of plants, and living creatures, more than you have in Europe (for we know what you have), the simples, drugs, and ingredients of medicines, must likewise be in so much the greater variety. We have them likewise of divers ages, and long fermentations. And for their preparations, we have not only all manner of exquisite distillations, and separations, and especially by gentle heats, and percolations through divers strainers, yea, and substances; but also exact forms of composition, whereby they incorporate almost as they were natural simples.

"We have also divers mechanical arts, which you have not; and stuffs made by them, as papers, linen, silks, tissues, dainty works of feathers of wonderful luster, excellent dyes, and many others, and shops likewise as well for such as are not brought into vulgar use among us, as for those that are. For you must know, that of the things before recited, many of them are grown into use throughout the kingdom, but yet, if they did flow from our invention, we have of them also for patterns and principles.

"We have also furnaces of great diversities, and that keep great diversity of heats; fierce and quick, strong and constant, soft and mild, blown, quiet, dry, moist, and the like. But above all we have heats, in imitation of the sun's and heavenly bodies' heats, that pass divers inequalities, and as it were orbs, progresses, and returns whereby we produce admirable effects. Besides, we have heats of dungs, and of bellies and maws of living creatures and of their bloods and bodies, and of hays and herbs laid up moist, of lime unquenched, and such like. Instruments also which generate heat only by motion. And further, places for strong insulations; and again, places under the earth, which by nature or art yield heat. These divers heats we use, as the nature of the operation which we intend requireth.

"We have also perspective-houses, where we make demonstrations of all lights and radiations, and of all colors; and out of things uncolored and transparent, we can represent unto you all several colors, not in rainbows, as it is in gems and prisms, but of themselves single. We represent also all multiplications of light, which we carry to great distance, and make so sharp, as to discern small points and lines. Also all colorations of light: all delusions and deceits of the sight, in figures, magnitudes, motions, colors; all demonstrations of shadows. We find also divers means, yet unknown to you, of producing of light, originally from divers bodies. We procure means of seeing objects afar off, as in the heaven and remote places; and represent things near as afar off, and things afar off as near; making feigned distances. We have also helps for the sight far above spectacles and glasses in use; we have also glasses and means to see small and minute bodies, perfectly and distinctly; as the shapes and colors of small flies and worms, grains, and flaws in gems which cannot otherwise be seen, observations in urine and blood not otherwise to be seen. We make artificial rainbows, halos, and circles about light. We represent also all manner of reflections, refractions, and multiplications of visual beams of objects.

"We have also precious stones, of all kinds, many of them of great beauty and to you unknown; crystals likewise, and glasses of divers kind; and among them some of metals vitrificated, and other materials, besides those of which you make glass. Also a number of fossils, and imperfect minerals, which you have not. Likewise loadstones of prodigious virtue: and other rare stones, both natural and artificial.

"We have also sound-houses, where we practice and demonstrate all sounds and their generation. We have harmony which you have not, of quarter sounds and lesser slides of sounds. Divers instruments of music likewise to you unknown, some sweeter than any you have; with bells and rings that are dainty and sweet. We represent small sounds as great and deep, likewise great sounds, extenuate and sharp; we make divers tremblings and warblings of sounds, which in their original are entire. We represent and imitate all articulate sounds and letters, and the voices and notes of beasts and birds. We have certain helps, which set to the ear do further the hearing greatly; we have also divers strange and artificial echoes, reflecting the voice many times, and as it were tossing it; and some that give back the voice louder than it came, some shriller and some deeper; yea, some rendering the voice, differing in the letters or articulate sound from that they receive. We have all means to convey sounds in trunks and pipes, in strange lines and distances.

"We have also perfume-houses, wherewith we join also practices of taste. We multiply smells which may seem strange: we imitate smells, making all smells to breathe out of other mixtures than those that give them. We make divers imitations of taste likewise, so that they will deceive any man's taste. And in this house we contain also a confiture-house, where we make all sweetmeats, dry and moist, and divers pleasant wines, milks, broths, and salads, far in greater variety than you have.

"We have also engine-houses, where are prepared engines and instruments for all sorts of motions. There we imitate and practice to make swifter motions than any you have, either out of your muskets or any engine that you have; and to make them and multiply them more easily and with small force, by wheels and other means, and to make them stronger and more violent than yours are, exceeding your greatest cannons and basilisks. We represent also ordnance and instruments of war and engines of all kinds; and likewise new mixtures and compositions of gunpowder, wildfires burning in water and unquenchable, also fireworks of all variety, both for pleasure and use. We imitate also flights of birds; we have some degrees of flying in the air. We have ships and boats for going under water and brooking of seas, also swimming-girdles and supporters. We have divers curious clocks and other like motions of return, and some perpetual motions. We imitate also motions of living creatures by images of men, beasts, birds, fishes, and serpents; we have also a great number of other various motions, strange for equality, fineness and subtilty.

"We have also a mathematical-house, where are represented all instruments, as well of geometry as astronomy, exquisitely made.

"We have also houses of deceits of the senses, where we represent all manner of feats of juggling, false apparitions, impostures and illusions, and their fallacies. And surely you will easily believe that we, that have so many things truly natural which induce admiration, could in a world of particulars deceive the senses if we would disguise those things, and labor to make them more miraculous. But we do hate all impostures, and lies, insomuch as we have severely forbidden it to all our fellows, under pain of ignominy and fines, that they do not show any natural work or thing adorned or swelling, but only pure as it is, and without all affectation of strangeness.

"These are, my son, the riches of Salomon's House.

"For the several employments and offices of our fellows, we have twelve that sail into foreign countries under the names of other nations (for our own we conceal), who bring us the books and abstracts, and patterns of experiments of all other parts. These we call merchants of light.

"We have three that collect the experiments which are in all books. These we call deprepators.

"We have three that collect the experiments of all mechanical arts, and also of liberal sciences, and also of practices which are not brought into arts. These we call mystery-men.

"We have three that try new experiments.

"Such as themselves think good. These we call pioneers or miners.

"We have three that draw the experiments of the former four into titles and tables, to give the better light for the drawing of observations and axioms out of them. These we call compilers. We have three that bend themselves, looking into the experiments of their fellows, and cast about how to draw out of them things of use and practice for man's life and knowledge, as well for works as for plain demonstration of causes, means of natural divinations, and the easy and clear discovery of the virtues and parts of bodies. These we call dowry-men or benefactors.

"Then after divers meetings and consults of our whole number, to consider of the former labors and collections, we have three that take care out of them to direct new experiments, of a higher light, more penetrating into Nature than the former. These we call lamps.

"We have three others that do execute the experiments so directed, and report them. These we call inoculators.

"Lastly, we have three that raise the former discoveries by experiments into greater observations, axioms, and aphorisms. These we call interpreters of Nature.

"We have also, as you must think, novices and apprentices, that the succession of the former employed men do not fail; besides a great number of servants and attendants, men and women. And this we do also: we have consultations, which of the inventions and experiences which we have discovered shall be published, and which not: and take all an oath of secrecy for the concealing of those which we think fit to keep secret: though some of those we do reveal sometime to the state, and some not.

"For our ordinances and rites, we have two very long and fair galleries: in one of these we place patterns and samples of all manner of the more rare and excellent inventions: in the other we place the statues of all principal inventors. There we have the statue of your Columbus, that discovered the West Indies: also the inventor of ships: your Monk that was the inventor of ordnance and of gunpowder: the inventor of music: the inventor of letters: the inventor of printing: the inventor of observations of astronomy: the inventor of works in metal: the inventor of glass: the inventor of silk of the worm: the inventor of wine: the inventor of corn and bread: the inventor of sugars; and all these by more certain tradition than you have.   Then we have divers inventors of our own, of excellent works; which since you have not seen, it were too long to make descriptions of them; and besides, in the right understanding of those descriptions you might easily err.   For upon every invention of value we erect a statue to the inventor, and give him a liberal and honorable reward.   These statues are some of brass, some of marble and touchstone, some of cedar and other special woods gilt and adorned; some of iron, some of silver, some of gold.

"We have certain hymns and services, which we say daily, of laud and thanks to God for his marvelous works. And forms of prayers, imploring his aid and blessing for the illumination of our labors; and turning them into good and holy uses.

"Lastly, we have circuits or visits, of divers principal cities of the kingdom; where as it cometh to pass we do publish such new profitable inventions as we think good. And we do also declare natural divinations of diseases, plagues, swarms of hurtful creatures, scarcity, tempest, earthquakes, great inundations, comets, temperature of the year and divers other things; and we give counsel thereupon, what the people shall do for the prevention and remedy of them."

And when he had said this, he stood up; and I, as I had been taught, knelt down; and he laid his right hand upon my head, and said, "God bless thee, my son, and God bless this relation which I have made.   I give thee leave to publish it, for the good of other nations; for we here are in God's bosom, a land unknown."   And so he left me; having assigned a value of about two thousand ducats for a bounty to me and my fellows.   For they give great largesses, where they come, upon all occasions.

THE REST WAS NOT PERFECTED.

CAMPANELLA'S

CITY OF THE SUN.

THE CITY OF THE SUN.

[A Poetical Dialogue between a Grandmaster of the Knights Hospitallers and a Genoese Sea Captain, his Guest.]

G. M.—Prithee, now, tell me what happened to you during that voyage?

Capt.—I have already told you how I wandered over the whole earth. In the course of my journeying I came to Taprobane, and was compelled to go ashore at a place, where through fear of the inhabitants I remained in a wood. When I stepped out of this I found myself on a large plain immediately under the equator.

G. M.—And what befell you here?

Capt.—I came upon a large crowd of men and armed women, many of whom did not understand our language, and they conducted me forthwith to the City of the Sun.

G. M.—Tell me after what plan this city is built and how it is governed?

Capt.—The greater part of the city is built upon a high hill, which rises from an extensive plain, but several of its circles extend for some distance beyond the base of the hill, which is of such a size that the diameter of the city is upward of two miles, so that its circumference becomes about seven. On account of the humped shape of the mountain, however, the diameter of the city is really more than if it were built on a plain.

It is divided into seven rings or huge circles named from the seven planets, and the way from one to the other of these is by four streets and through four gates, that look toward the four points of the compass. Furthermore, it is so built that if the first circle were stormed, it would of necessity entail a double amount of energy to storm the second; still more to storm the third; and in each succeeding case the strength and energy would have to be doubled; so that he who wishes to capture that city must, as it were, storm it seven times. For my own part, however, I think that not even the first wall could be occupied, so thick are the earthworks and so well fortified is it with breastworks, towers, guns and ditches.

When I had been taken through the northern gate (which is shut with an iron door so wrought that it can be raised and let down, and locked in easily and strongly, its projections running into the grooves of the thick posts by a marvelous device), I saw a level space seventy paces * wide between the first and second walls. From hence can be seen large palaces all joined to the wall of the second circuit, in such a manner as to appear all one palace. Arches run on a level with the middle height of the palaces, and are continued round the whole ring. There are galleries for promenading upon these arches, which are supported from beneath by thick and well-shaped columns, enclosing arcades like peristyles, or cloisters of an abbey.

But the palaces have no entrances from below except on the inner or concave partition, from which one enters directly to the lower parts of the building. The higher parts, however, are reached by flights of marble steps, which lead to galleries for promenading on the inside similar to those on the outside. From these one enters the higher rooms, which are very beautiful, and have windows on the concave and convex partitions. These rooms are divided from one another by richly decorated walls. The convex or outer wall of the ring is about eight spans thick; the concave three; the intermediate walls are one, or perhaps one and a half. Leaving this circle one gets to the second plain, which is nearly three paces narrower than the first. Then the first wall of the second ring is seen adorned above and below with similar galleries for walking, and there is on the inside of it another interior wall inclosing palaces. It has also similar peristyles supported by columns in the lower part, but above are excellent pictures, round the ways into the upper houses. And so on afterward through similar spaces and double walls, enclosing palaces, and

* A pace was $1\frac{9}{25}$ yards, 1,000 paces making a mile.

adorned with galleries for walking, extending along their outer side and supported by columns, till the last circuit is reached the way being still over a level plain.

But when the two gates, that is to say, those of the outmost and the inmost walls have been passed, one mounts by means of steps so formed that an ascent is scarcely discernible, since it proceeds in a slanting direction, and the steps succeed one another at almost imperceptible heights. On the top of the hill is a rather spacious plain, and in the midst of this there rises a temple built with wondrous art.

G. M.—Tell on, I pray you! Tell on! I am dying to hear more.

Capt.—The temple is built in the form of a circle; it is not girt with walls, but stands upon thick columns, beautifully grouped. A very large dome, built with great care in the center or pole, contains another small vault as it were rising out of it, and in this a spiracle, which is right over the altar. There is but one altar in the middle of the temple, and this is hedged round by columns. The temple itself is on a space of more than three hundred and fifty paces. Without it, arches measuring about eight paces extend from the heads of the columns outwards, whence other columns rise about three paces from the thick, strong and erect wall. Between these and the former columns there are galleries for walking, with beautiful pavements, and in the recess of the wall, which is adorned with numerous large doors, there are immovable seats, placed as it were between the inside columns, supporting the temple. Portable chairs are not wanting, many and well adorned. Nothing is seen over the altar but a large globe, upon which the heavenly bodies are painted, and another globe upon which there is a representation of the earth. Furthermore, in the vault of the dome there can be discerned representations of all the stars of heaven from the first to the sixth magnitude, with their proper names and power to influence terrestrial things marked in three little verses for each. There are the poles and greater and lesser circles according to the right latitude of the place, but these are not perfect because there is no wall below. They seem, too, to be made in their relation to the globes on the altar. The pavement of the temple is bright with precious stones. Its seven golden lamps hang always burning, and these bear the names of the seven planets.

At the top of the building several small and beautiful cells surround the small dome, and behind the level space above the bands or arches of the exterior and interior columns there are many cells, both small and large, where the priests and religious officers dwell to the number of forty-nine.

A revolving flag projects from the smaller dome, and this shows in what quarter the wind is. The flag is marked with figures up to thirty-six, and the priests know what sort of year the different kinds of winds bring and what will be the changes of weather on land and sea. Furthermore, under the flag a book is always kept written with letters of gold.

G. M.—I pray you, worthy hero, explain to me their whole system of government; for I am anxious to hear it.

Capt.—The great ruler among them is a priest whom they call by the name Hoh, though we should call him Metaphysic. He is head over all, in temporal and spiritual matters, and all business and lawsuits are settled by him, as the supreme authority. Three princes of equal power — viz, Pon, Sin and Mor — assist him, and these in our tongue we should call POWER, WISDOM and LOVE. To POWER belongs the care of all matters relating to war and peace. He attends to the military arts, and, next to Hoh, he is ruler in every affair of a warlike nature. He governs the military magistrates and the soldiers, and has the management of the munitions, the fortifications, the storming of places, the implements of war, the armories, the smiths and workmen connected with matters of this sort.

But WISDOM is the ruler of the liberal arts, of mechanics, of all sciences with their magistrates and doctors, and of the discipline of the schools. As many doctors as there are, are under his control. There is one doctor who is called Astrologus; a second, Cosmographus; a third, Arithmeticus; a fourth, Geometra; a fifth, Historiographus; a sixth, Poeta; a seventh, Logicus; an eighth, Rhetor; a ninth, Grammaticus; a tenth, Medicus;

an eleventh, Physiologus; a twelfth, Politicus; a thirteenth, Moralis. They have but one book, which they call Wisdom, and in it all the sciences are written with conciseness and marvelous fluency of expression. This they read to the people after the custom of the Pythagoreans. It is Wisdom who causes the exterior and interior, the higher and lower walls of the city to be adorned with the finest pictures, and to have all the sciences painted upon them in an admirable manner. On the walls of the temple and on the dome, which is let down when the priest gives an address, lest the sounds of his voice, being scattered, should fly away from his audience, there are pictures of stars in their different magnitudes, with the powers and motions of each, expressed separately in three little verses.

On the interior wall of the first circuit all the mathematical figures are conspicuously painted — figures more in number than Archimedes or Euclid discovered, marked symmetrically, and with the explanation of them neatly written and contained each in a little verse. There are definitions and propositions, etc., etc. On the exterior convex wall is first an immense drawing of the whole earth, given at one view. Following upon this, there are tablets setting forth for every separate country the customs both public and private, the laws, the origins and the power of the inhabitants; and the alphabets the different people use can be seen above that of the City of the Sun.

On the inside of the second circuit, that is to say of the second ring of buildings, paintings of all kinds of precious and common stones, of minerals and metals are seen; and a little piece of the metal itself is also there with an apposite explanation in two small verses for each metal or stone. On the outside are marked all the seas, rivers, lakes, and streams which are on the face of the earth; as are also the wines and the oils and the different liquids, with the sources from which the last are extracted, their qualities and strength. There are also vessels built into the wall above the arches, and these are full of liquids from one to three hundred years old, which cure all diseases. Hail and snow, storms and thunder, and whatever else takes place in the air, are represented with suitable figures and little verses. The inhabitants even have the art of representing in stone all the phenomena of the air, such as the wind, rain, thunder, the rainbow, etc.

On the interior of the third circuit all the different families of trees and herbs are depicted, and there is a live specimen of each plant in earthenware vessels placed upon the outer partition of the arches. With the specimens there are explanations as to where they were first found, what are their powers and natures, and resemblances to celestial things and to metals: to parts of the human body and to things in the sea, and also as to their uses in medicine, etc. On the exterior wall are all the races of fish, found in rivers, lakes and seas, and their habits and values, and ways of breeding, training and living, the purposes for which they exist in the world, and their uses to man. Further, their resemblances to celestial and terrestrial things, produced both by nature and art, are so given that I was astonished when I saw a fish which was like a bishop, one like a chain, another like a garment, a fourth like a nail, a fifth like a star, and others like images of those things existing among us, the relation in each case being completely manifest. There are sea urchins to be seen, and the purple shellfish and mussels; and whatever the watery world possesses worthy of being known is there fully shown in marvelous characters of painting and drawing.

On the fourth interior wall all the different kinds of birds are painted, with their natures, sizes, customs, colors, manner of living, etc.; and the only real phœnix is possessed by the inhabitants of this city. On the exterior are shown all the races of creeping animals, serpents, dragons and worms; the insects, the flies, gnats, beetles, etc., in their different states, strength, venoms and uses, and a great deal more than you or I can think of.

On the fifth interior they have all the larger animals of the earth, as many in number as would astonish you. We indeed know not the thousandth part of them, for on the exterior wall also a great many of immense size are also portrayed. To be sure, of horses alone, how great a number of breeds there is and how beautiful are the forms there cleverly displayed

On the sixth interior are painted all the mechanical arts, with the several instruments for each and their manner of use among different nations. Alongside the dignity of such is placed, and their several inventors are named. But on the exterior all the inventors in science, in warfare, and in law are represented. There I saw Moses, Osiris, Jupiter, Mercury, Lycurgus, Pompilius, Pythagoras, Zamolxis, Solon, Charondas, Phoroneus, with very many others. They even have Mahomet, whom nevertheless they hate as a false and sordid legislator. In the most dignified position I saw a representation of Jesus Christ and of the twelve Apostles, whom they consider very worthy and hold to be great. Of the representations of men, I perceived Cæsar, Alexander, Pyrrhus and Hannibal in the highest place; and other very renowned heroes in peace and war, especially Roman heroes, were painted in lower positions, under the galleries. And when I asked with astonishment whence they had obtained our history, they told me that among them there was a knowledge of all languages, and that by perseverance they continually send explorers and ambassadors over the whole earth, who learn thoroughly the customs, forces, rule, and histories of the nations, bad and good alike. These they apply all to their own republic, and with this they are well pleased. I learned that cannon and typography were invented by the Chinese before we knew of them. There are magistrates, who announce the meaning of the pictures, and boys are accustomed to learn all the sciences, without toil and as if for pleasure; but in the way of history only until they are ten years old.

Love is foremost in attending to the charge of the race. He sees that men and women are so joined together, that they bring forth the best offspring. Indeed, they laugh at us who exhibit a studious care for our breed of horses and dogs, but neglect the breeding of human beings. Thus the education of the children is under his rule. So also is the medicine that is sold, the sowing and collecting of fruits of the earth and of trees, agriculture, pasturage, the preparations for the months, the cooking arrangements, and whatever has any reference to food, clothing, and the intercourse of the sexes. Love himself is ruler, but there are many male and female magistrates dedicated to these arts.

Metaphysic then with these three rulers manage all the above-named matters, and even by himself alone nothing is done; all business is discharged by the four together, but in whatever Metaphysic inclines to the rest are sure to agree.

G. M.— Tell me, please, of the magistrates, their services and duties, of the education and mode of living, whether the government is a monarchy, a republic, or an aristocracy.

Capt.— This race of men came there from India, flying from the sword of the Magi, a race of plunderers and tyrants who laid waste their country, and they determined to lead a philosophic life in fellowship with one another. Although the community of wives is not instituted among the other inhabitants of their province, among them it is in use after this manner. All things are common with them, and their dispensation is by the authority of the magistrates. Arts and honors and pleasures are common, and are held in such a manner that no one can appropriate anything to himself.

They say that all private property is acquired and improved for the reason that each one of us by himself has his own home and wife and children. From this self-love springs. For when we raise a son to riches and dignities, and leave an heir to much wealth, we become either ready to grasp at the property of the state, if in any case fear should be removed from the power which belongs to riches and rank; or avaricious, crafty, and hypocritical, if anyone is of slender purse, little strength, and mean ancestry. But when we have taken away self-love, there remains only love for the state.

G. M.— Under such circumstances no one will be willing to labor, while he expects others to work, on the fruit of whose labors he can live, as Aristotle argues against Plato.

Capt.— I do not know how to deal with that argument, but I declare to you that they burn with so great a love for their fatherland, as I could scarcely have believed possible; and indeed with much more than the histories tell us belonged to the Romans, who fell willingly for their country, inasmuch as they have to a greater extent surrendered their private property. I think truly that the friars and monks and clergy of our country, if they were not weakened by love for their kindred and friends, or by the ambition to rise to higher dignities, would be less fond of property, and more imbued with a spirit of charity toward all, as it was in the time of the Apostles, and is now in a great many cases.

G. M. — St. Augustine may say that, but I say that among this race of men, friendship is worth nothing; since they have not the chance of conferring mutual benefits on one another.

Capt. — Nay, indeed. For it is worth the trouble to see that no one can receive gifts from another. Whatever is necessary they have, they receive it from the community, and the magistrate takes care that no one receives more than he deserves. Yet nothing necessary is denied to anyone. Friendship is recognized among them in war, in infirmity, in the art contests, by which means they aid one another mutually by teaching. Sometimes they improve themselves mutually with praises, with conversation, with actions, and out of the things they need. All those of the same age call one another brothers. They call all over twenty-two years of age, fathers; those who are less than twenty-two are named sons. Moreover, the magistrates govern well, so that no one in the fraternity can do injury to another.

G. M. — And how?

Capt. — As many names of virtues as there are among us, so many magistrates there are among them. There is a magistrate who is named Magnanimity, another Fortitude, a third Chastity, a fourth Liberality, a fifth Criminal and Civil Justice, a sixth Comfort, a seventh Truth, an eighth Kindness, a tenth Gratitude, an eleventh Cheerfulness, a twelfth Exercise, a thirteenth Sobriety, etc. They are elected to duties of that kind, each one to that duty for excellence in which he is known from boyhood to be most suitable. Wherefore among them neither robbery nor clever murders, nor lewdness, incest, adultery, or other crimes of which we accuse one another, can be found. They accuse themselves of ingratitude and malignity when anyone denies a lawful satisfaction to another, of indolence, of sadness, of anger, of scurrility, of slander, and of lying, which curseful thing they thoroughly hate. Accused persons undergoing punishment are deprived of the common table, and other honors, until the judge thinks that they agree with their correction.

G. M.—Tell me the manner in which the magistrates are chosen.

Capt.—You would not rightly understand this, unless you first learned their manner of living. That you may know then, men and women wear the same kind of garment, suited for war. The women wear the toga below the knee, but the men above. And both sexes are instructed in all the arts together. When this has been done as a start, and before their third year, the boys learn the language and the alphabet on the walls by walking round them. They have four leaders, and four elders, the first to direct them, the second to teach them and these are men approved beyond all others. After some time they exercise themselves, with gymnastics, running, quoits, and other games, by means of which all their muscles are strengthened alike. Their feet are always bare, and so are their heads as far as the seventh ring. Afterward they lead them to the offices of the trades, such as shoemaking, cooking, metalworking, carpentry, painting, etc. In order to find out the bent of the genius of each one, after their seventh year, when they have already gone through the mathematics on the walls, they take them to the readings of all the sciences; there are four lectures at each reading, and in the course of four hours the four in their order explain everything.

For some take physical exercise or busy themselves with public services or functions, others apply themselves to reading. Leaving these studies all are devoted to the more abstruse subjects, to mathematics, to medicine, and to other sciences. There is continual debate and studied argument among them, and after a time they become magistrates of those sciences or mechanical arts in which they are the most proficient; for every one follows the opinion of his leader and judge, and goes out to the plains to the works of the field, and for the purpose of becoming acquainted with the pasturage of the dumb animals. And they consider him the more noble and renowned who has dedicated himself to the study of the most arts and knows how to practice them wisely. Wherefore they laugh at us in that we consider our workmen ignoble, and hold those to be noble who have mastered no pursuit; but live in ease, and are so many slaves given over to their own pleasure and lasciviousness; and thus as it were from a school of vices so many idle and wicked fellows go forth for the ruin of the state.

The rest of the officials, however, are chosen by the four chiefs, Hoh, Pon, Sin and Mor, and by the teachers of that art over which they are fit to preside. And these teachers know well who is most suited for rule. Certain men are proposed by the magistrates in council, they themselves not seeking to become candidates, and he opposes who knows anything against those brought forward for election, or if not, speaks in favor of them. But no one attains to the dignity of Hoh except him who knows the histories of the nations, and their customs and sacrifices and laws, and their form of government, whether a republic or a monarchy. He must also know the names of the lawgivers and the inventors in science, and the laws and the history of the earth and the heavenly bodies. They think it also necessary that he should understand all the mechanical arts, the physical sciences, astrology and mathematics. (Nearly every two days they teach our mechanical art. They are not allowed to overwork themselves, but frequent practice and the paintings render learning easy to them. Not too much care is given to the cultivation of languages, as they have a goodly number of interpreters who are grammarians in the state.) But beyond everything else it is necessary that Hoh should understand metaphysics and theology; that he should know thoroughly

the derivations, foundations and demonstrations of all
the arts and sciences; the likeness and difference of
things; necessity, fate, and the harmonies of the universe; power, wisdom, and the love of things and of
God; the stages of life and its symbols; everything relating to the heavens, the earth and the sea; and the
ideas of God, as much as mortal man can know of him.
He must also be well read in the Prophets and in astrology.
And thus they know long beforehand who will be
Hoh.   He is not chosen to so great a dignity unless he has
attained his thirty-fifth year.   And this office is perpetual, because it is not known who may be too wise for it
or who too skilled in ruling.

G. M. — Who indeed can be so wise? If even anyone
has a knowledge of the sciences it seems that he must
be unskilled in ruling.

Capt. — This very question I asked them and they replied thus: "We, indeed, are more certain that such a
very learned man has the knowledge of governing, than
you who place ignorant persons in authority, and consider them suitable merely because they have sprung
from rulers or have been chosen by a powerful faction.
But our Hoh, a man really the most capable to rule, is
for all that never cruel nor wicked, nor a tyrant, inasmuch as he possesses so much wisdom.   This, moreover,
is not unknown to you, that the same argument cannot
apply among you, when you consider that man the most
learned who knows most of grammar, or logic, or of
Aristotle or any other author.   For such knowledge as
this of yours much servile labor and memory work is required, so that a man is rendered unskillful; since he has
contemplated nothing but the words of books and has
given his mind with useless result to the consideration
of the dead signs of things.   Hence he knows not in
what way God rules the universe, nor the ways and customs of Nature and the nations.   Wherefore he is not
equal to our Hoh.   For that one cannot know so many
arts and sciences thoroughly, who is not esteemed for
skilled ingenuity, very apt at all things, and therefore at
ruling especially.   This also is plain to us that he who
knows only one science, does not really know either that

or the others, and he who is suited for only one science and has gathered his knowledge from books, is unlearned and unskilled. But this is not the case with intellects prompt and expert in every branch of knowledge and suitable for the consideration of natural objects, as it is necessary that our Hoh should be. Besides in our state the sciences are taught with a facility (as you have seen) by which more scholars are turned out by us in one year than by you in ten, or even fifteen. Make trial, I pray you, of these boys." In this matter I was struck with astonishment at their truthful discourse and at the trial of their boys, who did not understand my language well. Indeed it is necessary that three of them should be skilled in our tongue, three in Arabic, three in Polish, and three in each of the other languages, and no recreation is allowed them unless they become more learned. For that they go out to the plain for the sake of running about and hurling arrows and lances, and of firing harquebuses, and for the sake of hunting the wild animals and getting a knowledge of plants and stones, and agriculture and pasturage; sometimes the band of boys does one thing, sometimes another.

They do not consider it necessary that the three rulers assisting Hoh should know other than the arts having reference to their rule, and so they have only a historical knowledge of the arts which are common to all. But their own they know well, to which certainly one is dedicated more than another. Thus Power is the most learned in the equestrian art, in marshaling the army, in marking out of camps, in the manufacture of every kind of weapon and of warlike machines, in planning stratagems, and in every affair of a military nature. And for these reasons, they consider it necessary that these chiefs should have been philosophers, historians, politicians, and physicists. Concerning the other two triumvirs, understand remarks similar to those I have made about Power.

G. M.—I really wish that you would recount all their public duties, and would distinguish between them, and also that you would tell clearly how they are all taught in common.

Capt.— They have dwellings in common and dormitories, and couches and other necessaries. But at the end of every six months they are separated by the masters. Some shall sleep in this ring, some in another; some in the first apartment, and some in the second; and these apartments are marked by means of the alphabet on the lintel. There are occupations, mechanical and theoretical, common to both men and women, with this difference, that the occupations which require more hard work, and walking a long distance, are practiced by men, such as plowing, sowing, gathering the fruits, working at the threshing-floor, and perchance at the vintage. But it is customary to choose women for milking the cows, and for making cheese. In like manner, they go to the gardens near to the outskirts of the city both for collecting the plants and for cultivating them. In 'fact, all sedentary and stationary pursuits are practiced by the women, such as weaving, spinning, sewing, cutting the hair, shaving, dispensing medicines, and making all kinds of garments. They are, however, excluded from working in wood and the manufacture of arms. If a woman is fit to paint, she is not prevented from doing so; nevertheless, music is given over to the women alone, because they please the more, and of a truth to boys also. But the women have not the practice of the drum and the horn.

And they prepare their feasts and arrange the tables in the following manner. It is the peculiar work of the boys and girls under twenty to wait at the tables. In every ring there are the suitable kitchens, barns, and stores of utensils for eating and drinking, and over every department an old man and an old woman preside. These two have at once the command of those who serve, and the power of chastising or causing to be chastised, those who are negligent or disobedient; and they also examine and mark each one, both male and female, who excels in his or her duties.

All the young people wait upon the older ones who have passed the age of forty, and in the evening when they go to sleep the master and mistress command that those should be sent to work in the morning, upon whom in succession the duty falls, one or two to separate apartments. The young people, however, wait upon one another, and that alas! with some unwillingness. They have first and second tables, and on both sides there are seats. On one side sit the women, on the other the men; and as in the refectories of the monks, there is no noise. While they are eating a young man reads a book from a platform, intoning distinctly and sonorously, and often the magistrates question them upon the more important parts of the reading. And truly it is pleasant to observe in what manner these young people, so beautiful and clothed in garments so suitable, attend to them, and to see at the same time so many friends, brothers, sons, fathers and mothers all in their turn living together with so much honesty, propriety and love. So each one is given a napkin, a plate, fish, and a dish of food. It is the duty of the medical officers to tell the cooks what repasts shall be prepared on each day, and what food for the old, what for the young, and what for the sick. The magistrates receive the full-grown and fatter portion, and they from their share always distribute something to the boys at the table who have shown themselves more studious in the morning at the lectures and debates concerning wisdom and arms. And this is held to be one of the most distinguished honors. For six days they ordain to sing with music at table. Only a few, however, sing; or there is one voice accompanying the lute and one for each other instrument. And when all alike in service join their hands, nothing is found to be wanting. The old men placed at the head of the cooking business and of the refectories of the servants praise the cleanliness of the streets, the houses, the vessels, the garments, the workshops and the warehouses.

They wear white undergarments to which adheres a covering, which is at once coat and legging, without wrinkles. The borders of the fastenings are furnished with globular buttons, extended round and caught up here and there by chains. The coverings of the legs descend to the shoes and are continued even to the heels. Then they cover the feet with large socks, or as it were half-buskins fastened by buckles, over which they wear a half-boot, and besides, as I have already said, they are

19

clothed with a toga. And so aptly fitting are the garments, that when the toga is destroyed, the different parts of the whole body are straightway discerned, no part being concealed. They change their clothes for different ones four times in the year, that is when the sun enters respectively the constellations Aries, Cancer, Libra and Capricorn, and according to the circumstances and necessity as decided by the officer of health. The keepers of clothes for the different rings are wont to distribute them, and it is marvelous that they have at the same time as many garments as there is need for, some heavy and some slight, according to the weather. They all use white clothing, and this is washed in each month with lye or soap, as are also the workshops of the lower trades, the kitchens, the pantries, the barns, the storehouses, the armories, the refectories, and the baths. Moreover, the clothes are washed at the pillars of the peristyles, and the water is brought down by means of canals which are continued as sewers. In every street of the different rings there are suitable fountains, which send forth their water by means of canals, the water being drawn up from nearly the bottom of the mountain by the sole movement of a cleverly contrived handle. There is water in fountains and in cisterns, whither the rain water collected from the roofs of the houses is brought through pipes full of sand. They wash their bodies often, according as the doctor and master command. All the mechanical arts are practiced under the peristyles, but the speculative are carried on above in the walking galleries and ramparts where are the more splendid paintings, but the more sacred ones are taught in the temple. In the halls and wings of the rings there are solar timepieces and bells, and hands by which the hours and seasons are marked off.

G. M.— Tell me about their children.

Capt.— When their women have brought forth children, they suckle and rear them in temples set apart for all. They give milk for two years or more as the physician orders. After that time the weaned child is given into the charge of the mistresses, if it is a female, and to the masters, if it is a male. And then with other young children they are pleasantly instructed in the alphabet, and in the knowledge of the pictures, and in running, walking and wrestling; also in the historical drawings, and in languages; and they are adorned with a suitable garment of different colors. After their sixth year they are taught natural science, and then the mechanical sciences. The men who are weak in intellect are sent to farms, and when they have become more proficient some of them are received into the state. And those of the same age and born under the same constellation are especially like one another in strength and in appearance, and hence arises much lasting concord in the state, these men honoring one another with mutual love and help. Names are given to them by Metaphysicus, and that not by chance but designedly, and according to each one's peculiarity, as was the custom among the ancient Romans. Wherefore one is called Beautiful (*Pulcher*), another the Big-nosed (*Naso*), another the Fat-legged (*Cranipes*), another Crooked (*Torvus*), another Lean (*Macer*), and so on. But when they have become very skilled in their professions and done any great deed in war or in time of peace, a cognomen from art is given to them, such as Beautiful the great painter (*Pulcher, Pictor Magnus*), the golden one (*Aureus*), the excellent one (*Excellens*), or the strong (*Strenuus*); or from their deeds, such as Naso the Brave (*Nason Fortis*), or the cunning, or the great, or very great conqueror; or from the enemy any one has overcome, Africanus, Asiaticus, Etruscus; or if any one has overcome Manfred or Tortelius, he is called Macer Manfred or Tortelius, and so on. All these cognomens are added by the higher magistrates, and very often with a crown suitable to the deed or art, and with the flourish of music. For gold and silver is reckoned of little value among them except as material for their vessels and ornaments, which are common to all.

G. M.— Tell me, I pray you, is there no jealousy among them or disappointment to that one who has not been elected to a magistracy, or to any other dignity to which he aspires?

Capt.— Certainly not. For no one wants either necessaries or luxuries. Moreover, the race is managed for

the good of the commonwealth and not of private individuals, and the magistrates must be obeyed. They deny
what we hold — viz, that it is natural to man to recognize his offspring and to educate them, and to use his
wife and house and children as his own. For they say
that children are bred for the preservation of the species
and not for individual pleasure, as St. Thomas also asserts.   Therefore the breeding of children has reference
to the commonwealth and not to individuals, except in
so far as they are constituents of the commonwealth.
And since individuals for the most part bring forth children wrongly and educate them wrongly, they consider
that they remove destruction from the state, and, therefore, for this reason, with most sacred fear, they commit
the education of the children, who as it were are the element of the republic, to the care of magistrates; for the
safety of the community is not that of a few.   And thus
they distribute male and female breeders of the best natures according to philosophical rules.   Plato thinks that
this distribution ought to be made by lot, lest some men
seeing that they are kept away from the beautiful women,
should rise up with anger and hatred against the magistrates; and he thinks further that those who do not deserve cohabitation with the more beautiful women, should
be deceived whilst the lots are being led out of the city
by the magistrates, so that at all times the women who
are suitable should fall to their lot, not those whom they
desire.   This shrewdness, however, is not necessary among
the inhabitants of the City of the Sun.   For with them
deformity is unknown.   When the women are exercised
they get a clear complexion, and become strong of limb,
tall and agile, and with them beauty consists in tallness
and strength.   Therefore, if any woman dyes her face,
so that it may become beautiful, or uses high-heeled
boots so that she may appear tall, or garments with
trains to cover her wooden shoes, she is condemned to
capital punishment.   But if the women should even desire them, they have no facility for doing these things.
For who indeed would give them this facility?   Further,
they assert that among us abuses of this kind arise from
the leisure and sloth of women.   By these means they

THE CITY OF THE SUN 293

lose their color and have pale complexions, and become feeble and small. For this reason they are without proper complexions, use high sandals, and become beautiful not from strength, but from slothful tenderness. And thus they ruin their own tempers and natures, and consequently those of their offspring. Furthermore, if at any time a man is taken captive with ardent love for a certain woman, the two are allowed to converse and joke together, and to give one another garlands of flowers or leaves, and to make verses. But if the race is endangered, by no means is further union between them permitted. Moreover, the love born of eager desire is not known among them; only that born of friendship.

Domestic affairs and partnerships are of little account, because, excepting the sign of honor, each one receives what he is in need of. To the heroes and heroines of the republic, it is customary to give the pleasing gifts of honor, beautiful wreaths, sweet food, or splendid clothes, while they are feasting. In the daytime all use white garments within the city, but at night or outside the city they use red garments either of wool or silk. They hate black as they do dung, and therefore they dislike the Japanese, who are fond of black. Pride they consider the most execrable vice, and one who acts proudly is chastised with the most ruthless correction. Wherefore no one thinks it lowering to wait at table or to work in the kitchen or fields. All work they call discipline, and thus they say that it is honorable to go on foot, to do any act of nature, to see with the eye, and to speak with the tongue; and when there is need, they distinguish philosophically between tears and spittle.

Every man who, when he is told off to work, does his duty, is considered very honorable. It is not the custom to keep slaves. For they are enough, and more than enough, for themselves. But with us, alas! it is not so. In Naples there exist seventy thousand souls, and out of these scarcely ten or fifteen thousand do any work, and they are always lean from overwork and are getting weaker every day. The rest become a prey to idleness, avarice, ill-health, lasciviousness, usury and other vices, and contaminate and corrupt very many families by hold-

ing them in servitude for their own use, by keeping them
in poverty and slavishness, and by imparting to them
their own vices. Therefore public slavery ruins them; useful works, in the field, in military service, and in arts,
except those which are debasing, are not cultivated, the
few who do practice them doing so with much aversion.
But in the City of the Sun, while duty and work is distributed among all, it only falls to each one to work for
about four hours every day. The remaining hours are
spent in learning joyously, in debating, in reading, in
reciting, in writing, in walking, in exercising the mind
and body, and with play. They allow no game which is
played while sitting, neither the single die nor dice, nor
chess, nor others like these. But they play with the ball,
with the sack, with the hoop, with wrestling, with hurling at the stake. They say, moreover, that grinding
poverty renders men worthless, cunning, sulky, thievish,
insidious, vagabonds, liars, false witnesses, etc.; and that
wealth makes them insolent, proud, ignorant, traitors,
assumers of what they know not, deceivers, boasters,
wanting in affection, slanderers, etc. But with them all
the rich and poor together make up the community.
They are rich because they want nothing, poor because
they possess nothing; and consequently they are not
slaves to circumstances, but circumstances serve them.
And on this point they strongly recommend the religion
of the Christians, and especially the life of the Apostles.

G. M. — This seems excellent and sacred, but the community of women is a thing too difficult to attain. The
holy Roman Clement says that wives ought to be common in accordance with the apostolic institution, and
praises Plato and Socrates, who thus teach, but the Glossary interprets this community with regard to obedience.
And Tertullian agrees with the Glossary, that the first
Christians had everything in common except wives.

Capt. — These things I know little of. But this I saw
among the inhabitants of the City of the Sun that they
did not make this exception. And they defend themselves by the opinion of Socrates, of Cato, of Plato, and
of St. Clement, but, as you say, they misunderstand the

opinions of these thinkers. And the inhabitants of the solar city ascribe this to their want of education, since they are by no means learned in philosophy. Nevertheless, they send abroad to discover the customs of nations, and the best of these they always adopt. Practice makes the women suitable for war and other duties. Thus they agree with Plato, in whom I have read these same things. The reasoning of our Cajetan does not convince me, and least of all that of Aristotle. This thing, however, existing among them is excellent and worthy of imitation — viz, that no physical defect renders a man incapable of being serviceable except the decrepitude of old age, since even the deformed are useful for consultation. The lame serve as guards, watching with the eyes which they possess. The blind card wool with their hands, separating the down from the hairs, with which latter they stuff the couches and sofas; those who are without the use of eyes and hands give the use of their ears or their voice for the convenience of the state, and if one has only one sense, he uses it in the farms. And these cripples are well treated, and some become spies, telling the officers of the state what they have heard.

G. M.— Tell me now, I pray you, of their military affairs. Then you may explain their arts, ways of life and sciences, and lastly their religion.

Capt.— The triumvir, Power, has under him all the magistrates of arms, of artillery, of cavalry, of foot soldiers, of architects, and of strategists, and the masters and many of the most excellent workmen obey the magistrates, the men of each art paying allegiance to their respective chiefs. Moreover, Power is at the head of all the professors of gymnastics, who teach military exercise, and who are prudent generals, advanced in age. By these the boys are trained after their twelfth year. Before this age, however, they have been accustomed to wrestling, running, throwing the weight and other minor exercises, under inferior masters. But at twelve they are taught how to strike at the enemy, at horses and elephants, to handle the spear, the sword, the arrow and the sling; to manage the horse; to advance and to retreat; to remain in order of battle; to help a comrade in arms; to anticipate the enemy by cunning; and to conquer.

The women also are taught these arts under their own magistrates and mistresses, so that they may be able if need be to render assistance to the males in battle near the city. They are taught to watch the fortifications lest at some time a hasty attack should suddenly be made. In this respect they praise the Spartans and Amazons. The women know well also how to let fly fiery balls, and how to make them from lead; how to throw stones from pinacles and to go in the way of an attack. They are accustomed also to give up wine unmixed altogether, and that one is punished most severely who shows any fear.

The inhabitants of the City of the Sun do not fear death, because they all believe that the soul is immortal, and that when it has left the body it is associated with other spirits, wicked or good, according to the merits of this present life. Although they are partly followers of Brahma and Pythagoras, they do not believe in the transmigration of souls, except in some cases, by a distinct decree of God. They do not abstain from injuring an enemy of the republic and of religion, who is unworthy of pity. During the second month the army is reviewed, and every day there is practice of arms, either in the cavalry plain or within the walls. Nor are they ever without lectures on the science of war. They take care that the accounts of Moses, of Joshua, of David, of Judas Maccabeus, of Cæsar, of Alexander, of Scipio, of Hannibal, and other great soldiers should be read. And then each one gives his own opinion as to whether these generals acted well or ill, usefully or honorably, and then the teacher answers and says who are right.

G. M.— With whom do they wage war, and for what reasons, since they are so prosperous?

Capt.—Wars might never occur, nevertheless they are exercised in military tactics and in hunting, lest perchance they should become effeminate and unprepared for any emergency. Besides there are four kingdoms in the island, which are very envious of their prosperity, for

this reason that the people desire to live after the manner of the inhabitants of the City of the Sun, and to be
under their rule rather than that of their own kings.
Wherefore the state often makes war upon these because,
being neighbors, they are usurpers and live impiously,
since they have not an object of worship and do not observe the religion of other nations or of the Brahmins.
And other nations of India, to which formerly they were
subject, rise up as it were in rebellion, as also do the
Taprobanese, whom they wanted to join them at first.
The warriors of the City of the Sun, however, are always
the victors.   As soon as they suffered from insult or disgrace or plunder, or when their allies have been harassed,
or a people have been oppressed by a tyrant of the state
(for they are always the advocates of liberty), they go
immediately to the council for deliberation.   After they
have knelt in the presence of God that he might inspire
their consultation, they proceed to examine the merits of
the business, and thus war is decided on.   Immediately
after a priest, whom they call Forensic, is sent away.   He
demands from the enemy the restitution of the plunder,
asks that the allies should be freed from oppression, or
that the tyrant should be deposed.   If they deny these
things war is declared by invoking the vengeance of God
—the God of Sabaoth—for destruction of those who maintain an unjust cause.   But if the enemy refuse to reply,
the priest gives him the space of one hour for his answer,
if he is a king, but three if it is a republic, so that they
cannot escape giving a response.   And in this manner is
war undertaken against the insolent enemies of natural
rights and of religion.   When war has been declared, the
deputy of Power performs everything, but Power, like
the Roman dictator, plans and wills everything, so that
hurtful tardiness may be avoided.   And when anything
of great moment arises he consults Hoh and Wisdom
and Love.

Before this, however, the occasion of war and the
justice of making an expedition is declared by a herald
in the great council.   All from twenty years and upward
are admitted to this council, and thus the necessaries are
agreed upon.   All kinds of weapons stand in the armories,

and these they use often in sham fights. The exterior
walls of each ring are full of guns prepared by their
labors, and they have other engines for hurling which
are called cannons, and which they take into battle upon
mules and asses and carriages. When they have arrived
in an open plain they inclose in the middle the provisions, engines of war, chariots, ladders and machines, and
all fight courageously. Then each one returns to the
standards, and the enemy thinking that they are giving
and preparing to flee, are deceived and relax their order;
then the warriors of the City of the Sun, wheeling into
wings and columns on each side, regain their breath and
strength, and ordering the artillery to discharge their
bullets they resume the fight against a disorganized host.
And they observe many ruses of this kind. They overcome all mortals with their stratagems and engines.
Their camp is fortified after the manner of the Romans.
They pitch their tents and fortify with wall and ditch
with wonderful quickness. The masters of works, of
engines and hurling machines, stand ready, and the
soldiers understand the use of the spade and the ax.

Five, eight, or ten leaders learned in the order of battle
and in strategy consult together concerning the business
of war, and command their bands after consultation. It
is their wont to take out with them a body of boys,
armed and on horses, so that they may learn to fight, just
as the whelps of lions and wolves are accustomed to blood.
And these in time of danger betake themselves to a place
of safety, along with many armed women. After the
battle the women and boys soothe and relieve the pain of
the warriors, and wait upon them and encourage them
with embraces and pleasant words. How wonderful a
help is this! For the soldiers, in order that they may
acquit themselves as sturdy men in the eyes of their
wives and offspring, endure hardships, and so love makes
them conquerors. He who in the fight first scales the
enemy's walls receives after the battle a crown of grass,
as a token of honor, and at the presentation the women
and boys applaud loudly; that one who affords aid to an
ally gets a civic crown of oak leaves; he who kills a
tyrant dedicates his arms in the temple and receives from

Hoh the cognomen of his deed, and other warriors obtain other kinds of crowns. Every horse soldier carries a spear and two strongly tempered pistols, narrow at the mouth, hanging from his saddle. And to get the barrels of their pistols narrow they pierce the metal which they intend to convert into arms. Further, every cavalry soldier has a sword and a dagger. But the rest, who form the light-armed troops, carry a metal cudgel. For if the foe cannot pierce their metal for pistols and cannot make swords, they attack him with clubs, shatter and overthrow him. Two chains of six spans' length hang from the club, and at the end of these are iron balls, and when these are aimed at the enemy they surround his neck and drag him to the ground; and in order that they may be able to use the club more easily, they do not hold the reins with their hands, but use them by means of the feet. If perchance the reins are interchanged above the trappings of the saddle, the ends are fastened to the stirrups with buckles and not to the feet. And the stirrups have an arrangement for swift movement of the bridle, so that they draw in or let out the rein with marvelous celerity. With the right foot they turn the horse to the left, and with the left to the right. This secret, moreover, is not known to the Tartars. For, although they govern the reins with their feet, they are ignorant nevertheless of turning them and drawing them in and letting them out by means of the block of the stirrups. The light-armed cavalry with them are the first to engage in battle, then the men forming the phalanx with their spears, then the archers for whose services a great price is paid, and who are accustomed to fight in lines crossing one another as the threads of cloth, some rushing forward in their turn and others receding. They have a band of lancers strengthening the line of battle, but they make trial of the swords only at the end.

After the battle they celebrate the military triumphs after the manner of the Romans, and even in a more magnificent way. Prayers by the way of thank-offerings are made to God, and then the general presents himself in the temple, and the deeds, good and bad, are related by the poet or historian, who according to custom was with the expedition. And the greatest chief, Hoh, crowns the general with laurel and distributes little gifts and honors to all the valorous soldiers, who are for some days free from public duties. But this exemption from work is by no means pleasing to them, since they know not what it is to be at leisure, and so they help their companions. On the other hand, they who have been conquered through their own fault, or have lost the victory, are blamed; and they who were the first to take to flight are in no way worthy to escape death, unless when the whole army asks their lives, and each one takes upon himself a part of their punishment. But this indulgence is rarely granted, except when there are good reasons favoring it. But he who did not bear help to an ally or friend is beaten with rods. That one who did not obey orders is given to the beasts, in an inclosure, to be devoured, and a staff is put in his hand, and if he should conquer the lions and the bears that are there, which is almost impossible, he is received into favor again. The conquered states or those willingly delivered up to them, forthwith have all things in common, and receive a garrison and magistrates from the City of the Sun, and by degrees they are accustomed to the ways of the city, the mistress of all, to which they even send their sons to be taught without contributing anything for expense.

It would be too great trouble to tell you about the spies and their master, and about the guards and laws and ceremonies, both within and without the state, which you can of yourself imagine. Since from childhood they are chosen according to their inclination and the star under which they were born, therefore each one working according to his natural propensity, does his duty well and pleasantly, because naturally. The same things I may say concerning strategy and the other functions.

There are guards in the city by day and by night, and they are placed at the four gates, and outside the walls of the seventh ring, above the breastworks and towers and inside mounds. These places are guarded in the day by women, in the night by men. And lest the guard should become weary of watching, and in case of a surprise, they change them every three hours, as is the custom with our soldiers. At sunset, when the drum and symphonia sound, the armed guards are distributed. Cavalry and infantry make use of hunting as the symbol of war, and practice games and hold festivities in the plains. Then the music strikes up, and freely they pardon the offenses and faults of the enemy, and after the victories they are kind to them, if it has been decreed that they should destroy the walls of the enemy's city and take their lives. All these things are done in the same day as the victory, and afterward they never cease to load the conquered with favors, for they say that there ought to be no fighting, except when the conquerors give up the conquered, not when they kill them. If there is a dispute among them concerning injury or any other matter (for they themselves scarcely ever contend except in matters of honor), the chief and his magistrates chastise the accused one secretly, if he has done harm in deeds after he has been first angry. If they wait until the time of the battle for the verbal decision, they must give vent to their anger against the enemy, and he who in battle shows the most daring deeds is considered to have defended the better and truer cause in the struggle, and the other yields, and they are punished justly. Nevertheless, they are not allowed to come to single combat, since right is maintained by the tribunal, and because the unjust cause is often apparent when the more just succumbs, and he who professes to be the better man shows this in public fight.

G. M. — This is worth while, so that factions should not be cherished for the harm of the fatherland, and so that civil wars might not occur, for by means of these a tyrant often arises, as the examples of Rome and Athens show. Now, I pray you, tell me of their works and matter connected therewith.

Capt. — I believe that you have already heard about their military affairs and about their agricultural and pastoral life, and in what way these are common to them, and how they honor with the first grade of nobility whoever is considered to have a knowledge of these. They who are skillful in more arts than these they consider still nobler, and they set that one apart for teaching the art in which he is most skillful. The occupations which require the most labor, such as working in metals and building, are the most praiseworthy among them. No one declines to go to these occupations, for the reason that from the beginning their propensities are well known, and among them, on account of the distribution of labor, no one does work harmful to him, but only that which is necessary for him. The occupations entailing less labor belong to the women. All of them are expected to know how to swim, and for this reason ponds are dug outside the walls of the city and within them near to the fountains.

Commerce is of little use to them, but they know the value of money and they count for the use of their ambassadors and explorers, so that with it they may have the means of living. They receive merchants into their states from the different countries of the world, and these buy the superfluous goods of the city. The people of the City of the Sun refuse to take money, but in importing they accept in exchange those things of which they are in need, and sometimes they buy with money; and the young people in the City of the Sun are much amused when they see that for a small price they receive so many things in exchange. The old men however, do not laugh. They are unwilling that the state should be corrupted by the vicious customs of slaves and foreigners. Therefore they do business at the gates, and sell those whom they have taken in war or keep them for digging ditches and other hard work without the city, and for this reason they always send four bands of soldiers to take care of the fields, and with them there are the laborers. They go out of the four gates from which roads with walls on both sides of them lead to the sea, so that goods might easily be carried over them and foreigners might not meet with difficulty on their way.

To strangers they are kind and polite; they keep them for three days at the public expense; after they have first washed their feet, they show them their city and its customs, and they honor them with a seat at the council and public table, and there are men whose duty it is to take care of and guard the guests. But if strangers should wish to become citizens of their state, they try them first for a month on a farm, and for another month in the city, then they decide concerning them, and admit them with certain ceremonies and oaths.

Agriculture is much followed among them; there is not a span of earth without cultivation, and they observe the winds and propitious stars. With the exception of a few left in the city all go out armed, and with flags and drums and trumpets sounding, to the fields, for the purpose of plowing, sowing, digging, hoeing, reaping, gathering fruit and grapes; and they set in order everything, and do their work in a very few hours and with much care. They use wagons fitted with sails which are borne along by the wind even when it is contrary, by the marvelous contrivance of wheels within wheels.

And when there is no wind a beast draws along a huge cart, which is a grand sight.

The guardians of the land move about in the meantime, armed and always in their proper turn. They do not use dung and filth for manuring the fields, thinking that the fruit contracts something of their rottenness, and when eaten gives a short and poor subsistence, as women who are beautiful with rouge and from want of exercise bring forth feeble offspring. Wherefore they do not as it were paint the earth, but dig it up well and use secret remedies, so that fruit is borne quickly and multiplies, and is not destroyed. They have a book for this work, which they call the Georgics. As much of the land as is necessary is cultivated, and the rest is used for the pasturage of cattle.

The excellent occupation of breeding and rearing horses, oxen, sheep, dogs, and all kinds of domestic and tame animals, is in the highest esteem among them as it was in the time of Abraham. And the animals are led so to pair that they may be able to breed well.

Fine pictures of oxen, horses, sheep, and other animals are placed before them. They do not turn out horses with mares to feed, but at the proper time they bring them together in an inclosure of the stables in their fields. And this is done when they observe that the constellation Archer is in favorable conjunction with Mars and Jupiter. For the oxen they observe the Bull, for the sheep the Ram, and so on in accordance with art. Under the Pleiades they keep a drove of hens and ducks and geese, which are driven out by the women to feed near the city. The women only do this when it is a pleasure to them. There are also places inclosed, where they make cheese, butter, and milk food. They also keep capons, fruit, and other things, and for all these matters there is a book which they call the Bucolics. They have an abundance of all things, since every one likes to be industrious, their labors being slight and profitable. They are docile, and that one among them who is head of the rest in duties of this kind they call king. For they say that this is the proper name of the leaders, and it does not belong to ignorant persons. It is wonderful to see how men and women march together collectively, and always in obedience to the voice of the king. Nor do they regard him with loathing as we do, for they know that although he is greater than themselves, he is for all that their father and brother. They keep groves and woods for wild animals, and they often hunt.

The science of navigation is considered very dignified by them, and they possess rafts and triremes, which go over the waters without rowers or the force of the wind, but by a marvelous contrivance. And other vessels they have which are moved by the winds. They have a correct knowledge of the stars, and of the ebb and flow of the tide. They navigate for the sake of becoming acquainted with nations and different countries and things. They injure nobody, and they do not put up with injury, and they never go to battle unless when provoked. They assert that the whole earth will in time come to live in accordance with their customs, and consequently they always find out whether there be a nation whose manner of living is better and more approved than the rest. They admire the Christian institutions and look for a realization of the apostolic life in vogue among themselves and in us. There are treaties between them and the Chinese, and many other nations, both insular and continental, such as Siam and Calicut, which they are only just able to explore. Furthermore, they have artificial fires, bat-

tles on sea and land, and many strategic secrets. Therefore they are nearly always victorious.

G. M.—Now it would be very pleasant to learn with
what foods and drinks they are nourished, and in what
way and for how long they live.

Capt.—Their food consists of flesh, butter, honey, cheese,
garden herbs, and vegetables of various kinds. They
were unwilling at first to slay animals, because it seemed
cruel; but thinking afterward that it was also cruel to destroy herbs which have a share of sensitive feeling, they
saw that they would perish from hunger unless they did
an unjustifiable action for the sake of justifiable ones,
and so now they all eat meat. Nevertheless, they do not
kill willingly useful animals, such as oxen and horses.
They observe the difference between useful and harmful
foods, and for this they employ the science of medicine.
They always change their food. First they eat flesh, then
fish, then afterward they go back to flesh, and nature is
never incommoded or weakened. The old people use the
more digestible kind of food, and take three meals a day,
eating only a little. But the general community eat twice,
and the boys four times, that they might satisfy nature.
The length of their lives is generally one hundred years,
but often they reach two hundred.

As regards drinking, they are extremely moderate.
Wine is never given to young people until they are ten
years old, unless the state of their health demands it.
After their tenth year they take it diluted with water,
and so do the women, but the old men of fifty and upward use little or no water. They eat the most healthy
things, according to the time of the year.

They think nothing harmful which is brought forth by
God, except when there has been abuse by taking too
much. And therefore in the summer they feed on fruits,
because they are moist and juicy and cool, and counteract the heat and dryness. In the winter they feed on dry
articles, and in the autumn they eat grapes, since they
are given by God to remove melancholy and sadness; and
they also make use of scents to a great degree. In the
morning, when they have all risen, they comb their hair
and wash their faces and hands with cold water. Then

20

they chew thyme or rock parsley or fennel, or rub their hands with these plants. The old men make incense, and with their faces to the east repeat the short prayer which Jesus Christ taught us. After this they go to wait upon the old men, some go to the dance, and others to the duties of the state. Later on they meet at the early lectures, then in the temple, then for bodily exercise. Then for a little while they sit down to rest, and at length they go to dinner.

Among them there is never gout in the hands or feet, no catarrh, no sciatica, nor grievous colics, nor flatulency, nor hard breathing. For these diseases are caused by indigestion and flatulency, and by frugality and exercise they remove every humor and spasm. Wherefore it is unseemly in the extreme to be seen vomiting or spitting, since they say that this is a sign either of little exercise or of ignoble sloth, or of drunkenness or gluttony. They suffer rather from swellings or from the dry spasm, which they relieve with plenty of good and juicy food. They heal fevers with pleasant baths and with milk food, and with a pleasant habitation in the country and by gradual exercise. Unclean diseases cannot be prevalent with them because they often clean their bodies by bathing in wine, and soothe them with aromatic oil, and by the sweat of exercise they diffuse the poisonous vapor which corrupts the blood and the marrow. They do suffer a little from consumption, because they cannot perspire at the breast, but they never have asthma, for the humid nature of which a heavy man is required. They cure hot fevers with cold potations of water, but slight ones with sweet smells, with cheese bread or sleep, with music or dancing. Tertiary fevers are cured by bleeding, by rhubarb or by a similar drawing remedy, or by water soaked in the roots of plants, with purgative and sharp-tasting qualities. But it is rarely that they take purgative medicines. Fevers occurring every fourth day are cured easily by suddenly startling the unprepared patients, and by means of herbs producing effects opposite to the humors of this fever. All these secrets they told me in opposition to their own wishes. They take more diligent pains to cure the lasting fevers, which they fear more, and they strive to counteract these by the observation of stars and of plants, and by prayers to God. Fevers recurring every fifth, sixth, eighth or more days, you never find whenever heavy humors are wanting.

They use baths, and moreover they have warm ones according to the Roman custom, and they make use also of olive oil. They have found out, too, a great many secret cures for the preservation of cleanliness and health. And in other ways they labor to cure the epilepsy, with which they are often troubled.

G. M.— A sign this disease is of wonderful cleverness, for from it Hercules, Scotus, Socrates, Callimachus and Mahomet have suffered.

Capt.— They cure by means of prayers to heaven, by strengthening the head, by acids, by planned gymnastics, and with fat cheese bread sprinkled with the flour of wheaten corn. They are very skilled in making dishes, and in them they put spice, honey, butter and many highly strengthening spices, and they temper their richness with acids, so that they never vomit. They do not drink ice-cold drinks nor artificial hot drinks, as the Chinese do; for they are not without aid against the humors of the body, on account of the help they get from the natural heat of the water; but they strengthen it with crushed garlic, with vinegar, with wild thyme, with mint, and with basil, in the summer or in time of special heaviness. They know also a secret for renovating life after about the seventieth year, and for ridding it of affliction, and this they do by a pleasing and indeed wonderful art.

G. M.— Thus far you have said nothing concerning their sciences and magistrates.

Capt.— Undoubtedly I have. But since you are so curious I will add more. Both when it is new moon and full moon they call a council after a sacrifice. To this all from twenty years upward are admitted, and each one is asked separately to say what is wanting in the state, and which of the magistrates have discharged their duties rightly and which wrongly. Then after eight days all the magistrates assemble, to wit, Hoh first, and with him Power, Wisdom and Love. Each one of the three

last has three magistrates under him, making in all
thirteen, and they consider the affairs of the arts pertaining
to each one of them; Power, of war; Wisdom, of the
sciences; Love, of food, clothing, education and breeding.
The masters of all the bands, who are captains of tens,
of fifties, of hundreds, also assemble, the women first and
then the men. They argue about those things which are
for the welfare of the state, and they choose the magistrates from among those who have already been named
in the great council. In this manner they assemble
daily, Hoh and his three princes, and they correct, confirm and execute the matters passing to them, as decisions
in the elections; other necessary questions they provide
of themselves. They do not use lots unless when they
are altogether doubtful how to decide. The eight magistrates under Hoh, Power, Wisdom and Love are changed
according to the wish of the people, but the first four are
never changed, unless they, taking council with themselves, give up the dignity of one to another, whom
among them they know to be wiser, more renowned, and
more nearly perfect. And then they are obedient and
honorable, since they yield willingly to the wiser man
and are taught by him. This, however, rarely happens.
The principals of the sciences, except Metaphysics, who
is Hoh himself, and is as it were the architect of all
science, having rule over all, are attached to Wisdom.
Hoh is ashamed to be ignorant of any possible thing.
Under Wisdom therefore is Grammar, Logic, Physics,
Medicine, Astrology, Astronomy, Geometry, Cosmography,
Music, Perspective, Arithmetic, Poetry, Rhetoric, Paint-
ing, Sculpture. Under the triumvir Love are Breeding,
Agriculture, Education, Medicine, Clothing, Pasturage,
Coining.

G. M.—What about their judges?

Capt.—This is the point I was just thinking of explain-
ing. Everyone is judged by the first master of his trade,
and thus all the head artificers are judges. They punish
with exile, with flogging, with blame, with deprivation
of the common table, with exclusion from the church and
from the company of women. When there is a case in
which great injury has been done, it is punished with

death, and they repay an eye with an eye, a nose for
a nose, a tooth for a tooth, and so on, according to the
law of retaliation. If the offense is willful the council
decides. When there is strife and it takes place unde-
signedly, the sentence is mitigated; nevertheless, not by
the judge but by the triumvirate, from whom even it
may be referred to Hoh, not on account of justice but of
mercy, for Hoh is able to pardon. They have no prisons,
except one tower for shutting up rebellious enemies, and
there is no written statement of a case, which we commonly call a lawsuit. But the accusation and witnesses are
produced in the presence of the judge and Power; the
accused person makes his defense, and he is immediately
acquitted or condemned by the judge; and if he appeals
to the triumvirate, on the following day he is acquitted
or condemned. On the third day he is dismissed through
the mercy and clemency of Hoh, or receives the inviolable rigor of his sentence. An accused person is recon-
ciled to his accuser and to his witnesses, as it were, with
the medicine of his complaint, that is, with embracing
and kissing. No one is killed or stoned unless by the
hands of the people, the accuser and the witnesses
beginning first. For they have no executioners and
lictors, lest the state should sink into ruin. The choice
of death is given to the rest of the people, who inclose
the lifeless remains in little bags and burn them by the
application of fire, while exhorters are present for the purpose of advising concerning a good death. Nevertheless,
the whole nation laments and beseeches God that his
anger may be appeased, being in grief that it should, as
it were, have to cut off a rotten member of the state.
Certain officers talk to and convince the accused man by
means of arguments until he himself acquiesces in the
sentence of death passed upon him, or else he does not
die. But if a crime has been committed against the liberty
of the republic, or against God, or against the supreme
magistrates, there is immediate censure without pity.
These only are punished with death. He who is about
to die is compelled to state in the presence of the people
and with religious scrupulousness the reasons for which
he does not deserve death, and also the sins of the others

who ought to die instead of him, and further the mistakes of the magistrates. If, moreover, it should seem right to the person thus asserting, he must say why the accused ones are deserving of less punishment than he. And if by his arguments he gains the victory he is sent into exile, and appeases the state by means of prayers and sacrifices and good life ensuing. They do not torture those named by the accused person, but they warn them. Sins of frailty and ignorance are punished only with blaming, and with compulsory continuation as learners under the law and discipline of those sciences or arts against which they have sinned. And all these things they have mutually among themselves, since they seem to be in very truth members of the same body, and one of another.

This further I would have you know, that if a transgressor, without waiting to be accused, goes of his own accord before a magistrate, accusing himself and seeking to make amends, that one is liberated from the punishment of a secret crime, and since he has not been accused of such a crime, his punishment is changed into another. They take special care that no one should invent slander, and if this should happen they meet the offense with the punishment of retaliation. Since they always walk about and work in crowds, five witnesses are required for the conviction of a transgressor. If the case is otherwise, after having theatened him, he is released after he has sworn an oath as the warrant of good conduct. Or if he is accused a second or third time, his increased punishment rests on the testimony of three or two witnesses. They have but few laws, and these short and plain, and written upon a flat table, and hanging to the doors of the temple, that is between the columns. And on single columns can be seen the essence of things described in the very terse style of Metaphysics — viz, the essences of God, of the angels, of the world, of the stars, of man, of fate, of virtue, all done with great wisdom. The definitions of all the virtues are also delineated here, and here is the tribunal, where the judges of all the virtues have their seat. The definition of a certain virtue is writtten under that column where the judges for the aforesaid virtue sit, and when a judge gives judgment he sits and speaks thus: O son, thou hast sinned against this sacred definition of beneficence, or of magnanimity, or of another virtue, as the case may be. And after discussion the judge legally condemns him to the punishment for the crime of which he is accused — viz, for injury, for despondency, for pride, for ingratitude, for sloth, etc. But the sentences are certain and true correctives, savoring more of clemency than of actual punishment.

G. M.— Now you ought to tell me about their priests, their sacrifices, their religion, and their belief.

Capt.— The chief priest is Hoh, and it is the duty of all the superior magistrates to pardon sins. Therefore the whole state by secret confession, which we also use, tell their sins to the magistrates, who at once purge their souls and teach those that are inimical to the people. Then the sacred magistrates themselves confess their own sinfulness to the three supreme chiefs, and together they confess the faults of one another, though no special one is named, and they confess especially the heavier faults and those harmful to the state. At length the triumvirs confess their sinfulness to Hoh himself, who forthwith recognizes the kinds of sins that are harmful to the state, and succors with timely remedies. Then he offers sacrifices and prayers to God. And before this he confesses the sins of the whole people, in the presence of God, and publicly in the temple, above the altar, as often as it had been necessary that the fault should be corrected. Nevertheless, no transgressor is spoken of by his name. In this manner he absolves the people by advising them that they should beware of sins of the aforesaid kind. Afterward he offers sacrifice to God, that he should pardon the state and absolve it of its sins, and to teach and defend it. Once in every year the chief priests of each separate subordinate state confess their sins in the presence of Hoh. Thus he is not ignorant of the wrongdoings of the provinces, and forthwith he removes them with all human and heavenly remedies.

Sacrifice is conducted after the following manner: Hoh asks the people which one among them wishes to give himself as a sacrifice to God for the sake of his fellows. He is then placed upon the fourth table, with ceremonies and the offering up of prayers: the table is hung up in a wonderful manner by means of four ropes passing through four cords attached to firm pulley blocks in the small dome of the temple. This done they cry to the God of mercy, that he may accept the offering, not of a beast as among the heathen, but of a human being. Then Hoh orders the ropes to be drawn and the sacrifice is pulled up above to the centre of the small dome, and there it dedicates itself with the most fervent supplications. Food is given to it through a window by the priests, who live around the dome, but it is allowed a very little to eat, until it has atoned for the sins of the state. There with prayer and fasting he cries to the God of heaven that he might accept its willing offering. And after twenty or thirty days, the anger of God being appeased, the sacrifice becomes a priest, or sometimes, though rarely, returns below by means of the outer way for the priests. Ever after this man is treated with great benevolence and much honor, for the reason that he offered himself unto death for the sake of his country. But God does not require death. The priests above twenty-four years of age offer praises from their places in the top of the temple. This they do in the middle of the night, at noon, in the morning and in the evening, to wit, four times a day they sing their chants in the presence of God. It is also their work to observe the stars and to note with the astrolabe their motions and influences upon human things, and to find out their powers. Thus they know in what part of the earth any change has been or will be, and at what time it has taken place, and they send to find whether the matter be as they have it. They make a note of predictions, true and false, so that they may be able from experience to predict most correctly. The priests, moreover, determine the hours for breeding and the days for sowing, reaping, and gathering the vintage, and are as it were the ambassadors and intercessors and connection between God and man. And it is from among them mostly that Hoh is elected. They write very learned treatises and search into the sciences. Below they never descend, unless for their dinner and supper, so that the essence of their heads do not descend to the stomachs and liver. Only very seldom, and that as a cure for the ills of solitude, do they have converse with women. On certain days Hoh goes up to them and deliberates with them concerning the matters which he has lately investigated for the benefit of the state and all the nations of the world.

In the temple beneath one priest always stands near the altar praying for the people, and at the end of every hour another succeeds him, just as we are accustomed in solemn prayer to change every fourth hour. And this method of supplication they call perpetual prayer. After a meal they return thanks to God. Then they sing the deeds of the Christian, Jewish, and Gentile heroes, and of those of all other nations, and this is very delightful to them. Forsooth, no one is envious of another. They sing a hymn to Love, one to Wisdom, and one each to all the other virtues, and this they do under the direction of the ruler of each virtue. Each one takes the woman he loves most, and they dance for exercise with propriety and stateliness under the peristyles. The women wear their long hair all twisted together and collected into one knot on the crown of the head, but in rolling it they leave one curl. The men, however, have one curl only and the rest of their hair around the head is shaven off. Further, they wear a slight covering, and above this a round hat a little larger than the size of their head. In the fields they use caps, but at home each one wears a biretto white, red, or another color according to his trade or occupation. Moreover, the magistrates use grander and more imposing-looking coverings for the head.

They hold great festivities when the sun enters the four cardinal points of the heavens, that is, when he enters Cancer, Libra, Capricorn, and Aries. On these occasions they have very learned, splendid, and as it were comic performances. They celebrate also every full and every new moon with a festival, as also they do the anniversaries of the founding of the city, and of the days when they have won victories or done any other great

achievement. The celebrations take place with the music
of female voices, with the noise of trumpets and drums,
and the firing of salutations. The poets sing the praises
of the most renowned leaders and the victories. Nevertheless if any of them should deceive even by dispar-
aging a foreign hero, he is punished. No one can
exercise the function of a poet who invents that which is not
true, and a license like this they think to be a pest of
our world, for the reason that it puts a premium upon
virtue and often assigns it to unworthy persons, either
from fear or flattery, or ambition or avarice. For the
praise of no one is a statue erected until after his death;
but while he is alive, who has found out new arts and
very useful secrets, or who has rendered great service to
the state, either at home or on the battlefield, his name
is written in the book of heroes. They do not bury
dead bodies, but burn them, so that a plague may not
arise from them, and so that they may be converted into
fire, a very noble and powerful thing which has its coming from the sun and returns to it. And for the above
reasons no chance is given for idolatry. The statues and
pictures of the heroes, however, are there, and the
splendid women set apart to become mothers often look
at them. Prayers are made from the state to the four
horizontal corners of the world. In the morning to the
rising sun, then to the setting sun, then to the south
and lastly to the north; and in the contrary order in the
evening, first to the setting sun, to the rising sun, to
the north, and at length to the south. They repeat but
one prayer, which asks for health of body and of mind
and happiness for themselves and all people, and they
conclude it with the petition " As it seems best to God."
The public prayer for all is long, and it is poured forth
to heaven. For this reason the altar is round and is divided crosswise by ways at right angles to one another.
By these ways Hoh enters after he has repeated the four
prayers, and he prays looking up to heaven. And then
a great mystery is seen by them. The priestly vestments are of a beauty and meaning like to those of
Aaron. They resemble Nature and they surpass Art.
   They divide the seasons according to the revolution of

the sun, and not of the stars, and they observe yearly
by how much time the one precedes the other. They
hold that the sun approaches nearer and nearer, and
therefore by ever-lessening circles reaches the tropics
and the equator every year a little sooner. They measure
months by the course of the moon, years by that of the sun.
They praise Ptolemy, admire Copernicus, but place Aris-
tarchus and Philolaus before him. They take great pains
in endeavoring to understand the construction of the
world, and whether or not it will perish, and at what
time. They believe that the true oracle of Jesus Christ
is by the signs in the sun, in the moon, and in the stars,
which signs do not thus appear to many of us foolish
ones. Therefore they wait for the renewing of the age,
and perchance for its end. They say that it is very
doubtful whether the world was made from nothing, or
from the ruins of other worlds, or from chaos, but they
certainly think that it was made, and did not exist from
eternity. Therefore they disbelieve in Aristotle, whom
they consider a logician and not a philosopher. From
analogies, they can draw many arguments against the
eternity of the world. The sun and the stars they, so to
speak, regard as the living representatives and signs of
God, as the temples and holy living altars, and they honor
but do not worship them. Beyond all other things they
venerate the sun, but they consider no created thing
worthy the adoration of worship. This they give to God
alone, and thus they serve him, that they may not come
into the power of a tyrant and fall into misery by undergoing punishment by creatures of revenge. They con-
template and know God under the image of the Sun and
they call it the sign of God, his face and living image, by
means of which light, heat, life, and the making of all
things good and bad proceeds. Therefore they have
built an altar like to the Sun in shape, and the priests
praise God in the Sun and in the stars, as it were his
altars, and in the heavens, his temple as it were; and
they pray to good angels, who are, so to speak, the intercessors living in the stars, their strong abodes.
For God long since set signs of their beauty in heaven,
and of his glory in the Sun. They say there is but one

heaven, and that the planets move and rise of themselves when they approach the sun, or are in conjunction with it.

They assert two principles of the physics of things below, namely, that the Sun is the father, and the Earth the mother; the air is an impure part of the heavens; all fire is derived from the sun. The sea is the sweat of earth, or the fluid of earth combusted, and fused within its bowels; but is the bond of union between air and earth, as the blood is of the spirit and flesh of animals. The world is a great animal, and we live within it as worms live within us. Therefore we do not belong to the system of stars, sun, and earth, but to God only; for in respect to them which seek only to amplify themselves, we are born and live by chance; but in respect to God, whose instruments we are, we are formed by prescience and design, and for a high end. Therefore we are bound to no Father but God, and receive all things from him. They hold as beyond question the immortality of souls, and that these associate with good angels after death, or with bad angels, according as they have likened themselves in this life to either. For all things seek their like. They differ little from us as to places of reward and punishment. They are in doubt whether there are other worlds beyond ours, and account it madness to say there is nothing. Nonentity is incompatible with the infinite entity of God. They lay down two principles of metaphysics, entity which is the highest God, and nothingness which is the defect of entity. Evil and sin come of the propensity to nothingness; the sin having its cause not efficient, but in deficiency. Deficiency is, they say, of power, wisdom or will. Sin they place in the last of these three, because he who knows and has the power to do good is bound also to have the will, for will arises out of them. They worship God in Trinity, saying God is the supreme Power, whence proceeds the highest Wisdom, which is the same with God, and from these comes Love, which is both Power and Wisdom; but they do not distinguish persons by name, as in our Christian law, which has not been revealed to them. This religion, when its abuses have been removed, will be the future mistress of the world, as great theologians teach and hope. Therefore Spain found the New World (though its first discoverer, Columbus, greatest of heroes, was a Genoese), that all nations should be gathered under one law. We know not what we do, but God knows, whose instruments we are. They sought new regions for lust of gold and riches, but God works to a higher end. The sun strives to burn up the earth, not to produce plants and men, but God guides the battle to great issues. His the praise, to him the glory!

G. M.—Oh, if you knew what our astrologers say of the coming age, and of our age, that has in it more history within a hundred years than all the world had in four thousand years before! Of the wonderful invention of printing and guns, and the use of the magnet, and how it all comes of Mercury, Mars, the Moon, and the Scorpion!

Capt.—Ah, well! God gives all in his good time. They astrologize too much.

www.ingramcontent.com/pod-product-compliance
Lightning Source LLC
Chambersburg PA
CBHW021215090426
42740CB00006B/238